F

How to Stop Your Relatives from Driving You Crazy

Strategies for Coping with
"Challenging" Relatives

DENISE LANG

A FIRESIDE BOOK
Published by Simon & Schuster
New York London Toronto Sydney Tokyo Singapore

F

FIRESIDE
Simon & Schuster Building
Rockefeller Center
1230 Avenue of the Americas
New York, New York 10020

First Fireside Edition 1992

FIRESIDE and colophon are registered trademarks
of Simon & Schuster Inc.

Designed by Richard Oriolo
Manufactured in the United States of America

10   9   8   7   6   5   4   3   2

Library of Congress Cataloging-in-Publication Data is available.

ISBN 0-671-78911-2

The publisher and author gratefully acknowledge permission to reprint an excerpt from
The Prince of Tides by Pat Conroy, copyright © 1986 by Pat Conroy, reprinted by
permission of Houghton Mifflin Company.

Originally published under the title *Family Harmony*.

For my sisters
Valerie Harnden and Michelle Kelly
with love always

ACKNOWLEDGMENTS

A book as broad in scope as *How to Stop Your Relatives from Driving You Crazy* could not have been completed without the help of some special people who demonstrated their sensitivity and dedication to family relationships through the generous gifts of their time and expertise.

I owe a debt of gratitude to John Kurtze of Edward Lowe Industries, Linda Martin, Barbara Moore, Dr. Melodie Moorehead, Rev. Tom Robinson, Msgr. John Ryan, and Dr. Richard Sostowski.

In addition, special thanks for many hours of support and clearheaded counsel goes to Dr. Sharon Ryan and to Stephen Sepaniak of Schenk, Price, Smith, and King.

Finally, a big hug to Larry, Chris, and Tiffany, my constant reminders of the importance of family, and to all who shared family stories and will remain nameless—I promise!

CONTENTS

Part III
THE MOST COMMON DIVIDERS: MONEY

Part IV
THE MOST COMMON DIVIDERS: VALUES

Part V
CONTRIBUTING CIRCUMSTANCES

INTRODUCTION

The first time my future husband (on a weekend visit from college) dined at my home, my parents got into a walloping argument and my father proved that Greeks don't hurl dishes at the wall only when they are happy. As my sister calmly asked this stunned beau to pass the butter, I was convinced he would realize that my family harbored deviant personalities and bolt for the door. Even if he made it through dinner, there were still the forty-seven posters of Donny Osmond that would be smiling brightly at him all through the night in my youngest sister's bedroom, which had been converted to a guest room for his use. I knew that I had a family tree with more than just a couple of nuts hiding in the branches and that everyone else's family was *normal*, but I had hoped to keep it secret.

I grew up a second-generation American in a Greek-Spanish household. My family's members waged war as frequently as some people visit the bathroom. I have witnessed fights worthy of ESPN coverage, and breaks in relations ranging from days to eleven years, including those involving money, care of an elderly parent, sibling jealousy, dictatorlike personalities, cultural clashes, morality issues, family business, and breaking tradition.

Despite that noisy beginning, Larry and I did get married. *His* family tree, though more subdued, included adult sibling rivalries, conflicts concerning care for aging relatives, remarriages, pot-stirring personalities, and numerous communication gaps (while my family yelled out their feelings, his rarely revealed them). Through the ensuing eighteen years of marriage, we have dealt with continuing feuds and evolving personalities and come to a major realization—we are not alone! *Every* family is a little bit nuts, because we are all human. It's how we deal with our families that determines whether we will reap the best kernels of our heritage or the chaff.

As I researched my last book, *The Phantom Spouse: Helping You and Your Family Survive Business Travel and Relocation,* one theme kept popping up: the extended family's influence over how people cope with other stresses in their lives, whether that be change of job, relocation, or relationships. That recurring theme and my family experiences motivated me to set out on a new quest. For more than a year, I traveled across the country gathering family stories that run the gamut of conflicts and feuds and illustrate either how people cope or go nearly crazy trying. Since few people wanted to point to their own flesh and blood and expose them publicly (although more than a few begged me to do it—"Would serve that S.O.B. right!"), for the sake of honesty and consistency, all names have been changed in the anecdotes to protect both the innocent and the guilty. Only the professional counselors quoted are referred to by their real names. Should a particular story and name sound like *your* family, the coincidence is purely accidental and shows how universal our family conflicts are.

Some people have questioned whether we can, in fact, achieve harmonious relationships with family members who seem to know instinctively the shortest route to driving us crazy. The answer is an optimistic *yes,* but it will take building some muscle.

Just as a group of individual islands, towns, or even opportunities are linked through a system of roadways and bridges, so too individual family members can remain connected through psychic bridges, those pathways that cross gaps in communication or obstacles of personality and understanding. For that reason, I will use the extended metaphor of "building bridges" for means of traversing those obstacles. The image is a dynamic one and reflects my view of that family *is* important and worth the effort it takes to smooth out those conflicts and head them off when possible. The bridge-building supports I'll offer are designed to do just that, while helping you retain your dignity and sanity. In addition to those supports is a wealth of information, both legal and psychological, which also helps construct bridges across gaps in understanding.

I am not a psychologist. My degree from the University of Florida was in journalism and communications with a double minor in psychology and education. While I have taken a number of graduate courses in behavior and psychology, my credentials for writing this book lie elsewhere. While my inspiration may spring from my experiences as a family member and as a journalist and author who has conducted thousands of interviews, I have also had access to, and the enthusiastic cooperation of, some outstanding professionals in the fields of psychiatry, sociology, law, the ministry, business, and addiction rehabilitation. All these experts could speak from a personal as well as professional perspective with sensitivity and humor. That was important to me because families *are* funny—and crazy, and yes, sometimes maddening.

Building bridges to achieve family harmony is an ongoing process that has a curious effect. Not only are two family members connected, but the one doing the building grows stronger. Just as a construction worker's muscles grow and develop through the repeated lifting of heavy steel and blocks, so will your emotional muscles grow as you use the tools provided to build bridges to the very people who make you crazy. You will both be the richer for it.

Part I

MONKEYS IN THE FAMILY TREE

1

A Real Cast of Characters

It is a treasured American image: smiling Grandma is proudly placing an overstuffed turkey on a laden table; Grandpa, carving knife nearby, is aglow with love as his children and grandchildren snuggle 'round the table to receive the rich bounty amid the family love and camaraderie. It is this Norman Rockwell image to which we aspire, which we envy and attempt to duplicate. And for a few, it may even materialize . . . sometimes.

The actual scenario may more realistically find Grandma, harried and grumbling since early morning because, once again, the responsibility for preparing the family dinner has been dumped on *her* and, of course, no one can get there early to give her a hand. Grandpa is aglow—with the bourbon he's been sipping while listening to Grandma bitch all morning— and by the time the family arrives, he may be sliding under the table if he isn't propped up. No one is about to trust him with a carving knife.

Son Joe is gritting his teeth at his younger, and financially more successful, brother Ted's pompous bragging about everything from his new BMW to his upcoming ski vacation. Daughter Susan keeps looking at her watch wondering, "Oh God, how long do I have to stay before I can go meet Donald?" (with whom she's just moved in, but doesn't dare bring to dinner, because her father has already declared that he would rather she walk the red-light district than associate with Don).

Teenage grandchildren are sitting out back in the snow, possibly sharing a beer and comparing notes on their impossible parents. And Aunt Tess, whom nobody can stand anyway because she's constantly criticizing and

3

always brings lima beans (also despised) to family dinners, has a few too many Manhattans and starts dragging out injustices committed against her by Grandma thirty years earlier. This prompts a razor-sharp verbal exchange, which takes the heat off Joe's wife Cindy, who can't bear to listen to sister-in-law Janet's lectures on child-rearing, because, of course, Janet's children never do *anything* wrong.

And so it goes. By the time dinner is served, warm family camaraderie centers on passing the condiments and keen interest on watching the dog lick himself in unmentionable places. Yet ask any member, "Why not just skip it?" and you'll get an incredulous look, a shake of the head, and the reply, "Because—it's my family."

Ah, families! No other social group is as loved, despised, imposed upon, bragged about, concealed, revered, dissected, ignored, or elevated. They can triple our pleasure or devastate a holiday or special occasion. Families are our links to the past, the very core of our identities, and the silent navigators, good or bad, that steer us into the future. It is within the family that we first learn to be social, observe value structures, and glean some semblance of self-worth. But the ride is not an easy one. It is rife with the pitfalls that are inevitable when you throw dozens of different personalities together with the lifetime admonition that they must get along.

While some may paraphrase comedian Henny Youngman's refrain, "Take my family—please," most recognize that we are as bound to our extended families as we are to our own toes and they are just as necessary to our existence if we are to meet life's challenges sure-footedly. When we are in the midst of a family battle, however, anyone else's family can always look better.

One of the country's foremost family therapists, Dr. Salvador Minuchin, once commented dryly, "Everyone knows that *other* families' problems are well-handled and logically resolved." It is only our own that are crazy, aggravating, overemotional, picky, or uptight. Right? Wrong!

While prominent families such as the Johnsons, Guccis, Pulitzers, and Von Bülows make headlines by washing their dirty linen in public, the rest of the nation's 64.5 million families are embroiled in their own conflicts. No one is immune. The revered Albert Einstein had problems with a meddling mother, an illegitimate daughter, and a mentally ill son. Even the notable portrayer of idyllic American life, Norman Rockwell, had his share of family strife. One of his three wives was a psychiatric patient who burned down their house; surely even *he* had to learn to dance a diplomatic two-step in order to get along with three sets of extended-family members.

* * *

THE CANDY APPLE FAMILY

No matter what your family is like, it is important to recognize that we are surrounded by illusions regarding family life today.

In the days when extended families were bound together by the need for survival, members focused on a common challenge, be that poverty, life in a new country, a hostile environment, or hostile neighbors. Family provided an integral sense of pride, belonging, continuity, and victory over the odds. Since a family was surrounded by other families undertaking similar challenges, there was a shared sense of purpose and the families who "made it" were the ones who triumphed over very practical hurdles.

Today our families are scattered. The challenge for survival is not so much one that pits us against the elements, as it is a struggle for economic success, a household free from substance abuse, and one in which the members respect or simply have time for each other.

The families that are held up as those who have "made it" are products of the electronic media. From "Leave It to Beaver" to "The Waltons" to "The Cosby Show" we are given a message that television families are what a family ought to be like. And we, comparing our own members— from our picky aunt who brings her own food in Tupperware bowls to family dinners (in case she doesn't like what's being served) to our siblings who know which buttons to push to make us crazy—come up very short. Of course, we *know* that our family is the only one that can't get along like the Waltons.

Our illusions regarding what families ought to be like remind me of the day my thirteen-year-old son Chris, in the throes of adolescent angst, complained that "Everybody else always looks so together. Nobody seems to have worries about friends or about themselves. I'm the only one who's miserable." The only one indeed! We are culturally programmed to present a happy face to those around us. Both individually and as families, we strive to look our best to the outside world, belying the stresses, problems, and anxieties boiling inside.

"Where I grew up, we called it being a street angel and house devil," said Doris, a redheaded Irish woman from Brooklyn. "Out on the street, we were to be polite and kind, particularly to family members, but once a person got home and hung up their good clothes, wham! Anything could happen, including violence, and nobody on the outside would suspect it."

Looking around us and comparing our family, with all of its idiosyncrasies and characters, to the "perfect" families around us is a little like buying a candy apple at the fair. How many of us can pass that tray of bright, shiny, red, perfectly round apples and not buy one? The promise of a fresh, crispy apple inside that candy confection is hard to pass up. So we give in. First we have to get past that shiny candy coating, and that's tough to crack. We finally crunch through and . . . very often, instead of the fresh, crisp apple the packaging seduced us into buying, we find the apple is stale, mushy, and maybe even rotten. Yet who would have known, looking at the tray, where each apple looked more perfect than the next?

We have been seduced into thinking that other families are perfect. Other families must handle their problems with logic and ease because they all look so good. Each of us presents a facade as bright and shiny as a carnival candy apple. Of course, were we to crack through that enticing candy apple coating, we might find that other families have the same brown spots and mushy places as ours.

Your family, with all its nuttiness, *is* normal, but that doesn't necessarily make it easier to cope with when a conflict arises.

THE RHYME AND REASONS FOR FAMILY DIVISIONS

Sometimes huge family arguments are sparked by what seem like insignificant incidents or actions. In discussing family frictions and the ensuing struggle for harmony, it is important to point out that there are as many types of feuds as there are reasons for them.

At one end of the spectrum, we have the type that can be classified as a persistent irritation brought about because of a clash of personalities, values, traditions, desires, or mores within the extended family structure. Jane's situation is one of these types of feud. It sleeps below the surface of relationships until someone steps on it, bringing forth a roar of resentment.

Although to most people, it looks as if Jane "has it all," she is constantly berated or needled by extended family members. Her hours are long in the advertising business she has built, and she has had to miss a couple of her children's school events due to business trips. But for the most part, Jane and her husband and children are happy with their lifestyle. Conversations with family members, however, are riddled with "How is poor Charlie doing now that you have to travel?" or "Are you sure you are giving the children enough of your time? I'm sure they'd rather have you make cupcakes for their birthdays at school than buy them new designer sweatshirts!" That continual nudging (pronounced *noodging* and accompanied by a smirk) can wear a person out.

At the other end of the spectrum is the type of feud that actually divides family members, causing rifts that can last from weeks to years. We might think that only catastrophic incidents cause this type of feud, but just as many families are divided over something as seemingly trivial as the selection of a name for their offspring, as those brought about by money, illness, and differences in values. Such was the case with Pat and Ben.

Pat and Ben, brother and sister, lived next door to each other. Ben had to rise early in order to make his shift at the glassworks, while Pat enjoyed sleeping a little later. Ben had the habit of revving his car's engine to warm it up, thus awakening Pat at 5:20 A.M. Pat made a few nasty comments to Ben, who seemingly ignored her protests. So one morning while Ben was revving his engine, Pat calmly filled a large cooking pot with ice water, trudged over to Ben's car, knocked on the window and, when he rolled it down, threw the entire contents of the pot into his face . . . and all over him and his car. What ensued was not only a juvenile screaming match but the involvement of numerous family members, each taking sides and dividing loyalties. Nearly two years later, Ben and Pat are still not speaking to each other and family relations are strained.

"Why do we need to take this so seriously?" you might ask. "After all, it's just your family you're talking about. The people you don't hesitate to tell what you think, like 'God, you look awful!' or 'Henry, you always were such a cheapskate!' or 'That color makes you look so fat!' " Family is where you "let it all hang out" and you don't get thrown out of the club. As one man told me, "Family is where I can say or do anything I want, and they have to forgive me and take me in."

This is true to a large extent. There are few things more powerful than the family bond, but for that very reason, the liberties we take, the impositions we make, and the expectations we levy all tend to spark fireworks. At the root of most feuds, however, are four basic challenges: the struggle for power, a lack of communication, unrealistic expectations, and the lack of good negotiating skills. These are the four challenges that will be addressed through our bridge-building skills.

THE NEED TO BUILD BRIDGES

The Florida Keys stretch like pearls in a necklace for 150 miles from the tip of the Florida peninsula into the Gulf of Mexico. Though they are similar in vegetation and physical composition, each has nonetheless a unique character. These islands are connected by the Overseas Highway and forty-two bridges, including one that is seven miles long. If not for these bridges, the individual properties of these wonderful tropical islands would be unavailable to most of us.

A family in conflict or in the midst of a feud is like the Florida Key chain. Each member displays an inherent "family resemblance," yet each is an individual, standing alone. The bigger the conflict, the wider the gulf that separates them and no matter how strong your voice, you cannot resolve a conflict over a gulf. Unless you have a bridge, that is.

Like the bridges that link the Florida Keys, the bridges that we build to each of our family members provide a means of conveying our attention, skills, and emotions over the sometimes choppy waters that divide us. Some bridges, like the Seven-Mile Bridge, have to traverse great spans of water that swirl with unseen currents and are teeming with sharks and barracudas. These bridges must be resilient, and so must our emotional bridges, because the emotional waters are also teeming with currents and sharks that threaten to separate us.

In order to build bridges that will satisfactorily traverse deep emotional waters and connect two sparring people, a series of cables and supports must be put in place. Some of these cables are comprised of factual information, such as educational, legal, and medical options. Other cables are emotional growth lines, which are strengthened by our resolve and self-esteem. Serving as the foundation for the bridge building are five major supports that hold the bridges in place.

FIVE BRIDGE-BUILDING SUPPORTS

Communication, or a lack of it, lies at the heart of many family feuds.

Jack and his father cannot be in the same room for more than a couple of hours before they get into a fight. Although Jack is now in his thirties, with four children of his own, old patterns of relating to each other surface, followed by comments beginning with "Well, you always . . ." or "You never . . ." Soon, anyone else within earshot is dragged into the argument and, more than once, a visit has been broken up because of this inability to communicate civilly.

Building communication skills among family members is a challenge that takes time, patience, and forethought. *Planned communication* is the first key support to building a bridge.

Choose the right time to make announcements. One wouldn't go into a business meeting to present an important decision or complaint without doing a little planning ahead as to the most propitious time and method for presentation. Yet we drop verbal bombs on our family with little thought as to the listener's ability to handle the subject matter at that precise moment. Throwing a temper tantrum at age forty-one, when your mother has just had a bad day at the office, only reinforces her old method of dealing with you.

Avoid generalizations when talking with family members. These include using phrases beginning with "You always . . ." and "You never . . ."

because there are few accusations that put people in a combative mood more than those. Your listener's mind will selectively eliminate anything said following those phrases. Instead of hearing you, they'll be off on another argument in retaliation.

Finally, planned communication involves continual communication, whether by family newsletter, regular telephone calls, or letterwriting. More misunderstandings arise when one faction of the family is not informed of a major or minor occurrence in another. This is particularly important today as families are scattered across the country.

The second key bridge-building support is to dump the "supposed to's" and *adjust your expectation level.*

It is amazing that even normally sane people have unrealistic expectations of their families and go through a continual spiral of disappointment. I call these the "supposed to's" of family life that drag us down and perpetuate the Candy Apple Family myth. For example: A mother is *supposed to* be warm and nurturing; a father is *supposed to* be a strong guide; we are *supposed to* get together with our loved ones around the dinner table in sweet harmony; our grandparents are *supposed to* accept us unconditionally; our siblings are *supposed to* be supportive of our life choices; our parents are *supposed to* be interested in our lives and those of our children, willing to drop what they're doing when we need them.

The list can go on forever. There are so many artificial "supposed to's" that we consciously or subconsciously employ when dealing with our relatives that we rarely take into consideration who and what they really are as people. As a result, when they disappoint us by not following our personal script for them, emotional chaos reigns.

Coupled with the system of "supposed to's" is the fact that we desire only the very best for those closest to us, be that financial success or the most wonderful relationships. But we are prisoners of our own and others' expectations. When we are given a gloriously wrapped present, it may spark our imagination to expect an incredible treasure inside, yet we often find when we tear off the wrapping that the gift cannot live up to our imaginations. Neither can our loved ones. If we lower our level of expectation, we will enjoy the pleasure our relationships can bring us.

Which brings us to the third key support, *tolerance versus endorsement.*

Because we care for our family members, we tend to want to have their choices coincide with what we consider best for them. Since we are dealing with a kaleidoscope of personalities and desires, that tendency to direct others can aggravate a feud. Learning that tolerance of another's actions does not necessarily mean we gladly endorse their choice lays the foundation for good communication building and a productive relationship.

When twenty-five-year-old Eve decided to follow the racing car circuit with Rob, a forty-year-old chief mechanic for a well-known driver, her sisters were upset. Not only did they not like Rob's supercilious reverse snobbery toward their more conventional lives but his intrusion into the family entailed keeping Eve busy traveling when family events took place. There were hurt feelings on both sides as the sisters turned a cold shoulder toward Rob, and Eve seemed to abdicate all family responsibilities and traditions.

"We finally realized that if we wanted to keep any sort of relationship with our sister, we would just have to accept the fact that she was living her own life and that she was the one who would have to live with the consequences," says Jenny. "We miss having Eve as an active part of our family, but at some point you have to set a priority."

The fourth key bridge-building support, the *humor warp*, is engaged nearly every day, but we use it in relation to others more than with our own family.

Have you ever roared with laughter when a friend regales you with a story about Aunt Violet, who considered it her solemn duty to diagnose the worst possible diseases when family members had an unusually long bout with the common cold? And who once—even funnier—"helpfully" brought a catalog of caskets over to a family member's house who was getting on in years, in order to help him make the right decision.

What makes the story funny is that it happened to someone else. Professional comedians know this and regularly include "family horror stories" in their act. Now if *you* were the one worried about a mysterious pain, or were in the throes of a particularly virulent flu, it wouldn't be funny if Aunt Violet were knocking at *your* door. Time to engage the humor warp.

This is a simple mind game, in which you take two steps back from your particular family "thorn"—perhaps your brother who goes through elaborate rituals to convert everyone to his religion, or your aunt who always dredges up the story about the time you passed gas when she introduced you to her neighbor's hunk of a seventeen-year-old son—and pretend that these people belong to someone else's family. That's right, give them away. And then laugh. When you get really good at laughing at the characters in your family tree through the humor warp, you may find yourself laughing, instead of tensing, in the midst of them, and appreciating their diversity.

The last bridge support is the adoption of a *surrogate family*.

Part and parcel of the illusion of the Candy Apple Family is the idea that our family members should satisfy all our needs. The perfect mom or dad should always be willing to listen attentively, give sage advice, never interfere when we choose to diverge from the family pathway, and always be on hand to dust us off and buoy us up when we need help, emotional or financial. Siblings should always be the perfect backdrop for our talents, humbly supportive yet so accomplished in their own arenas that we would proudly introduce them anywhere.

However, in our families, we have frail humans, who will not always satisfy our every need. That perfect family only exists in our imaginations, but our needs for all those family supports are very real.

Rather than make demands on our mothers, fathers, and siblings that they may not be able to meet, adopt a surrogate family. This does not have to be just one family, but an idealized family composed of people who meet those specific needs.

If you need a sister who is noncompetitive and low-key, go out among your friends and find one. If you need a father who will not try to dominate your life, go find an older friend whose personality meshes with your need. That way, when your own father needles you or your sister is aggressive, you can look beyond that aspect of their personality and minimize the stress build-up, because you have your "perfect" surrogate family members waiting in the wings.

Since a family gathering is often the site of combat—where the "you nevers" and "you're supposed to's" can instantly decimate a "happy occasion"—let's take a look at how to appreciate our family's longevity while minimizing its tendency to go for the jugular.

COPING WITH
THE FAMILY GATHERING

Whether a family is gathering for a holiday feast, a religious celebration, a birthday, or just a Sunday dinner, the simple fact that the family is gathering often sets the stage for myriad subdramas. People often pick that specific time to drop bombshell announcements—pregnancies, marriages, divorces, cohabitations, and so on. Then they have to take the consequences when other family members "shoot from the hip."

Before you know it, a simple disagreement takes on global proportions with relatives wetting their lips in anticipation of getting in a few licks themselves. Attacks become more personal, and a dig about not remembering to give niece Sally a birthday present winds up spawning warfare over why Uncle Jack's family never wanted him to marry into yours because not one of them has any common sense. Pretty soon, even Henry Kissinger would find himself slinking out the back door rather than trying to negotiate a peaceful settlement.

The step from snide remark to family crisis is a slippery one where most of us have taken a tumble. We wind up glaring at each other across a ravine of angry words and hurt feelings.

Every time Marsha has the family gather at her house, she develops a migraine headache. "I can feel it coming on as I'm shopping for the food," she says. "I may be picking out potatoes, but my mind is on whether my brother and father will get into a fight. Over at the liquor section, I worry about my uncle who always drinks too much and gets into an argument. By the time I'm preparing food at home, the telephone starts ringing with relatives asking who else will be here and is so-and-so's fat son still as obnoxious as ever. And I know that no matter what I fix, my sister will manage to find something to criticize. What should be a happy time just completely frazzles me," says Marsha. "By the time they get here, my head hurts so much that I have to lie down in a room by myself. And I know they are probably talking about my avoiding them!"

In dealing with family conflicts, perhaps we can take a cue from the Chinese symbol for crisis, which is composed of two characters; one representing danger and the other representing opportunity. Each crisis has the potential for both. We should try to concentrate on turning those family crises into opportunities for growth and for building emotional bridges across those angry ravines. Toward this end, there are several ways you can partially control the stress of each family gathering itself, long before family members gather.

First, decide what you want from the gathering. Many people approach each family gathering with the idea that they are "going to get it right this time." If that's what you're thinking—forget it! Those people who can drive you nuts in a microsecond have probably not changed since the last time you thought you were going to "get it right." Adjust your expectation level realistically: Are you going to get together because there are *some* members you would like to see, despite the stresses? Because you want the children to know their cousins, aunts, or grandparents despite all the warts? Be honest!

Second, consider some diet and nutrition principles. If you know your family members tend toward the dramatic and hyperreactive, limit the amount of salt and caffeine you serve. I know your dad swears that caffeine doesn't affect him, but I bet if you substitute decaffeinated coffee for regular, his nerves will be noticeably calmer when his brother makes a critical remark.

If you have a drinking family, try making a "very special punch" with a higher content of fruit juice than alcohol to celebrate your time together. Most relatives will at least try the punch so your feelings won't be hurt.

By the time they are all there, you can put your third coping technique to work: Introduce another stress. That's right, another *stress.*

When relatives gather at your home, do you just plan the food and let the amusements take care of themselves? Is it any wonder then that the source of entertainment often becomes picking on each others' weaknesses? In his bestseller *The Joy of Stress,* Dr. Peter Hanson advocates indulging in a stressful activity, in order to relax from a stressful life. The key is that the new stress must be different from the one causing the problem. The professional baseball player, for example, would not find it particularly relaxing to go out and play ball on his day off. But he might really enjoy bowling, golf, or skiing.

During the days of American Camelot, the Kennedys' touch football games became legendary, but the games served to do more than just make good Sunday newspaper copy. Consider the strong personalities included in a large family such as the Kennedys. Do you think a family that produced a president, an ambassador, two senators, a number of human resource leaders, and troops of people talented in the arts would have a gathering where members would meekly surrender the floor to others?

In order to relieve the potential conversational hazards arising from being cooped up for an extended period of time with little to do but eat, drink, and dwell on both real and imagined hurts, introduce a *safe stress.* If touch football or frisbee is beyond your group, try the old standby parlor game of charades or the new version where teams must draw, not act out, their clues. All the popular television game shows have home varieties that lend themselves to team play, as do many electronic games.

If you are really feeling creative, spend some time putting together a personal family trivia game, asking little-known facts about various relatives, both alive and deceased. With this one, however, be careful that embarrassing information doesn't leak out under the guise of good fun.

The main idea is to spend a little time treating your family members like guests—not in the stuffy sense, but in the sense that some thought is given to constructive or entertaining activities instead of leaving everyone to fend for themselves. More than a tactic to please everyone, it is a means of self-defense. But then, sometimes despite all of our efforts, a family member insists on showing his or her true colors.

WHO IS WHO?

The bridge supports and cables will be highlighted throughout the book, but when you talk about families driving you crazy, it inevitably comes down to a discussion of the personalities of the people involved. Often our roles are already scripted for us before we arrive on the scene. These are roles that we assume as children and play into adulthood, polishing and perfecting the form whether we are comfortable with them or not.

When you refer to a relative who is making you crazy, how do you describe him or her? A real dictator type? A pot-stirrer? Could they be describing *you* the same way? When the battle lines are drawn, where do you stand? Sometimes, we don't even realize the parts we play and those parts may be different depending upon which branch of the family you're dealing with. Take the following test to find out.

WHAT ROLE DO YOU PLAY?

Part One: *Situations*

Select the answer that best describes your reaction to the given situation.

1. Your brother is marrying a woman from a culturally different background. Your parents and several relatives have spoken out against the marriage. You . . .
   a. have a strong talk with your brother about what a mistake he's making and issue an ultimatum that if he insists on going through with the marriage, you'll attend the ceremony but will have little to do with him afterward.
   b. take your brother aside and joke about his rebel stand, and ask him what time the wedding is.
   c. call the relatives who oppose the marriage; collect their opinions and make an appointment to present their views in a rational manner to your brother.
   d. listen to what your relatives have to say, but don't offer an opinion to your brother unless he asks.
   e. go out of your way to befriend your brother's fiancée because you know how she must feel—you are usually the one in hot water.
2. Your newly divorced, college-professor cousin introduces a much younger blue-collar worker as her new live-in at a special family anniversary dinner. Tension mounts all evening as she flaunts the relationship. You . . .
   a. tell her she's making a fool of herself and embarrassing her parents on this special night.
   b. stay at dinner for the minimum acceptable amount of time, then make an excuse and leave before tempers flare.
   c. are polite to your cousin and her companion, but let everyone

know the following day what you thought of her behavior while soliciting their opinions.

   d. try to keep the dinner rolling along without incident by acting as a buffer between your cousin and her parents.

   e. keep a low profile but welcome the new companion.

3. Your aging father has just been diagnosed as having Alzheimer's disease. He lives in another state, near one of your married sisters. (Your mother is deceased.) You have two other siblings, also in scattered locales. You . . .

   a. draw up a plan of adjustment concerning your father's living arrangements and the disposal of his property as well as assigning financial and other responsibilities to be assumed by your siblings and yourself. Then you inform the rest of the family concerning what their actions should be.

   b. manage to pay your father a visit and then keep a low profile.

   c. call your siblings and other relatives, relaying everyone's feelings and concerns. You also offer your own solution to the question of who should take responsibility for your father.

   d. find yourself being called upon to investigate options and make the decisions because you are levelheaded and are usually on good terms with all those concerned.

   e. find that nobody is asking your opinion about what should be done and your father doesn't want you to visit.

4. Your conservative uncle decides to quit his banking job, divorce his wife of twenty years, and become a resort boat captain in the Bahamas. You . . .

   a. spend considerable time and money to try to talk him out of his hairbrained scheme.

   b. make plans to sail aboard his boat.

   c. decide to serve as a go-between for your uncle and the rest of the relatives who think he's lost his senses.

   d. are asked to try to "talk sense" into him by everyone from your mother to your cousin. You secretly admire his decision, however.

   e. are jealous that he is getting so much attention for his rebellious act.

5. Your mother and sister, who live in different towns, are having an argument over what your mother feels was a deliberate snub by your sister. You . . .

   a. tell them both exactly what you think of the situation, their actions, and how you would resolve it.

   b. keep your answering machine on so you don't have to listen to either of them complain.

    c. feel important that they have both used you for a sounding board and try to make each see the other's point of view. You also tell other relatives what's going on so they don't get involved.

    d. receive frantic phone calls from both your mother and sister. After listening to the story, you point out the breakdown in communication and suggest they patch it up with each other.

    e. find yourself blamed for the animosity between your mother and sister.

6. While your brother is out of town on business, you accidentally stumble across your sister-in-law passionately embracing another man at the local shopping mall's parking garage. She does not see you. You . . .

    a. give her time to get home, then confront her, and threaten to tell your brother.

    b. walk away and make no mention of the incident, since, after all, there may be a simple explanation.

    c. go home and call your mother and other brother and ask for advice on how to handle the situation.

    d. try to spend more time with your brother and sister-in-law to determine if you can detect marital turmoil. At some point, you mention to your sister-in-law that you were at the shopping mall that day and see what develops.

    e. feel it serves your brother right, he's so cold. You file the information away for future use.

7. You've just moved into a new home that took your life's savings. To celebrate, you invite the entire family, which includes several very young children. During the party, one of the two-year-olds runs a red magic marker up and down your new beige loveseat. You . . .

    a. go crazy! You point out the parents' lack of supervision and demand payment for the cost of reupholstering the loveseat.

    b. wouldn't have invited the whole family over at the same time in the first place. You're not nuts!

    c. through clenched teeth, accept the parents' apologies and their promise to make restitution. Then, the next day, pass the word through the grapevine to exclude the offenders from future gatherings until they gain control of their child.

    d. minimize the damage and work out a reasonable settlement while choking back your tears.

    e. swallow hard and absorb the loss. After all, it was your fault for not childproofing the house.

8. Your divorced brother, single parent to two young children, is in financial trouble again. Various members of the family, including you,

have bailed him out before over a five-year period, but he keeps coming back for more. He pleads with you for help. You . . .

a. agree to help him but set down rules he must follow both financially and personally to set his life in order.
b. tell him you'd love to help him out again but just can't—you're short of cash yourself. Tell him to let you know, though, how he works it out.
c. decide to lend him the money needed, but make sure everyone else in the family knows you've done your part.
d. examine his financial needs, offer to lend him part of the necessary funds, and then put him in touch with a social service agency that assists people in need of financial guidance.
e. say "Hell, no!" You've already helped out more than anyone's helped you. Tell him to go ask Mother.

Part Two: Attitudes

1. You are standing in a grocery check-out line. The clerk is very new and slow. You . . .
   a. are very agitated and offer suggestions on how to use the cash register and bag groceries properly.
   b. begin to joke with the other customers in line to relieve the tension.
   c. turn to those nearest you and exchange disparaging comments.
   d. empathize with the clerk about how tough being new is.
   e. feel sorry for the clerk but do nothing.
2. When facing an unfamiliar social situation, you . . .
   a. plunge in confidently. After all, what's not to like?
   b. view the event as an opportunity to make new connections.
   c. become uptight and generally hang back until someone else makes friendly overtures.
   d. are nervous and proceed slowly, gradually engaging a few people in conversation.
   e. are scared stiff but try to make yourself useful so people will like you.
3. You view getting older as . . .
   a. an opportunity to exercise your judgment without having to explain your actions.
   b. a death knell.
   c. a time to surround yourself with loved ones.

d. a gateway to freedom from responsibility.

e. a peaceful plateau, but you doubt you'll make it.

4. If you are stuck at home with a long illness, you . . .

a. keep track of all those who did not help you, for future reference.

b. feel extremely sorry for yourself and begin to get frantic.

c. spend a lot of time on the telephone maintaining outside contact.

d. welcome the solitude but make a special mental note to return kindnesses done for you.

e. feel depressed because you probably did something to deserve feeling so lousy for so long.

5. You view your whole family as . . .

a. the spokes of a wheel with you at the center to keep it balanced.

b. a place to ground yourself for a while before moving on.

c. a network of people whom you try to bring closer together.

d. groups of individuals in a constant state of struggle and change.

e. a group of people whose expectations you are constantly trying to live up to and very often failing.

TO SCORE: Add up your letter totals. You will probably find that you have more of one than any other letter. Here is what those letter totals mean.

Mostly A's. You are one aggressive person. The positive aspect of this personality is that you would probably be a huge success at the helm of U.S. Steel. Family members, however, may view you as a Dictator, the classic example of the relative who gives ulcers rather than gets them. Because you are competent, you are convinced that your way is the right way and can't understand why others don't always agree, but accept this because you learned early how to make other dance to your tune—most of the time!

Mostly B's. Others in the family may envy the fact that you don't have to put up with all the emotional garbage that is afloat in family relationships, Butterfly. Your tendency is simply to fly away! You certainly don't want to be embroiled in anyone else's problems. You don't mind hanging around for the fun occasions but find family arguments so unproductive. Besides which, they cramp your carefree style. You do tend to drive others crazy with your unreliability, however. They just don't realize how anxious you really are behind that clown mask.

Mostly C's. You should be publishing your own newspaper because you truly have the knack for keeping the news flowing in many different directions at once, Pot-Stirrer, you busy thing! Constantly stirring away in the pot, you delight in watching the action even if you have to help it along. You are probably the best-informed family member, because you make it your business to be involved.

Mostly D's. You are often viewed as the sane one of the family. The cool one. The Diplomat. The one to whom others turn for guidance, whether you want them to or not. You have a knack for making others feel good about themselves, but the constant call to arms may cause you stress. You don't really want to say no to a call, though, do you? After all, there is a certain prestige and satisfaction invested in the position. If only you could duck those hysterical, late-night phone calls, without feeling guilty.

Mostly E's. Poor thing, you get blamed for everything, don't you, Scape-goat? From the time you can remember, you have been in trouble, even when the situation was only remotely connected to you. Always vigilant about sensing changing moods, you battle with trying to do the "right" thing by just giving up, since you have been taught to have a low opinion of yourself. If you could just break out of your victim's bonds, the rest of the family would be surprised at just how strong you are.

There you have them: the Dictator, the Butterfly, the Pot-Stirrer, the Diplomat, and the Scapegoat. All those relatives you know and love so well. These roles are by no means static, and people can take on more than one depending upon the situation.

Labeling personalities and dealing with them on a regular basis while maintaining your sanity is another story. For this reason, prior to any discussion of the causes of family conflicts and the building of bridges across those troubled waters, we will examine each of the personality roles in depth.

2

All Hail
the Dictator

Look for the happiest, most energized person in an extended-family gathering, and very often you will find the Dictator doing what Dictators do best—anything he or she wants to! Control is the name of the game for this active relative, who sees every family situation as an opportunity to exercise power. The old adage "A man's home is his castle" was written for this character who is likely to boil you in oil verbally if you displease him.

Kenneth spent most of his life building a successful restaurant business. His ebullient personality, dark good looks, and hard work not only drew enthusiastic patrons to his establishment but also carried him through difficult economic times and industry fluctuations. At home, however, that public affability was transformed into an egomania that permeated every aspect of his family's life.

As his five children grew, he determined their schools, clothes, friends, and activities. When his wife disagreed, Kenneth would rage until he felt his control was unquestioned. No child's grade or achievement was "good enough" for him, and he relentlessly pushed his children and compared their small achievements to his own (idealized in many cases). He had to approve his children's choice of mates, and even the names of his grandchildren. Now retired, he revels in manipulating his children's—and even his grandchildren's—activities.

"And the thing is, we let him do it," says one of his sons. "Here I am, a forty-three-year-old banker, responsible for millions of dollars and a staff of employees, and I'm like a ten-year-old child when I'm around him—still trying to please him, and making sure that my family pleases him."

If you plan to play board games with the Dictator, you had better make sure that he picks the game and that you aren't partial to observing the rules, because if he's losing, he'll probably change them.

"I can't stand playing games when the whole family gets together, but it's a Sunday after-dinner tradition," sighs Sandy, a thirty-four-year-old mother of two. "First we have dinner, then Dad drags out anything from Monopoly or Risk to one of those psychological games like Scruples. It always winds up in a fight. And when he discovered Trivial Pursuit—well, even if we drag out all the reference books and show him he's wrong on a particular answer, he'll argue that the reference material is faulty! We try to teach our boys that good sportsmanship is more important than winning, but they get a different message from their grandpa, whom they adore, by the way. I keep hoping each time that it will be different, but I guess I'm a jerk for believing that it might be."

Dictators are usually at the center of activity, and if, by chance, attention shifts, they are masterminds at creating diversions both good and bad that will, once again, place them at the epicenter. Dictators come in all shapes, sizes, colors, socio-economic levels, and genders. And ones like Crazy Catherine take control to its ultimate conclusion.

"She gathered all of the family members around her because she said she was dying," recalls a granddaughter. "She then proceeded to go around the room, recounting old hurts—some of them stretching back to childhood. She told each one of us what she thought of us, our lifestyles, and our families, and when half the room was in tears and the other half ready to strangle her, she died. Right then and there!"

WHO DIED AND
LEFT THEM BOSS?

Most family members seem to have a basic belief that the Dictator, like Frankenstein's monster, was made from the body parts of several people and infused with the life force of a lightening bolt that ricocheted off a satellite dish into hell and back.

The truth is much more mundane. Very often, Dictators are the firstborn of their families and learned the tricks of the trade at the knee of their own family's Dictator. A family legacy, you might say. Unlike the other characters in the family, the Dictator type is almost exclusively a parent or a sibling who was cast in the parental role upon a parent's death. While ethnic backgrounds sometimes play a role in the development of this type of personality (see chapter 20), Dictator Jr. takes this role model to heart by observing the apparent power and homage afforded Dictator Sr. According to family therapists Dr. Melodie Moorehead, Dr. Joan Di-Gregorio, and Dr. Richard Garvine of Ft. Lauderdale, Florida, this power is just one of several myths surrounding the Dictator. Their association, which sees clients with problems ranging from abuse and AIDS to separation disorders, is headquartered in the sunny land of palm trees and balmy breezes where many Dictators go to retire and orchestrate their families from afar.

"While the Dictator can be either male or female, we typically see that the Dictator is often the father who selects a passive spouse," says Moorehead. "The weak person is often attracted to the dominant personality in an attempt at equilibrium. The firstborn also makes an attempt at equilibrium, but finds him- or herself growing up in an environment that affords very little power, because the Dictator has it all. Therefore, in order to survive, the child identifies with the aggressor and learns to be a mini-Dictator."

While the child must remain subservient in his father's house, he becomes a full-blown Dictator in his own right because that is the only way he has observed that one can exercise power. But that power is a myth, and the Dictator is really a scared kid.

Children all pass through the "terrible twos" on their road to healthy development. Think back to that stage when the toddler first attempted to control his environment. There is a story about my younger sister Valerie that has become a family joke. When Val was two, she threw a yelling, screaming, kicking temper tantrum when she could not get her way. Stomping out of the room, she went to hers and began kicking her stuffed animals out of her path. She soon found herself facing the opposite wall of the room and finally, in a rage, screamed "Move wall!" Of course, the wall did not move and Val kicked it too. As you can imagine, she learned a valuable lesson.

Unfortunately, Dictators haven't met their "walls." They made the leap from being a two-year-old kicking stuffed animals out of the way to, as an adult, kicking people out of the way in order to maintain some control. But that control lasts only as long as those around them allow themselves to be kicked.

While the Bully Dictator is the most common, there is another type that is just as exasperating. This is the Martyr Dictator, whose silken bonds are in some ways more difficult to break.

Peg's mother-in-law, Jean, is in a wheelchair. A victim of polio in her youth, she nevertheless married and had three children. Family events center around Jean's desires to such a point that Peg feels completely displaced.

"She uses that wheelchair like a club," says Peg, a slender black woman with closely cropped hair and stylish clothes. "Her three children all went into the professions she selected for them, because she would say 'I want to die easy knowing you are trying to make your mama happy.' At family dinners, she'll sit there like a mouse and order people around in this little, tinny voice, and then half giggle and say, 'I'm handicapped, you know.' Handicapped—baloney! Her children are the handicapped ones. I know I must sound mean, but it makes me crazy to see everyone in the family breaking their backs and shifting priorities (we even had to come home early from our first vacation in three years because she decided to schedule a special retirement party) to please Mama who will probably live to bury the rest of us!"

In their book *Invisible Loyalties*, authors Dr. Ivan Boszormenyi-Nagy and Geraldine Spark say that the Martyr Dictator controls offspring with guilt. "Martyrlike parents can produce in their child an enduring longing, combined with bitter resentment, guilt-laden obligations, and a highly developed capacity for manipulating others' guilt."

Poor Dictator. They have never learned that they could be loved and treated as equals and have more power than they ever imagined in a healthy relationship. "Ha! Easy for me to say," you shrug. "What am I supposed to do, feel *sorry* for the person who is driving me up the wall with their demands?"

Well, there is a reason Dictators live happily ever after while the rest of us rush for the Mylanta. We let them.

WHY DO THEY GET AWAY WITH IT?

In traveling across the country and speaking with people about their family members, I asked those complaining about Dictator personalities, "Why do you let them get away with it?" The response was overwhelmingly the same. A shrug of the shoulders and a sad, "What can I do? That's just the way he [she] is."

This perpetuates both the myth and the Dictator. It's acceptable to rage and throw a temper tantrum to get one's way because that's just the way it is. That's baloney.

Marilyn is a fifty-two-year-old widow whose day centers around cleaning her mother's house, taking her mother to the doctor or shopping, and cooking for her mother and her mother's friends. If Marilyn makes an infrequent date with a friend to go to a movie, her mother may throw a house-shaking tantrum, reminding Marilyn of years of sacrifice for her children until Marilyn, beaten and guilty, capitulates and cancels the date.

Robert's family is generally viewed as one of those Candy Apple families. People who have known them for years marvel at how both children, now in their teens, still spring to attention when Robert points his finger, just as they did when they were small. What Robert doesn't know—yet—is that his son is on drugs and his daughter is a borderline anorexic.

Mark is a former marine sergeant. He has always used physical punishment with his family members. Now in his late fifties, he still thinks nothing of reaching out and roughing up one of his grown sons if they do something to displease him.

"When you have the forty-three-year-old banker or the fifty-two-year-old woman who are turning their own lives upside down still trying to please Mommy or Daddy and feel some self-worth, that's a sure sign that individuation did not take place in the family," says Dr. Moorehead. "Dysfunction occurred during maturing years and if those grown, adult children continue to operate in that system, they feed that system and keep the Dictator going."

One of the myths under which the Dictator operates is one that I call the *myth of the hourglass*. Dictators view the family as a closed system, such as an hourglass, with the grains of sand representing particles of power. The object, for them, is to retain all of the power by turning the family upside down so all the particles of power stay in the Dictator's lap. If, by chance, the hourglass is flipped over and particles stray, the Dictator firmly flips the glass again.

What Dictators don't seem to realize is that the family is not a closed system and that power is unlimited. Just as working out in a gym to develop pectoral muscles is not draining strength away from your legs but increasing the total strength of your entire body, a family member gaining strength of personality and identity does not drain strength from the whole. On the contrary, he or she increases the strength and power of the entire family. The insecure Dictator, however, sees this only as a threat—a threat of loss of power—and that scares the Dictator silly.

Robert, mentioned earlier, still treats his teenage children as if they were toddlers. He cannot bring himself to realize that his role as a parent has changed from all-powerful, do-everything Dad to strong guide, as his children reached an age when they needed to test their own individuality. So his kids have learned to play the game. They still want to please Dad on the surface, but have found other outlets to gain some measure of control over their lives. Unfortunately, they have chosen negative outlets.

So now we have a little understanding of what makes Dictators tick, but that doesn't solve the problem of how to cope with them without losing our own self-esteem and sanity. Take heart—it *can* be done, but it requires tremendous motivation and consistency on our part.

RETRAINING THE DICTATOR

Nearly everyone has a "bully" story in his or her childhood bank of memories. Billy the Bully was the terror of my son's preschool. Larger than most kids, Billy commanded the playground like a Nazi field marshal, dispensing kicks, derogatory barbs, or favors at his whim. My son Chris, on the small side, came in for his share of grief until one day when he decided to draw the line. My husband and I had taken a trip to Hawaii and brought Chris a special T-shirt, which he proudly wore to school. During the course of the day, Billy taunted Chris about the shirt and finally decided to twist it off his back. The teacher, in relaying the story to me later, said that suddenly she could see something snap in Chris's eyes as he drew himself up to his full forty-inch height, swung his arm around, and punched Billy square in the nose. There was blood and punching initially, but Billy left Chris alone after that. He had given Billy a boundary.

Dictators are like Billy the Bully—insecure and used to flexing their muscles and getting their way. It is easy to say that you just have to stand up to them. (No, I'm not advocating punching Dad in the nose!) But we all know that family relationships, particularly those with parents, have more complexities and involve more guilt and long-term patterns of behavior than one with the playground bully. True, but the bottom line is the same: In order to retrain the Dictator, you must retrain yourself to give him or her a boundary.

When we were children, we depended upon our parents for survival. We needed food, clothing, and shelter as well as approval. Children want to please their parents, and that is commendable. But take a look at yourself now. Do you still depend upon your parents for food, clothing, and shelter—in short, survival? Chances are, you don't. In fact, aside from the invisible bonds of relationship, you really don't need them anymore for survival. What's the worst that can happen if you just say no? Somebody will get mad at you? So what? Will it alter the course of your life? Or will you simply feel guilty because you are unused to being your own person?

Retraining the Dictator means establishing priorities in your life and saying no when necessary. I won't kid you. Sometimes, initially, there will be emotional bloodshed.

Bill's parents had a summer cottage that they expected all four of their grown children and their families to visit each summer. Other relatives would float in and out and invariably sibling rivalries would surface and arguments would break out. Bill and his family attended these summer gatherings for years, despite the fact that no one except Bill's father looked forward to them. Finally Bill and his wife decided to take the kids on a cross-country trip instead of the annual family gathering. "You would have thought I was betraying the family heritage," says Bill, a deeply tanned and athletic high school coach. "My father went crazy. He told me that he lived for the summers when we all got together and I would be the only one not there this year. My sister got into the act and told me that Dad doesn't have many years left and if he got a heart attack this summer, it would be my fault. I mean, you wouldn't believe the crisis this caused—all because I just couldn't take the bickering and bullying anymore.

"Well, we went on our cross-country trip and had a ball. My wife and I and our two children haven't been this close in years. I was the outcast in my extended family for a few months—my father wouldn't speak to me on the telephone and my mother kept telling me that he was heartbroken. But along came Thanksgiving and we all got together again and you know what? Everything went on as usual—with one difference. My father actually asked my opinion on a couple of matters. This may sound crazy to you, but he's never asked my opinion, ever. Now I find it easier to exert a little more of my personality and independence without feeling the guilt I had always felt if I went against my father. It may have taken me thirty-eight years, but I feel as though I've finally grown up."

That growing-up process is tough with a Dictator in the house, because his or her opinions and decisions influence everything, including the self-esteem of the other family members. But that is the second step in dealing with a Dictator: Realize that no one can take your self-esteem away from you. The only power anyone can have over you is the power you give them.

In dealing with family members, be they the Dictator or anyone else, someone is usually jockeying for this ever-elusive and much-desired power. I would suggest that we begin thinking in terms of *strength*, which comes from within, rather than *power*, which is mostly fantasized, both by the authority figure and by those who suffer under him.

Abigale was the Dictator in her family. She was verbally abusive of her husband and children on a regular basis. When she emotionally devastated one of her daughters, her husband would follow behind, making excuses for her and generally trying to smooth things over . . . until her husband died of a ruptured ulcer.

"Suddenly Dad wasn't there to clean up Mom's emotional shotgun blasts," says one daughter. "I remember shortly after Dad died, Mom went on a rampage with me over not rushing over to help her clean out some papers when she decided she wanted it done. She called me all kinds of names and told me never to bother calling her again, because I was nothing but a fair-weather daughter. Well, in the past, Dad would apologize for her and I would feel guilty and think that if I was a good daughter I'd do what she wanted. But this time it was different. Maybe it was because of all the stress of Dad's death, but I thought, Enough is enough. I'll do exactly what she said.

"I didn't call her—just as she had requested. I was told by other relatives that she called all of them and told them how rotten and selfish I was. This went on for three months. I held my ground. Finally, out of the blue one day, she called as if nothing had happened. Then about two months later, she made a casual reference to that time as 'our little spat' and that's been it. I don't know how long it will last, but for the first time in years, she hasn't called me names or hung up on me if we disagree over something."

Many people continually give in to the Dictator, hoping that they will be loved more, accepted, and favored. They continually set themselves up for disappointment because the Dictator, as I have said above, is afraid of change, loss of power, and loss of love. In order to retrain the Dictator, we must reassure him or her that we love them and that our "rebel stand" has nothing to do with rejecting him or her personally.

The Dictator thrives on myths: the hourglass myth, the myth that their approval is needed for our survival, and the myth that they have real power over us and our self-esteem. Our task, in dealing with them and eventually building a strong bridge to them, is to decide whether we want to continue operating with them from the position of victim or the position of strength.

3

The Pot-Stirrer's
Tempest

Family Pot-Stirrers could have great careers going if only they would channel their energies into professional reporting endeavors. Pot-Stirrers love to be at the center of the action as the reporter or catalyst, not the focus. If there is little in the way of family rumblings, the Pot-Stirrer will doggedly pursue family members by telephone or visit, playing the devil's advocate and then rushing to disseminate the information.

When Jennifer was a senior in college, her father died. After graduation, Jennifer married her college sweetheart and moved more than a thousand miles away from home. A year later, Jennifer's mother, who had remained in her small midwestern hometown, announced her intentions to marry Jennifer's high school boyfriend, Brad, who was seventeen years younger than she. Jennifer was shocked.

Entering into this explosive situation was Jennifer's older sister Cassie. Cassie, who had never gotten along with their mother and was jealous of Jennifer's relationship with her, found herself in the powerful and entertaining position of being friends, apparently, with both Brad and Jennifer. She seduced both into trusting her and dropped tidbits of information that caused each to rail against the other, planted half-truths, and told outright lies that critically damaged the relationship between Jennifer and her mother.

It was like a soap opera as Cassie carried "the latest" news to other shocked and gossiping family members, carefully chronicling verbal assaults and engineering subversive actions. The highlight of her pot-stirring occurred on the eve of her mother's wedding. Having snooped and discovered some apparently forgotten photo albums, she had come across a high school photograph of Jennifer and Brad clutching in a passionate embrace. Cassie placed the photo in her mother's packed suitcase so she would find it on the honeymoon. It took more than five years and tremendous feats of bridge-building communication between Jennifer, her mother, and Brad before the culprit and the extent of her pot-stirring were revealed.

Pot-Stirrers firmly believe that knowledge is power. They are desperate for power but don't have the position within the family hierarchy to grab it as aggressively as the Dictator does. And while the underlying motivation for the Dictator is anxiety and insecurity, the underlying emotion of the friendly Pot-Stirrer is anger. Now this may come as a surprise as you think fondly of your own Pot-Stirring members—You mean Aunt Agatha, you think, with her chatty, outgoing, *helpful* ways is really angry? Why, she serves an important function in the family—she really keeps everyone going! Of course, now that you mention it, Aunt Agatha has been known to pass along supposedly confidential information, and she does seem to be involved in every family hullabaloo—but usually as a communicator. Well, she *did* exaggerate Uncle Bill's relationship with his secretary when his wife was in the hospital, and cousin Janice is still angry over the time Aunt Agatha told her that cousin Melanie was angling to get Grandma's handmade lace tablecloths and the silver candlesticks that belonged to her great-grandmother . . . but still . . . Aunt Agatha is so good at talking to everyone and "keeping the family together."

Believe it! There's a certain poetry in being a Pot-Stirrer. William Shakespeare immortalized the image in his play *Macbeth* with the three witches feverishly stirring the pot while intoning "Double, double, toil and trouble; / Fire burn, and cauldron bubble." Against the backdrop of their predictions, Macbeth changes from a man of strong though imperfect moral sense to a man who will stop at nothing to get and keep what he wants.

Although "eye of newt" and "scale of dragon" are no longer in vogue, the three witches have nothing on modern family Pot-Stirrers who ply their trade under the guise of being everyone's friend. Therein lies the myth of the Pot-Stirrer: The Pot-Stirrer is just being helpful. And while their communications may not inspire murder, family relationships can be fractured or even severed if the Pot-Stirrer is not identified.

Since the job of matriarch or patriarch in the family is taken, the Pot-Stirrer is usually (but not always) a sibling. Some unlucky families have two Pot-Stirrers, with a generation skipped in between. In such a situation all bases are covered. Operating under the tenet of "loyalty to family," the Pot-Stirrer will make the rounds, ingratiating her- or himself, encouraging confidences and passing them on.

"I know my brother is a Pot-Stirrer, but it's hard to resist talking with him," says Carlee, a professional woman in her thirties. "I'm so busy that I often feel remote from the family and Don seems to know just when to call. He has caused some problems for me in the past, but I don't think he means to do it and it's nice to know that somebody in the family cares."

How Pot-Stirrers View Themselves

"Yes, I'm the Pot-Stirrer in my family, I admit it," giggles Natasha. A vibrant mother of two, she is unusual in her Cuban refugee family in that she stays at home full-time while the other women in her family work outside the home. "I feel as though I am the only one who has the courage to address problems and see that something gets done," she said. "For example, my brother was having money problems. He is a very proud man and didn't want our father to know because our father has worked very hard since coming from Cuba. Our *padre* feels that anyone can make it in the United States. Well, my brother is not very lucky. So what are we going to do about it? Why should my brother and his wife and *niños* eat beans and rice when my father has plenty of money. We are *familia* after all, not strangers!

"So, I asked my sister's opinion. She, as usual, was too busy to be involved and she said to do nothing. My husband said to do nothing. But I couldn't do nothing. I went to my father and told him the situation and I'm glad I did. He loaned my brother some money. Of course, it was a surprise to him that my brother was having problems. My father thinks my brother is perfect."

This Pot-Stirrer sees herself as the bastion of family loyalty and, like most Pot-Stirrers, will question the actions of other family members in terms of their loyalty to the family as a whole. They rarely, if ever, see themselves in a negative light. And they will rarely, if ever, admit that the "supposed to's" of family life that have disappointed them are the cause of their anger and jealousy, and the motivation for their stirring up the emotions of other family members. In fact, they will loudly proclaim themselves to be the only people in their families who believe in honesty. This just perpetuates the "helpfulness" myth.

While most family members will proudly announce their character roles, Pot-Stirrers often view themselves as anything but what they are. If they do admit it, they will only admit that they might be erroneously perceived as Pot-Stirrers by others.

"I guess I could be called a Pot-Stirrer," says Jackie, "but I prefer to think of myself as the Communicator of the family. No one in this family talks to the others—we are so spread out across the country. In fact, only three of us live in the same general area. If I didn't pass along information, who would?"

Joyce says that both she and her husband are Pot-Stirrers. "We alternate in this role. Sometimes I instigate talking or doing something about a problem; sometimes he does. But I see myself as the hub of the family."

Of the hundreds of people I interviewed for this book, only six admitted to being Pot-Stirrers, although I was often offered "Communicator" as an alternative. A significant difference between true Communicators and Pot-Stirrers, however, is the effect their information has on their listeners. After talking with a Communicator, the listener usually feels better and more fully informed. After talking with a Pot-Stirrer, the listener usually feels more informed but worse off in some way. It is a subtle difference, but subtlety is one of the attributes that makes a family Pot-Stirrer so effective.

HOW THEY DO WHAT THEY DO

The seductive voice pours soothingly through the telephone line. "I know you're having trouble with so-and-so. I can't believe this is happening to you, of all people. Why don't you tell me about it?" What a wonderful opening line! Someone is actually interested. Someone cares about my side of the story. Someone is actually taking the time to ask my opinion. Why shouldn't I open up and really let them know how I feel?

Why not, indeed. If the person calling you is the relative with whom you are having a disagreement—great. Let it all out. But if the person on the other end of the line is just fishing for information—look out. You are the tuna about to be reeled aboard and hung out for the rest of the family to see!

Pot-Stirrers are successful because they know which buttons to push to make you and everyone else crazy. They think of themselves as providing a service, but they are highly manipulative and use the role as an outlet for their own hostilities. Why else would they go out of their way to stir up the anger and emotions of other family members, thereby raising the overall anxiety level until, very often, a blow-up is inevitable. Like the treacherous currents that swirl below the surface of the water, the Pot-Stirrer's stirring is often invisibly separating family members.

Take the case of Darlene and Pat. Pat and her mother were having an argument. In fact, the argument had developed to the point where the pair were not speaking to each other. Enter Darlene, who usually did not get along with mother and was secretly jealous of Pat, the "good one" of the family. Darlene called her mother to get her side of the story, then carried the hostilities to Pat under the guise of being on her side. Not content to let it rest there, Darlene decided that she had not been in communication with other extended family members for a long time, so she called "just to say hi" and "by the way, did you hear what's happening between Mother and Pat?" Pretty soon, relatives from other states were lining up behind either Pat or her mother, and the argument was blown out of proportion.

The late Dr. Virginia Satir was a world-famous family therapist who devised a set of terms for communication behaviors. Using the Satir modes in her book *The Gentle Art of Verbal Self-Defense,* author Suzette Haden Elgin describes one form of communicator as the Leveler. This is the person who appears to be completely honest and on the level. "But" says Elgin, "a phony Leveler is more dangerous than all the other categories combined, and very hard to spot." A Pot-Stirrer is a phony Leveler. You think you are speaking to someone who is up-front and honestly interested. What you don't see are their hidden agendas.

Another reason Pot-Stirrers are successful is that they count upon the lack of communication among other family members. Since they become the source of information—or misinformation—they are in control and wield power. In both Darlene's and Cassie's situations (at the beginning of this chapter), the principal players in the drama were not on good terms with each other. In addition, other family members were not in daily contact and could not make accurate judgments as to the validity of the Pot-Stirrers' information. Therefore, the information was believed wholeheartedly.

Besides, when it comes right down to it, people love to gossip about each other, especially in families. But beware: The one who carries gossip *to* you will also gossip *about* you. No one in the family is sacred! No one.

LIMITING THE POT-STIRRER'S POWERS

Studies done by faculty at the State University of New York at Buffalo on caucuses show that there is far more criticism of an opponent's behavior and more character assassination when researchers meet with each side separately in a dispute than when both aggrieved parties meet face-to-face.

It doesn't take a study of the psychological findings to bear that out in your family. Of course, Aunt Aggie is going to say nasty things about your mother and vice versa, if someone is there to provide the attentive, eager, and drooling audience. Take away the audience and what happens? Maybe Mom and Aunt Aggie will confront each other and work out their dispute.

How do we stop the Pot-Stirrer from fanning the flames? As with retraining the Dictator, it will take some risk and strength on your part. First of all, you have to identify the Pot-Stirrer in any given situation. Most of the time, it will be one particular personality in the family, though as I have said above, these roles are fluid and someone can assume the role of Pot-Stirrer at a moment's notice.

Joan Howard, a family therapist in Thousand Oaks, California, and former president of the Stepfamilies Association of America, points out that awareness of the pot-stirring modus operandi is half the battle in protecting yourself against being sucked into the game.

"Pot-Stirrers operate out of a need to feel involved, important, and alive, but people can be damn toxic sometimes and we have a responsibility as adults to protect ourselves from toxic people," says Howard. "It doesn't mean we have to club them over the head—just limit our involvement with them. Limit the information you share with them; remember it can come back to haunt you. Also, if you recognize the role the Pot-Stirrer is playing, you can control yourself from reacting angrily to the information that's passed on to you."

So what do you say when your mom calls with a juicy bit of news that she got from Aunt Bertha? Try to break the gossip chain, but do it lovingly. Try saying, "Mom, you know our family is important to me and I really don't think this is very healthy for the family. When Aunt Bertha gives you information like this, I wish you'd just say that you don't want to hear about it. And Mom, I really don't want to hear about it either."

But what happens then, you wonder, when Mom shoots back, in a hurt voice, "What's the matter with you? This is important. Don't you care about the family?"

You have not only just been given the loyalty test, you've been put on the line. What do you say? Dr. Melodie Moorehead suggests holding a discussion at this point. You have to consider whether talking about the particular issue is really going to produce anything productive for the person involved. After all, sometimes your help *is* needed. But if the answer is no, then this is just conversation and the Pot-Stirrer is deriving some satisfaction out of spinning the conversational wheel—time to act from a position of strength, rather than that of a victim. "I know how you feel about this, but I'd rather stay out of the situation and leave it to those involved to solve," you say firmly. Be prepared for the chilly silence that follows, but it's worth taking the risk for peace of mind and maintenance of your sanity.

If the Pot-Stirrer in your family has an abundance of time on his or her hands (and Pot-Stirrers usually do have more time than others), try to rechannel their energies. Suggest a family newsletter or a reunion that the Pot-Stirrer might spearhead.

And if you are the object of a Pot-Stirrer's frantic helpfulness, be firm in deflecting his or her efforts at serving as a go-between. Too often, however, the objects of the Pot-Stirrer's attention aren't even aware of the activity on their behalf. The stronger the bridges of communication we build to other family members, however, the less likelihood of falling into the Pot-Stirrer's tempestuous current.

4

The Butterfly's
Flutter

The Butterfly, whether single or married, is sometimes considered the "black sheep" of the family. This phantom relative promises everything but rarely delivers. The Pied Piper of Hamelin could have had no more charisma than the Butterfly, seducing listeners with a magical charm. Although this person is usually fascinating and wears a Day-Glo T-shirt with the capital letters F U N emblazoned on the front and back, parents and siblings gnash their teeth over the Butterfly's seeming lack of compassion and responsibility.

Marcus was always considered special by his mother. He looked like beloved Uncle Henry and, while still an infant, a lung ailment almost cost him his life. Naturally, as he was growing up, he couldn't be saddled with the same responsibilities as his two sisters and brother because he was "delicate." When he got into the usual young boy's mischief, his pleading "Uncle Henry eyes" would normally be enough to melt his mother's resolve and grease the way for his escape.

Is it any wonder that years later, Marcus still could rarely be counted upon in times of family need? Flitting from one endeavor to another, he fancied himself an adventurer—something not viewed favorably by his two ex-wives. Talented, charming, and witty, he was a desired party guest and interesting acquaintance—someone to be enjoyed but not someone to depend upon.

When his father needed critical cancer surgery, Marcus was vacationing in the South Pacific and "couldn't get away," but his postcards said "Let me know what happens." During holidays, family gatherings, financial strains, or when his sister's family was plunged into chaos after an automobile accident, Marcus was elsewhere. When he did grace the family with his presence, he'd capture the hearts of his nieces and nephews, promising trips and gifts before he flew off once again in search of fun. Of course, the trips and gifts rarely materialized. Family members learned to tolerate Marcus's cavalier attitudes until his mother's death. Despite the fact that he was in town, Marcus avoided the wake and all his relatives. He did not appear until the actual burial ceremony at the cemetery. No one has spoken to him since.

The Butterfly, who is usually a sibling, or sometimes a divorced parent (often referred to as either a "good time Charlie" or simply "that irresponsible S.O.B.") was trained early in his or her role by Mom or Dad. For some reason, that child was designated as "special." Like Marcus, he or she could resemble a favorite relative or have required special handling because of an illness.

Until the time Lisa was seven years old, she spent more time in hospitals than she did in school. Born with congenital heart defects, she required several operations. Although the operations were successful and doctors assured her parents that Lisa could lead a normal life, she was treated like a princess by both parents. Little, if anything, was required of her in terms of normal family responsibilities, other than a big smile. Lisa learned that a smile was her key to acceptance. Now an adult, Lisa drives her two siblings crazy with her flaky approach to life and lack of commitment.

Lisa may be flaky, but Elton is described by his sister Corey as "oblivious" to anything going on in the family. Elton is ten years younger than his sister, the son of their widowed mother and her second husband. "I'm the responsible one," says Corey. "I'm the one they call when they need help or Mom's lonely or Aunt Beth needs to be driven to the doctor. Elton's never around. He usually even forgets to send birthday cards—a lousy card, for chrissakes. But let him show up and—boom! The sun rises and sets where he stands. I just don't understand it."

A small number of Butterflies learned the same techniques to avoid abusive home situations. In cases of parental alcoholism or physical violence, a Butterfly may learn an escapist routine and continue it throughout adult life. (For more on this aspect, see chapter 15.)

But whether the Butterfly avoids family commitments, responsibilities, and gatherings because he or she is "flaky," "oblivious," or "chicken," the net result is the same. You go crazy and the Butterflies are happy-go-lucky . . . or are they?

* * *

ANXIETY MADE THEM DO IT!

"I was in the hospital having my third child," says Gina. "My sister was supposed to come and help take care of the other two children for a couple of days. It's easy for her because she doesn't work and doesn't have any children. As it turned out, I really did need help more than I anticipated because I wound up having a Caesarean section, then contracted an infection, and the baby was jaundiced. So there I was in the hospital, hooked up to all kinds of things, with a raging fever, upset about the baby, and my sister called to say she couldn't come, but she'd call every day to see how we were getting along.

"Can you imagine? I've had to move around a lot because of my husband's job and we don't have any family around us. I really needed her, counted on her, but she let me down—again. It really is typical. I realized I could never depend on her again after that."

Why do they let you down? Surely they know someone is depending on them. Are they just scatterbrained? Not likely. The myth in operation with the Butterflies is that they avoid responsibility because they just don't give a damn. Nothing could be further from the truth. The Butterfly cares more than you know. And although his or her inconsistency drives you nuts, the Butterfly is really more to be pitied than hated.

When you were toting garbage cans to the street . . . they were watching television. When you were babysitting, delivering newspapers, cooking for younger siblings . . . they were out playing. While you were learning to compromise over everything from clothing to television shows . . . they got their way. When you broke a vase, dented a fender, or were caught skipping school and had to take the consequences . . . they were excused.

Wait a minute, you say. So far, it sounds like *you* got the short end of the stick and *they* got off easy. Take a closer look. When you were learning responsibility, commitment, coping skills, and the consequences of your actions, they were learning avoidance.

Dr. Richard Garvin, a Ft. Lauderdale family therapist, feels that Butterflies are the least equipped members of the family to face life's tribulations, and that scares them. "They were really very cheated growing up. They never learned coping skills, how to accomplish getting their needs met. In most cases, they never had the one-to-one relationship with a parent who could help them learn healthy, flexible rules for dealing with complex life situations."

Just imagine if you were terrible at math when you were growing up. As an adult, would you gravitate toward tasks where you had to use calculus or would you avoid them? Family situations that call upon our skills in human relations represent calculus to Butterflies. They scare them silly because they have never developed the skills to survive. Therefore, they avoid them.

The Butterfly usually is not the oldest sibling, who tends to be "the responsible one." The Butterfly could be the baby or the clown, or better yet, the one who does crazy things. That way, even though they may not be considered responsible, they can prove that they have a distinctive identity. Being a Butterfly also inspires a certain amount of attention. Being a family "conversation piece" is a role filled early in life.

Doesn't your family talk about the Butterfly that way? "Tell me what little Montague is doing now!" chortles Uncle Sam. Little Montague is the one you saw on the evening news, rappelling down the side of the Eiffel Tower, or taking a militant stand for the protection of Gypsies as an endangered species, or just announcing his fifth wedding in fourteen years. Of course, little Montague may now be forty-eight years old and living under a bridge by the overpass, but he's still the talk of the family. And everyone feels so much better that *they* aren't living under the bridge by the overpass and what could you expect of Montague anyway?

Butterflies are not angry family members. In fact, it is their desperate need to be liked and accepted that contributes to what drives everyone crazy around them.

PROMISE THEM ANYTHING

Famous last words uttered by Butterflies: "Sure I'll be there early to help you set up for Mom and Dad's big dinner"; "Of course I'll call"; "Sure I'll be there early"; "I'll send it to you right away"; "Sure I'll be there."

Butterflies would never think of just saying no. It might cause an argument and they cannot cope with that. So they agree, agree, and agree. And then they avoid the situation. In his book, *Coping with Difficult People*, Dr. Robert Bramson calls this type of character a "Super-Agreeable." Super-Agreeables always tell you things that are satisfying to hear. They are difficult people precisely because they leave you believing they are in agreement with your plans, only to let you down. "The tragedy is that if Super-Agreeables were straightforward to begin with, you could put up with some minor unpleasantries, the problem could more easily be resolved, and much bad feeling could be avoided."

But how do you say to your sister or brother, "No, I am not going to be at the funeral because death scares me and I don't want to see Aunt Jillian in the coffin"? It's so much easier to say, "Sure, I'll be there," because that is what is expected and will not be questioned. Then it is just as easy to avoid the unpleasant situation and all the people involved for a long time, thereby perpetuating the myth that the Butterfly just doesn't care.

"What really drives me crazy with my brother is that he promises things to my son, who adores him, and then he doesn't come across," says Gloria. "I've tried to tell him not to make unrealistic promises about taking him fishing or buying him a radio-controlled plane, because Billy believes him and counts on him. I have learned to ignore half of what my brother says, but it hurts me to see my son disappointed over and over again."

So how do we build a bridge to this poor "puppy-dog" relative who fades in and out of our lives?

COPING MEANS EMPATHY

As with most family situations, you are not going to change the Butterfly . . . not really. But you can grow in empathy and change your behavior toward him or her.

Realize first and foremost that you cannot count on the Butterfly. No amount of laying down the law, outlining your expectations, or delivering a sermon on "supposed to's" is going to do it. What you need to do is change your expectation level for this relative, and you will be much less crazy over his or her lack of responsibility. And then give yourself a chance to grieve over the loss of the idealized brother or sister you would like to have.

You can call a Butterfly after a disappointment (and should call—they should be held accountable for their actions) and relay your feelings, but remember that this character will avoid any confrontation. If you really want an answer, you will have to make being honest less confrontational. For example, sister Peggy was supposed to attend your daughter Susan's big dance recital. She never showed. When you call her, tell her how you felt. Tell her what you needed specifically from her and then toss the ball into her court. Ask her what you should do about it in the future.

You are not responsible for a sibling's irresponsibility, nor should it color your life. Remember, the Butterfly faces many demons that, to you, are insignificant little toads.

5

━━━

Diplomats Never Sleep

A Diplomat's work is never done. Ambassadors to Third World nations carry no heavier responsibility for peacekeeping efforts than the family Diplomat. Family Diplomats are easy to spot at any gathering. They are the serious ones, the responsible ones who pick up other people's plates and glasses on the way to the kitchen.

They are the ones maniacally attempting to keep all volatile personalities at opposite ends of the rooms and their mouths full of potato salad. Their trademarks are bags under their eyes from receiving late-night phone calls from feuding relatives, and the nervous tendency to jump if someone loudly yells, "Oh yeah?"

When Aunt Lily accused Susan's mother of murdering their elderly, comatose father because she had allowed doctors to turn off the life-support systems, Susan was the only one who could serve as intermediary between feuding family factions. When her two brothers, embroiled in an age-old battle of verbal jousting, looked for a logical, fair mediator, Susan was the one they both turned to. And when her in-laws were in the process of dividing into camps over the rumor that a nephew had contracted AIDS and his family was keeping it quiet, it was Susan who got to the bottom of the rumor and allayed fears by dispensing the correct information.

The Diplomat's life is the Pot-Stirrer's in reverse. Instead of seeking out the battlefronts, the warring parties seek out the Diplomat, sweeping him or her and the immediate family into another maelstrom of family drama. Dale Carnegie must have been his family's Diplomat, because the chapter headings in his world-renowned book *How to Win Friends and Influence People* reads like a credo for family Diplomats ("If You Want to Gather Honey, Don't Kick Over the Beehive," "Do This and You'll Be Welcome Anywhere," or "Make the Fault Seem Easy to Correct" are just a few examples!).

In fact, I'll venture a guess that *you* are your family's Diplomat or at least have strong diplomatic leanings. Who else in the family would spend the time, effort, and money to purchase and read a book on how to build up and maintain your family ties without going crazy? You are the master bridge-builder who is constantly seeking out "graduate courses" in engineering those tricky relationships.

Being a family Diplomat is a noble avocation. Even the Bible says "Blessed are the peacemakers, for they shall be called the children of God." They shall also be called at any hour of the day or night, come rain, snow, or tornado to mediate and argue. They are also very likely to be the firstborn. You know the type: serious, super-responsible, always trying to please, the overachiever. The one Mom and Dad always relied upon to get the job done and get it done right. Sound like someone you know?

Politics and diplomacy come naturally to this firstborn character who has had to learn to avoid the fallout of parental explosions while growing up, and perhaps even diplomatically protect younger siblings from that fallout. In his popular *The Birth Order Book*, Dr. Kevin Leman suggests that a firstborn becomes either a Dictator personality (look at J. R. Ewing of television's "Dallas") or a Peacemaker. The Peacemaker "is the person with the hard-driving personality, is often quite proud of the way he gets things done, but he pays the price. If his body doesn't break down, relationships with his family or friends usually do."

Therein lies a significant point of difference between the Diplomat and other family roles. While the others may drive you crazy, the Diplomat is the one most likely to go crazy—much to the surprise of family members who operate under the myth that the Diplomat can handle anything for anyone. Since the Diplomat is usually perceived as "the strong one," the "calm one," the "rational one," or the "capable one," everyone is shocked when he or she develops ulcers, nervous tics, borders on a complete nervous breakdown, or pulls a real switch and runs off to Australia to live in the Outback. "What happened?" they cry. To understand what happened is to try and understand what makes a Diplomat the master juggler.

* * *

WHAT MAKES THE
DIPLOMAT RUN?

There is a communication game designed by Dr. Larry Hall and Dr. Michael Livesay of the Edward Lowe Foundation. You can either imagine this exercise or you can have the whole gang act it out. Give everyone in your extended family a small rubber ball and have them all stand in a circle. Now on the count of three, everyone should toss their ball to the one person in the family with whom they can and do communicate the best. One, two, three . . . toss. What do you have?

Chances are, you will find that one person in the family has been tossed most of the balls and is struggling to hang on to them all. That person is the family Diplomat.

While few people are willing to admit that they are Dictators or Pot-Stirrers, most who hold the Diplomat position are proud of the fact. Being the Diplomat makes you valuable, needed, and looked up to. It is a position that earns you approval—and that is something Diplomats need from their families even at the risk of missed meals, sleep, and peace of mind. Their patterns of caretaking began early in life and as adults continue to include not only their immediate families of origin but extended families and often adopted families as well. As illustrated by the ball-toss game above, one person cannot effectively handle all those balls.

"My husband is the oldest son in a large Italian family," says Jean. "There is always someone who is fighting with someone else—so much so, that it's almost comical. He was raised with a very strong sense of family and loves them, but he is constantly drawn into their battles because he is so sensible. He would never turn a family member down if he could help. Sometimes that means we take our vacations with other family members and they spend lots of time talking, fighting, and talking. He winds up exhausted instead of relaxed. The one time he tried to avoid a family argument, he felt so guilty, he wound up jumping in."

Good old guilt—that's another part of what makes the Diplomat run. Generally the Diplomat does have good communication and people skills and is confident of those abilities. Family is also of prime importance, and so is the desire for peace and harmony. When someone in the family is struggling or feuding and those skills are needed, it is easier for the Diplomat to lend those abilities already honed than force other members to develop their own.

"Yes, being a Diplomat can drive people crazy, but it's usually your spouse that goes crazy, rather than your other family members," says Bonnie. "My husband loves my family but he cringes every time the phone rings late at night, because it's usually someone with a problem for me to solve. But he should have known what he was in for the day we got married. There I was, walking down the aisle and instead of keeping my eyes on him, I was nervously watching to make sure my mother didn't go across the aisle to punch out his mother.

"Why do I do it?" Bonnie asks herself. "Because it makes me feel needed and important. I like it most of the time. Sometimes I have to admit, I'd just like to take the phone off the hook and go on vacation without letting anyone know where I am. Sometimes it does get to be too much, but I don't want to hurt anyone's feelings."

TAKING A RISK

Someone who takes on so much responsibility could hardly be called an escapist. Or could they? Carol Kurtz, a Washington, D.C., psychotherapist, sees the Diplomat as an escapist of a different sort. While the Butterfly avoids any kind of conflict by simply removing himself from the bosom of the family, the Diplomat avoids conflict by taking care of others. Focusing on the pressures and problems in a family allows the caretaker to escape from himself.

"Part of caretaking is a way to avoid being your own person," says Kurtz. "Diplomats do this because they really need others' approval for their self-esteem. They don't feel as though they are really good enough. In the hierarchy of family life, if you are the caretaker, or the Diplomat, that removes you a step. You cannot be honestly intimate with anyone, because you are very busy taking care of everyone else."

The Diplomat rarely communicates one-to-one with anyone in the family. Instead, he or she is usually a part of a triangular communication process. A and B cannot talk to each other, so they bring C into it. Diplomats may find themselves in so many triangles that they may have to check to see if their heads are pointed.

The challenge for Diplomats is to remember that they can decide how much they want to be in a relationship with extended family members. They don't have to be shackled to them just because they are related. The ideal response to a "war declaration" phone call is: "Don't pull me into this argument. It won't help resolve the problem. You need to talk to each other."

Your relatives may not be happy, but it isn't the Diplomat's job in life, contrary to the experience of years of reinforcement, to make sure all the relatives are happy. This calls for developing some emotional karate moves to deflect relatives and situations that threaten your peace and your household. When your cousin calls in the middle of your son's birthday party or just as you are walking out the door for a much-earned evening with just your spouse, don't feel guilty about telling Cousin Nell that you will call her back. If it is truly an emotional situation for her, suggest an alternative support system. It is difficult for the Diplomat, but priorities must be set.

Another coping mechanism for restyling the Diplomat is to remember that, believe it or not, the family will go on without you. The role of Diplomat was thrust upon you, and you chose to wear the mantle, but the weight of all those family squabbles can get heavy. Reassessing your priorities, teaching others a few of those interpersonal skills that come so easily to you, and shrugging off the Diplomatic cape can be a scary process, because it forces you to redefine your role in the family structure. But that is also a mechanism for growth.

The Diplomat, like the other family roles, may be the public persona. Who you really are and what you really want in the family must come from inside you. Even the strongest and most capable bridge builders need their rest in order to re-energize themselves and be productive. If you take the risk and rest every now and then, I bet those nervous tics will fade away.

6

Family Scapegoats Do It All

Family Scapegoats can be as humorous as Neil Simon's character Eugene in *Brighton Beach Memoirs*, who wails "Guess who's going to be blamed for the war in Europe?" But often, they are tragic.

The difference between a healthy family and a dysfunctional one is that in the healthy family, the system meets the needs of the individuals involved. For example, if one child has an aptitude for music and another for athletics, and the father is an attorney and the mother a writer, a healthy family would make room for all those individual interests, talents, and time requirements to the best of its ability.

In a dysfunctional family (a family that is not functioning properly), the individuals take on roles to meet the needs of the sick system. A family Scapegoat role is assigned in childhood by parents, or an older sibling with the parents' cooperation, and serves as a smoke screen for other problems that exist in the family. "If that damn daughter of mine weren't always getting into trouble, then I wouldn't be so nervous that I have to drink" might be the reasoning in a dysfunctional family. Each of the members would then revolve their activities and energies around the anticipation of Dad's drinking to excess and blaming daughter Sue as the cause. The Scapegoat is the one the rest of the family labels as "the bad guy," but he or she is usually just different in some way.

Six months after Irene was adopted, her new mother discovered that she was pregnant. Irene was a colicky baby; her new sister Lisa was not. Irene hit the terrible twos with a vengeance; Lisa was reasonably placid. By the

45

time another sister was added and the girls entered their teens, the pronounced personality differences drove their parents, who themselves were experiencing marital difficulties, to distraction. And Lisa had learned to use the differences to her advantage.

"I was labeled the troublesome one," says Irene. "I was blamed for everything from my youngest sister falling out of the tree and breaking her arm, to the back door sticking, to my mother's asthma and father's ulcers. That was my role, and stupidly, I fulfilled all of their dire predictions. I got involved with drugs and a crummy crowd. I cracked up the car and ran away from home—my mother found me hiding in a girlfriend's closet. Finally when my grandmother, whom I was always close to, died, I got the blame for that as well. It just about did me in."

The family Scapegoat is rarely the firstborn, but can be an only child, the baby of the family, or one who had the misfortune to be born during a particularly stressful time in the parents' marriage. Through no fault of their own, they are assigned the task of bearing the brunt of the family's ups and downs. For all concerned, this is much easier than having to face and deal with the problems that may range from alcoholism to marriage tensions. If everyone can focus negative attention on the Scapegoat, they can avoid facing everything else.

"I was the Scapegoat growing up in my family, and I wound up being the Scapegoat in my marriage as well," says Lee, who was raised in a small West Coast harbor town. "I was the quiet, sensitive one in a family full of aggressive leaders. My mom and sister used to criticize me all the time, saying that I wasn't good enough to be in their family. I needed glasses, which my mother wouldn't buy, because she said it would make me look more dowdy. My hair color was different and I always had a weight problem, unlike my sister and my mother who, in her day, won a lot of beauty contests at both the local and state level. But I learned that to get along with my mother, or to get any kind of attention, this was the role I had to fill. Even negative attention meant I was being noticed."

Although you would expect the Scapegoats to do their best to escape the situation at the earliest possible moment, therapists have found that Scapegoats feel they serve an important function in the family.

An Important Part of the Family System

In Biblical days, after the sacrificial goat had been offered (but not slaughtered) on the altar, the high priest would lay his hands on the goat's head and confess all of the sins of the people. Then the goat was led away into the desert or some other solitary place, bearing away the sins. The people felt better and went on with life as usual, until sins became so plentiful once more that another scapegoat was needed to absorb their evildoing.

Today's family Scapegoat isn't so much different from the Biblical predecessor. Instead of family members cleaning up their own emotional garbage, they kick it under the fence into the Scapegoat's yard and then complain that if only the Scapegoat would clean up his or her yard, it would be a nice neighborhood. It's his or her fault the place looks like a dump!

Scapegoats take it on the chin, both literally and figuratively, for everything from the car breaking down and the myriad family illnesses to items that can't be found and the crabgrass growing in thicker.

"I used to get blamed for every lost thing around our house," says Rachel. "You'd think, to hear my mother talk, that I had a black market business going, selling her stockings, scissors, books, kitchen utensils, and my dad's tools. I even got blamed for things my sister lost. For example, when it came time for my high school senior picnic, I asked Mom if I could take a bowl of potato salad and the serving spoon. She flew into a rage and said no, because my sister—who did no wrong—lost her bowl and utensils on the last picnic so, of course, I would too. This would then contribute to her going broke buying new bowls and utensils for irresponsible children!"

Dr. C. R. Snyder of the University of Kansas has studied the psychology of excuses and blaming. "Without excuses, we would be exposed and vulnerable; they protect our self-esteem," he says in a magazine interview. A man or woman who continually blames unacceptable behavior on an addiction or problem—and Scapegoat children are considered problems—finds that all future transgressions are also blamed on that problem. A change in system comes, says Snyder, only when the self-protective excuse is broken down and they are made to face the link between themselves and their actions. When that happens, the Scapegoat's supposed shortcomings fade in importance.

Chances are, if you have a Scapegoat in your family, it would help to take a good, hard look at the family system and see who is having the real problems. This is not to say that the Scapegoat is completely innocent of wrongdoing ever, but wrongdoing can vary in definition from family to family as well.

"Looking back, I realize I was the Scapegoat in my family," says Jim. "I had two sisters and I was the only son. My father's favorite speech was one I call the 'All for you' speech. Both he and my mother would remind me of how he went to work at fourteen to help support his family. Then after he and Mom had us, he gave up his dream of becoming a lawyer to work on an assembly line so we could have a better life. He never took vacations, worked at night, and saved money for our college tuitions. And he did it 'all for me.'

"The fact that he had cirrhosis of the liver from hard drinking, the fact that he and mom hadn't slept together in years, or that he was fired from his job just before he was to be vested in his pension is all my fault, because of all the years of sacrifice. And what did I do? I realized that I was very good with my hands and wanted my own carpentry business instead of going to college," says Jim. "When I finally told him what I wanted to do, he picked up a chair and tried to break it over my head. A lot of years have passed, and we see each other on holidays, but he never fails to mention that all the problems in his life were due to 'what he did for me.' "

Our family circle is the first unit from which we draw our identities and self-esteem. Children perceive their parents as larger than life and all-knowing. Therefore, says the Scapegoat, if Mom says I'm to blame, it must be right. By the time children have matured and have some outside feedback, and have perhaps realized that there is help outside the immediate family, they have absorbed the Scapegoat role so thoroughly that they agree with their parents that they are the "weak link" in the family chain.

SHEDDING THE SCAPEGOAT IMAGE

The way most Scapegoats get help—if they do get help—is quite by accident. They may be the ones dragged into a therapist's office by the scruff of the neck. "Fix him!" demands the father. "Fix her!" demands the mother. Even the siblings are chanting, "Fix him! Fix her!" and then supposedly, everything in the family will be right again.

But a curious thing happens. While the initial focus is on the child who is causing "all the problems" by acting out or with drug and alcohol abuse, the rest of the family comes under close scrutiny and the other underlying illnesses are laid bare.

That is really an ideal scenario. Sometimes, another member of the family or a compassionate outside authority figure will step in and bring the Scapegoat's downtrodden role to the attention of the parents or a mental health practitioner. Most Scapegoats will tell you, however, that they struggled into adulthood with very little support. Only through almost superhuman self-examination, therapy, and self-discipline were they able to break out of the old patterns of family life.

Irene, mentioned at the beginning of the chapter, finally sought help as an adult, joined Adult Children of Alcoholics, married, and had two children of her own.

"Two weekends ago my mother told us to come for dinner to see a distant relative," she says. "Even though I understand what went on in my family, I still always get a headache in anticipation of going back there. I always feel I don't look good enough or the kids don't look good enough. I walk in the door with apologies already on my lips.

"Anyway, it was a relatively pleasant dinner, no pun intended. Two days later, the relative called to say goodbye and told me all kinds of neat things about myself. I really needed to be reaffirmed. She was telling me all those things I knew about myself but wished someone would see. I have learned to forgive myself for being human, because we beat ourselves up pretty well."

In some dysfunctional families, the Scapegoat role is hereditary and the child of the Scapegoat is blamed and treated by the grandparents with the same disdain that was once reserved for his or her parent. Sometimes, this is what it takes for the original Scapegoat to say "Enough is enough."

"I was the Scapegoat in my family," says Lizette, now a fifty-two-year-old grandmother herself. "I took it the entire time I was growing up—my mother blaming me for things because I was really the unwanted child. A few years ago, when I saw how my mother was treating my twenty-four-year-old daughter, I realized that she had transferred that Scapegoat role onto her. No way was I going to sit by and put up with that!" she says. "My daughter had done nothing to deserve that kind of treatment. I guess I didn't either, but I had been used to it. I have just about cut off relations with my mother for now. There's a lot of guilt involved, but I couldn't bear to see this treatment passing down to another generation."

As children, we are dependent upon our parents. We need them. But as adults, we have to decide, "What do I need now?" The Scapegoat is in desperate need of family members' building strong bridges to him or her. For the Scapegoat, the bridges are more than emotional ties, they are a lifeline. Scapegoats need help in viewing their parents as people, and imperfect people at that. Scapegoats need help in setting realistic expectations of their immediate family members, as well as support in mourning the loss of their ideal family and in adopting strong surrogate family members.

Scapegoats tend to have highly developed sensitivities that have helped them survive unhealthy family situations. Fortunately, sensitivity and awareness can be turned inward and used as a means for growth, to break out of the Scapegoat mold once and for all.

Part II

The Most Common Dividers: Relationships

7

You *Do* Marry
a Family

Although those famous Kentucky feuding families, the Hatfields and the McCoys, spent the better part of fifty years intent on decimating each other with bullets, our contemporary soldiers on the family battlefield use an array of psychological weapons that deliver blows so painful that a bullet might be considered more merciful. And despite the fact that, ideally, a marriage takes place between two individuals, no couple is an island, to paraphrase John Donne. Differences in age, class, education, religion, culture, race, and even politics serve as fertile ground for miscues, misunderstandings, and outright hostilities.

Meg and Jim get along fine most of the time. It's their families that make them crazy. Jim's blue-collar parents are incensed over their attorney daughter-in-law's retaining her maiden name, heavy travel schedule, and lack of interest in domestic matters (including cooking for their son) or having children. Meg's family keeps their construction supervisor son-in-law at arm's length, barely tolerating his rough social skills, liberal political views, and lack of interest in the family business, a well-known clothing firm. It is not unusual for Meg and Jim to attend a party at her parents' home and not be introduced. Or if Meg is introduced, Jim is ignored or relegated to help serve drinks. "I sometimes feel I need to suit up in armor—name brand, of course—before even speaking to members of Meg's family," sighs Jim. "We've been married six years but the barbs just keep flying at an incredible pace, whether we're there in person or on the telephone. I'm almost through trying to make it better. Almost . . . not quite."

When Louie announced to his family that he planned to marry Cynthia, a twenty-six-year-old divorcée with a three-year-old daughter, Louie's mother waged an increasingly hysterical battle to impede the relationship. She would burst into tears if he tried to speak to her and refused to speak to Cynthia, although she had welcomed the girl and her daughter into the house when the pair were dating. Since twenty-four-year-old Louie lived at home, his mother would leave him letters on his bed, in his closet and bathroom, and prompted the family priest to call him at work to discuss the matter. She finally demanded he observe a midnight curfew. That resulted in Louie's moving in with Cynthia until their wedding six months later. After four years of marriage, Louie's mother only speaks to Cynthia when spoken to, turns a cold shoulder to Cynthia's daughter while showing affection for the twins born to Louie and Cynthia, and still cries when her son attempts to discuss the situation with her.

Gary's sister Felicia laughed when Gary told her, "Guess who's coming to dinner?" When she met Tara—tall, slender, well dressed, and black— she was speechless. "I guess Gary felt comfortable in that relationship in New York, but you're talking a small, Indiana town here," says Felicia. "They did get married and we're all trying to deal with it, but it's tough. A lot of Tara's family refused to go to the wedding, even though it was in their own hometown. I have an aunt in Oregon who began sticking pins in voodoo dolls to 'break the spell,' as she put it. You can say that color doesn't make a difference, but there's so much more to it than that. There are social issues, different perceptions and frames of reference, and even interests. I think we have all grown in some ways, but will it ever be a 'normal' relationship? I don't know."

Celebrating these differences, stretching to grow in unfamiliar ways, and the sharing of cultures *should* be what a true marriage is all about. But as Marlene, a woman who moved with her husband to Alaska to escape the bulldoglike jaws of their respective families says, "Norman Rockwell lied!" For even if the couple is a model of compromise and marital bliss, it may be difficult to cope with other family members who are not as receptive to those differences and are far from being *silent* navigators.

For the first time in years, the divorce rate in the United States is declining, and it is both fashionable and desirable to be married. Nearly 2.4 million weddings took place in 1988, according to the Department of Health and Human Services. More than merely a reflection of individual liaisons, these statistics represent the binding of millions more through the in-law relationship, a relationship that can ultimately cause the dissolution of those marriages. According to a survey by *Cosmopolitan* magazine, in-law relationships were cited as the number one problem by 25 percent of those couples seeking marital counseling, and as the secondary problem by

another 60 percent. As one woman said, "There should be some sort of premarital in-law counseling before two people get married. I had no idea what I was getting into and how closely bound my husband is to his family, although when we were dating, he used to say he wasn't very close. I'm at a point now where I'm just trying to figure out how to put a muzzle on a few of the relatives. You can talk psychology all you want but I've had the urge to strangle more than once."

Few of us, in the excitement of courtship, know what we're getting into where families are concerned. Then again, some can see the potholes in the road ahead before the wedding day.

IT STARTS WITH A WEDDING

Linda and Barry were almost the boy and girl next door. Their families shared a cabana at the beach club, and they ran in the same social circles. Linda admired Barry's stylish and flamboyant mother, and his mother told tomboyish Linda that she was her favorite. But then Linda and Barry "discovered" each other in their twenties and began dating. That's when everything changed.

"All of a sudden, she began acting jealous that I was taking over her son," says Linda, now married to Barry for eighteen years. "When Barry went to Annapolis, his mother withdrew socially and mourned the loss of her son. She went in for some stomach surgery, and I was the only one there in the waiting room for her. I brought her a big bouquet of flowers after the surgery, and when she opened her eyes and saw me, she said 'Oh, shit.' When Barry and I finally got engaged, he was afraid to tell his parents, because when his brother had announced his engagement just the month before, his mother had thrown a hysterical fit and stated she wouldn't attend any of her sons' weddings. I wish she had stuck to that. She made our engagement period hell and kept saying her son was too young to get married. He was twenty-eight! We had a very large, formal wedding, which we paid for ourselves. Her moment of glory came at the wedding rehearsal dinner. Came the moment that Barry lifted his glass and toasted me, his mother stood up, threw her champagne glass on the floor, and screamed 'Bullshit!' She ran off to the ladies room, which is where she stayed for the rest of the evening. I guess you might say that she has remained in the same frame of mind for eighteen years."

Although the bride and groom like to think that they are going to plan their wedding, the real architects of the event are the mothers, and herein lies the first source of potential conflict. Issues of separation, differences in background, and power struggles all rear their ugly heads during this very emotional and stressful period. Not only is one forced to confront tremen-dous change in the immediate family but weddings mean contact with extended-family members, coupled with the promise or threat of a whole new extended family from the other side. This is added to the already bubbling potpourri of unresolved hurts and issues in each family.

While the joining of two people should be the focus of the day, the wedding's importance is often viewed as an opportunity to display one's material success, to accept or reject relatives socially, or simply to use as a club to get one's way. One woman threatened her sister, saying that unless her entire family was invited, including her husband's family, she and her daughters would wear black to her niece's wedding (this was before black was considered fashionable at weddings). Another woman who had op-posed her son's marriage arrived at the wedding wearing her bowling league slacks and shirt, spent the entire ceremony seated by herself weeping con-spicuously, and then trotted off to her bowling match after the church service, bypassing the reception.

Some parents may take an active role in impeding the wedding. Such was the case with Dan's parents when he planned to marry his high school sweetheart, Gail. His parents blamed Gail's influence for Dan's attendance at Harvard instead of MIT, "the family school," and they objected to Gail's articulate, independent personality. So they attempted to bribe the minister not to marry the couple, making up lies about Gail's background and their son's "instability." The minister deflected their attempts and proceeded with the wedding. During the ceremony, the fateful question was asked if there was anyone who could show just cause why the two should not be married. Fulfilling every bride's nightmare, Dan's mother stood up and announced to her son in front of the entire congregation that if he backed out, she was prepared to sign over their summer home and a sizable income.

"Would you believe that even after we had been married a year, his mother called—on Christmas, no less—and told him it wasn't too late to get out of the marriage," says Gail. "I used to get upset, but now I have to laugh at her predictability. I am just glad that Dan had the strength to separate from his family on his own. He has a thirty-four-year-old brother, never married and still living at home, still pleasing Mom and Dad."

Generally, parents do what they perceive to be the best for their child, so they feel the need to endorse their child's choice of mate. On occa-sion, that adult child will select someone who is perfectly molded to his family of origin. More often than not, however, that future spouse presents some very real differences, which were, perhaps, part of the attraction. But family members, feeling they must guide the errant child back to right-eousness, pull out all the stops to awaken their offspring to the "terrible mistake" that is being made. What they wind up doing is widening the gulf that is forming between them.

This is not to say that parents and relatives should not step in to educate a member who is involved in a violent or destructive situation, but most conflicts center around personality and background.

THE US-VERSUS-THEM CONFLICT

From the time children are very young, they are given a sense of belonging to a very special unit: the family. The very name they bear is a family name. Their birthright is a family history, and many spend enormous amounts of time and money tracing those important roots (witness Alex Haley). They grow up learning interpersonal and social skills as taught by generations of the family. Family loyalty is not only prized but expected, and a definite distinction is made between what is "family business" and what can be told to "outsiders." Styles of communication, values, and expectations are transmitted.

By the time children reach adolescence, they may realize that there are other ways to do things and may flaunt this newfound knowledge, but only in the most dysfunctional of homes will you find children absolutely turned against their families. The idea of family, of "us" versus "them," is too integral a part of our identity.

At some point, children grow up, go out, and select a mate—one of "them" to incorporate into the family pool. Even in the healthiest of families, there have to be areas of compromise and negotiation. Some families, however, do not recognize that through marriage "the two shall become one."

"It gets to me every time she says it, although you'd think I'd be used to it after six years," says Erin, a vivacious blonde who manages a children's clothing store. "The first time my mother-in-law called a family meeting to discuss my father-in-law's ill health, she said she only wanted 'family' to attend. That meant, she told me, just my husband and not me. It irked me, but I thought okay, it's *his* father. I can accept that. But this pattern has continued. The straw that broke the camel's back, so to speak, was just six months ago, when she threw an anniversary party for herself and excluded all of her five children's spouses and included the grandchildren, because she just wanted 'family' there. I don't even speak to her when she calls on the telephone anymore. After all, if I'm not family, why should I bother?"

Erin is standing on one side of a gulf and her mother-in-law is standing on the other. In the gulf are issues of separation, a Dictator-like personality, and expectations that are not being met and may never be met. It is one thing to understand intellectually the bridge-building supports, and it is another thing to put them into practice after having been verbally slapped in the face. Emotions cloud our reasoning powers, and conflicts that may seem insignificant are the ones that wind up pushing us further apart. But then, it is usually the small rock and rarely the mountain that trips us up.

"The light switch, would you believe that?" demands Elizabeth. "My father-in-law is not speaking to me because of the damned bathroom light switch. In his house, the bathroom mirror can switch lights from high to low. When I go in, it is usually set for low, and I'd switch it to high because I hate the feeling of being in a poorly lit room. Usually, I'd forget to switch it back to low. The last time we went for a visit, he had put tape over the 'high' switch, and he and other family members sat around smirking. All he had to do was tell me 'Would you mind switching the lights back to low when you leave?' But no, he taped the light as though I were two years old. It was humiliating and, I admit it, I blew my cool."

Since holidays and special life events are the focus of family life, so is gift giving. Differences in gift-giving styles can be a source of conflict when one family traditionally celebrates and gives gifts lavishly, while another ignores such things as birthdays, anniversaries, religious milestones, and academic achievements.

"I came from a family where we spent a lot of thought and time on each person's gift," says Palmyra. "My mother-in-law drives me crazy when she recycles old gifts so she doesn't have to buy anything, or just buys whatever happens to be on sale, whether that fits the person or not. I don't mean to sound materialistic, because what you spend on a gift is not the point. I feel a gift is an expression of love or whatever you think of the person who will receive it. I wouldn't care if she spent $3.98 on a pair of pantyhose that I like. But she doesn't bother. I have seen her give away presents that I gave her the year before. Or I have received things, like a sweater, that she received from someone else—and we are completely different sizes. I nearly lost it when she gave me a two-cup coffee maker that I know she received as a promotional thing at work. I don't drink coffee, don't like it, and never will. And she's known this for ten years!"

Changing one's expectation levels and a sense of humor might help Palmyra select gifts for her mother-in-law that she, herself, would like, so that when the gift is recycled, it will be welcome. A little trickier situation is the one in which Alan and Sally find themselves.

Alan was an only child. Sally came from a large family of seven brothers and sisters. While Sally is gregarious and emotional like her family, Alan is quieter and more analytical. Both families have difficulty accepting the differences in style Alan and Sally presented, but real conflict came over a possession.

"We were doing well financially and decided to buy a small condo in Aspen," says Alan. "We worked hard for it and looked forward to enjoying it. As soon as Sally's family heard what we had done, they all began making reservations to use it, join us on weekends, and even bring friends. I am in a very high-pressure job and this was supposed to be our weekend getaway, but in Sally's family, the philosophy is, 'What's yours is mine and what's mine is mine.' Being an only child, I was used to having my own things—not having to pool everything I owned. I've tried to make many accommodations to their way of thinking, but this is one area where I had to put my foot down. I told them they could come visit when they were invited. Several of them have given us the cold shoulder ever since."

PREJUDICE

Prejudice is one of the most classic forms of "us versus them." It can be found in the Archie Bunker type of relative who constantly uses pejorative slang words for ethnic groups, like "spic," "kike," "mick," and "wop," despite the fact that he is insulting in-laws of those backgrounds. Or the woman who vociferously boycotts French products, because she feels that the French didn't help the United States during World War II, and who likewise remonstrates against Japanese products because of the bombing of Pearl Harbor. Differences in age inspire family barbs and boycotts, and in some bizarre circumstances, differences between couples are supported by law.

For example, as late as 1987, interracial marriages were still against the law in Mississippi. Although they did not live in Mississippi, Fiona, who is white, and Will, who is black, had to face the prejudice of, not only outsiders, but family members as well when they decided to marry. They met when twenty-eight-year-old Fiona was giving horseback-riding instruction and thirty-nine-year-old Will went riding where she worked. After many weeks of pleasant exchanges, the two began dating.

"I admired his sense of humor," says Fiona. "He was confident and could laugh at himself. The color difference was invisible when we were together." But it wasn't invisible to relatives when the two announced their engagement. Although the couple expected Fiona's family to be upset, they were surprised when her family attempted to adjust and Will's family was the one to throw up roadblocks every step of the way. Few attended the wedding. Complicating the situation was the fact that Will's father became a bedridden invalid, and Will, an only child, brought his father to live with them. Several years of nursing her father-in-law did nothing to bring about Fiona's acceptance into the family. On the contrary, Will's large network of aunts and cousins would drop by the house without calling and walk in without knocking. They snooped through drawers and circulated false stories.

When Will's father died, several of the aunts called Fiona to tell her that black people's funerals were more casual than white people's. "They actually told me to wear jeans, and they told me other supposed traditions that, had I listened to them, would have made me look very bad and foolish," says Fiona, shaking her head. "Fortunately, I used my common sense instead of listening. Of course, they arrived dressed to the nines. Afterward, since we had so many people back to the house, I had put out styrofoam cups for coffee. One of Will's aunts loudly announced that she just couldn't drink coffee from a paper cup—she wasn't raised that way.

"I have learned to cope over the years by maintaining my self-esteem and always acting like a lady. Our friends, who accept both Will and myself, have become our close family. I have learned that prejudice is not just a white man's error and that, as in any relationship, you have to know your strengths and weaknesses. I have learned to expect little and enjoy each day when I can, and I limit my contact with those people who are very upsetting. It would be nice to think we could be one big happy family, but I realize it probably won't ever happen."

FAMILY SECRETS

Another facet of the us-versus-them syndrome is the area of family secrets. What youngster hasn't heard that "you don't wash the family's dirty linen in public"? Well, the linen does not really have to be dirty, and the public may be the new relative who must either buy into the secret, ignore the secret, or perpetuate the secret—or risk ridicule. Just as in the children's story "The Emperor's New Clothes," a person may find him- or herself innocently pointing out a glaring discrepancy that family members just ignore or take for granted.

"Very often, there are no spoken rules in families, only things that are not talked about," says Dr. Richard Garvine. "The outsider comes in and doesn't know the rules of the game and will point to the secret and say 'Look at that.' It may be that a daughter grew up liking to watch Daddy get dressed in the morning, a practice they never bothered to stop. It was just not something that was spoken about. Maybe a relative had an illegitimate child and put it up for adoption; maybe brother Bill has a criminal record. Whatever it is, bringing it out into the open can be hell on the one who dares to speak about it."

Family secrets can revolve around taboos or even death. Brothers Nigel and James were very close growing up. James left England to seek his fortune in the United States, leaving most of his family behind. He and Nigel grew steadily apart over the years, as both endured economic ups and downs and couldn't visit easily. Both were extremely poor at writing letters and telephoning. When James was fifty-eight and suffering from high blood pressure, he had a massive heart attack. During this same time, Nigel suffered a stroke and died almost immediately. Since James's hold on life was tenuous, the family decided to shield him from the fact of his brother's death. Even as he grew slowly stronger, they were afraid the news would precipitate another heart attack. Three years passed and James, who had recently lost his wife, wanted to pay one last visit to his brother Nigel before he died. The family kept discouraging the visit.

This is the stuff that soap operas are made of. Some families attempt to conceal a death, forcing members to pretend that the relative is busy, traveling, working, showering and can't come to the telephone—for years on end! Others attempt to conceal the fact that someone is still very much alive, as in the case of Letitia, who was told that her father had died shortly after her birth. The truth of the matter was that Rinaldo left his wife and daughter and ran off to the Bahamas, where he started a new life—which included a new wife. Most senior members of the family knew of Rinaldo's whereabouts and said "Good riddance!" Letitia's mother lived with the secret until a month before her death; she then decided to tell George, her grandson, that his grandfather was probably still alive and sunning himself in the Bahamas. Initiating other relatives into the secret places the burden on them to support the "family position," or else. "I feel rotten," George says. "I think my Aunt Letitia has a right to know about her father, but I don't know that it's my place to tell her. I feel guilty that my grandmother told me, and I feel guilty when I talk to my aunt. I wish I was still ignorant of the whole situation."

Even when everyone supports the secret, eventually it is uncovered, and the consequences can cause more chaos than there would have been without the concealment. Matthew, a forty-six-year-old businessman, has just found out that his favorite aunt, who died recently, was really his mother, and that the woman whom he regarded as his mother was really his grandmother. "It has been a conspiracy of silence in the family for all these years," says his wife, "and Matt is fighting mad as well as emotionally devastated. It was an old story of a young girl in the South getting pregnant very young, and Mama saying that she would raise the child. Of course, everyone else in the family knew but never said anything. When he finally found out, through his 'aunt's' will, he confronted family members who all said, 'Oh, we just assumed you knew.' "

Mix Them Up
and Blend Well

It seemed to work out all right for Macon Leary in Anne Tyler's novel *The Accidental Tourist*. His sister Rose not only invited Macon's ex-wife Sarah to her wedding but asked her to be the maid of honor. Macon showed up with his new live-in Muriel and her son, and everyone behaved in a very civil manner. It seems as if they could have been from the original cast of "The Brady Bunch," that happy, supportive, beautifully *blended* family of Mom, Dad, and six kids from previous marriages.

Never did the Brady kids line up against each other in an us-versus-them confrontation. Never did the celebration of holidays, traditional family activities, different brands of consumables, or views on spending money cause a problem. Moreover, the Bradys lived in a cocoon devoid of extended family—for good reason. Had the show's writers shown what family life in a newly blended family was really like, complete with relatives vying for time, feuds over broken traditions, and invitations to significant others from Bob and Carol's past, then few viewers would have had the courage to make a marriage work the second time around.

"The Brady Bunch" is to remarried couples what "The Waltons" are to first-time families. Everyone is on their best behavior all the time, something that the more than 11 million blended families in this country will tell you is truly fiction.

According to the census bureau, approximately one-third of all the marriages occurring in the United States each year are between couples of which at least one partner was previously married. This means that many couples enter a new marriage with not one but two sets of relatives on each side to exacerbate all of the aforementioned stresses.

Joan Howard, family therapist and former president of the Stepfamily Association of America, says that the sheer number of people involved can generate family frictions. "In a first marriage, a man and woman come together from their families of birth bearing certain ideas, values, and traditions. They then develop some new values and traditions together or reassess their old ones—keeping some and discarding others.

"In a stepfamily, that process has already been done at least once before. In addition, traditions and ways of doing things may have been refined during the time the adult was a single parent, so that when two people remarry, particularly if they are parents, they bring these previous histories to the new marriage. There is another 'step' thrown into the equation.''

And it is those extra steps that magnify frictions and make the individuals involved vulnerable to various family members. Imagine being in a family with three Dictators and four Pot-Stirrers. It is enough to make your head spin, yet millions of families are facing such a situation on a daily basis. And even if the immediate blended family can negotiate a harmonious household, there are still those times when four sets of relatives make their presence known, and sometimes in a divisive way.

"My family is driving me crazy," says Dorothy, mother of two, who divorced Ted three years ago and recently married Steven. "My parents said that just because I couldn't live with Ted, they didn't want to just cut him off after having him in the family for fifteen years, so they still include him in some family gatherings. This is really uncomfortable for me and even more so for Steve. On the other side of the coin, I can't separate the kids from Ted's parents—they are still their grandparents, after all, and they are very put out if I don't visit them as well. The last time I sent the kids to visit Ted's parents, while Steve and I celebrated Thanksgiving with Steve's parents, the kids returned with all kinds of expensive toys and electronics that I had declined to buy them. When I tried to return them, the kids accused me of trying to divorce their grandparents. No matter what I do, I can't seem to win."

Loyalties to divorced or deceased spouses can cause frictions when extended family members continue to maintain the old loyalties, and the new spouse becomes the "them" in the us-versus-them conflict. "My wife's family is Italian and all of them speak fluent Italian," says Mark. "I only speak English. It is so aggravating to be at a family dinner or event when they start to speak Italian in front of me, particularly if my wife is out of the room. I feel so left out and insulted. When I try to make a humorous remark, reminding them that I feel as though I am at a foreign film, her sister says 'Oh, that's right. We keep forgetting, because Tony'—her ex-husband—'used to speak the language.' If I hear that one more time, I may hit something."

KEEPING SANE WHILE THOSE
AROUND YOU ARE ACTING CRAZY

You have probably multiplied the anecdotes in this chapter by a dozen of your own. On paper, it may seem amazing that any of us can get along with each other at all in close quarters. What saves us is our capacity to be adaptable, resilient, and motivated. By laying down all of the key bridge-building supports discussed in chapter 1, strong connections can be made in this most complicated of all involvements, marriage.

One of the first negotiation techniques taught to business students is to identify the real problem and address it. This sounds so logical and simple, yet within the family context, we often do anything but that. Communications can center around shooting barbs at others and character assassination instead of focussing on the specific friction that makes us crazy.

Is your brother-in-law an insufferable pig, or, specifically, is it his boasting about his new material possessions that makes you want to punch him? Communicating specifics and then discussing what can be done to rectify them is where most family members are lacking, says Carol Kurtz.

"Saying what you feel is very different from saying what you need in a relationship. You need to say, This is what is making me angry (or driving me crazy) and this is what I want (what will help)," she says. "It's that last part of the equation that most people leave off. They stop with, 'You make me angry!' You have to finish it for the listener if you expect anything productive to come out of the exchange."

Barriers to good communication are easy to understand if you buy into the "supposed-to" myth. We tend to treat relatives as if they were mind-readers who are "supposed to" know what will make us happy, comfortable, or welcome. Not so. Spell it out for them, and if they still don't get it—or if they choose to ignore it—adjust your expectation level. If you don't, the one who will be miserable is you.

Remember that it would be nice if we could always have our family's approval, but it is not necessary to our daily existence or our self-esteem. In those situations where you know beforehand—such as a family gathering or visit with the in-laws—that frictions will occur, operate from a position of strength. That is, visualize the realities of the situation, not the way you would like it to be, decide how much you are willing to be exposed to, and then limit your time. If your mother-in-law wants to come and stay for five days after Thanksgiving, and you know you'll go crazy because all she does is criticize, tell her that your schedule permits only one or two days after the holiday. You won't change your mother-in-law, but by taking a more active part in the decision making (in setting a limit) and thereby shifting strength into your hands, you will be better prepared to tolerate the frictions.

Which brings me to the point that families are a long-term relationship. The old adage about "winning the battle but losing the war" could apply to the family battlefield as well. When families lived in close proximity, they learned to tolerate each other's shortcomings because they had to. Today, many people must drive or fly across hundreds or thousands of miles to be with family members. If a conflict occurs while apart, we can cut a person off on the telephone by simply hanging up and—poof!—they disappear. We don't learn tolerance anymore. There are times when operating from a position of strength means that you tolerate another's choices, although they be different from your own. It can also mean extending the hand of friendship first, even if you are convinced, for example, that your sister-in-law changes the ingredients in the recipes you've given her and then blames you when the meal turns out inedible. Kurtz calls it, "acting as if."

Since most people get nervous when preparing to make a speech, experts will advise the speaker to "act as if" you are confident and in control of the situation. If you playact the fantasy, the truth will not be far behind. In the family friction arena, acting from a position of strength sometimes means acting "as if" you are confident and prepared to acquiesce on certain points to retain harmony among your immediate and extended families.

Once that emotional hurdle is vaulted, you can then concentrate on getting your emotional strokes from those who become part of your surrogate family. This isn't to say that you will actually replace your mother, father, sister, or brother with an "outsider," but if you have adjusted your expectation levels, then your blood relatives' lack of support will become less important and easier for you to deal with—the real key for staying sane.

Finally, try to laugh, because families *are* funny. If you find little to laugh about with individual characters, then give yourself the opportunity to laugh at their aggravating predictability, as Gail did earlier, with the mother-in-law who spent years trying to break up her marriage.

If we build strong bridges across the many differences involved in the marital web of relationships, then we can use those differences as pathways to growth rather than as schisms.

8

Children in the Eye of the Storm

More than a hundred years ago, President Abraham Lincoln said that the fate of humanity rested in the children's hands. So does the fate of the family.

Children sail into the future like sleek schooners, bearing the colors and sails of their families. Below deck is a repository of family traditions, identities, and secrets. Their bridges, polished with our values and dreams, silently send navigational signals to guide them through the cresting waves. They are the link between our quickly fading past and our expectations of tomorrow. They are the bloodline. And for these reasons, children are often a major source of conflict within extended families.

Newspaper and magazine advice columns are full of letters such as these: "My mother-in-law refuses to childproof her home when my young boys come for a visit. She gets hysterical and vindictive if they break something, and tells everyone in the family as well as her friends what awful things they've done. Yet she complains to everyone that I'm uncaring if I don't bring them over."

Or, "I married a divorced man with two children. I came into the marriage prepared to love his children and be a good stepmother, but it seems I can't do anything right in their eyes. They are constantly throwing their mother up to me, and then they turn around and make up stories to tell the rest of the family. My husband seems oblivious to all of this, and if I point it out, we wind up in a fight. When his mother called to report what the boys had told her, it was the last straw. I don't think I can take any more."

Or, "My husband and I tried for years to have children. We finally adopted an adorable Korean girl. We are delighted, but some of our rela-

66

tives are the problem. They treat her very differently from her cousins in the family—as if she weren't there. She's getting to an age where she is beginning to notice the difference in treatment. We've always been a close family, but this is breaking us up."

Children can bring out a variety of behaviors in the extended family. Perhaps Mom and Dad were very rigid in raising their children, with little time or inclination to play. But by the time they are grandparents, they may have realized what they missed and attempt to "atone" by overindulging the grandchildren and criticizing their own youngsters' parenting styles. The result? Conflict.

Or sometimes, due to personality and life's circumstances, one sibling's children are raised with very different value and discipline structures from their cousins—and their behavior shows it. Put those people together in a family gathering and you have the sparks to ignite a roaring conflict.

Or maybe a child's behavior is not the central issue; rather, the child is a bargaining chip in a custody battle or an old, unresolved conflict across generational lines. In a continuing struggle for power, grandparents may contradict everything the child's parent says, putting the parent—the supposed authority figure—in a bad light. The result? Conflict on two fronts: grandchild versus parent; parent versus grandparent.

Whatever the particular situation, in order to see the bloodline beast in your relatives emerge, you must have a child to throw into the equation. For many, having, or not having, children is itself the first source of conflict.

THE PRESSURE
TO REPRODUCE—ON DEMAND!

Mike and Sharon had been married for three years when relatives began dropping hints that it was time for them to start a family. At five years, the hints took on a more aggressive tone. By six years, Sharon's mother was openly lamenting that her daughter was not a very nurturing person and Mike's mother would make it a point to call and announce every pregnancy of Mike's childhood friends and distant cousins. Sharon's father took Mike aside and told him that if it was a matter of money, he would take care of expenses and give the child a generous monthly allowance from birth. Mike's mother took to giving her two daughters and their children very lavish gifts, but only trinkets to Sharon who, she said, wasn't concerned with family matters, "so why bother?"

Mike's father went so far as to give the couple a weekend at a lake resort for an anniversary present and then proceeded to instruct his son on the rudiments of sexual intercourse, just in case that was the problem. Mike swears his father was in the bushes outside the bedroom window on Saturday night of that weekend. Needless to say, "it" didn't occur.

"The crazy thing about it was that by the time we had been married for six years, we were ready to get pregnant but couldn't," says Sharon. "We kept trying to be good sports about the teasing, the barbs, the sometimes vulgar insinuations that everyone felt free to express, but we couldn't tell them that we were failing. We went to a fertility expert and after a lot of testing, we found that Mike's sperm count was very low, so it was going to be difficult, though not impossible, to get pregnant. One day, after an offhand comment by one of Mike's sisters, I got hysterical, told everyone what bastards I thought they were, and the whole story came out. Then my parents blamed Mike, as though it was his fault. He felt guilty and miserable, and it began to affect our relationship—a relationship that had always been very good. I finally said, 'Whoa, enough's enough.' We laid down the law to all of our relatives in a letter and followed it up with a phone call. We assured them of our love for them, our love for each other, and the fact that whatever happened was our business; that we would appreciate their support, but it wasn't necessary to our existence. They all got the point—some more easily than others. And a year later, they were all happy when I finally got pregnant, but I'll never forget what we went through. Why do families do that to each other?"

Why do they do it? Because each of us is an extension of our parents, aunts, uncles . . . just as surely as the branches of a tree are an extension of the trunk. Our relatives feel that if the branch looks bad, the tree looks bad. (By the same token, if a particular branch looks good, all the other branches are quick to make their close association widely known!) But "bad" doesn't have to mean a prison record. It could be behavior that deviates from what the family expects—and they are quick to shake the branch that dares to sway to its own breeze.

Nothing threatens the life of that tree more than the refusal of the branches to multiply and be fruitful. "Would you believe that my mother-in-law started buying baby clothes, both boy's and girl's, after I had been married just a year?" said Robin. "I couldn't believe it when Christmas or my birthday would come and I would open her present, expecting to find perfume or a blouse and inside would be a silver rattle or sleepsack. I decided that I could really go nuts, get resentful, and ruin an otherwise pleasant relationship, or I could laugh at her. I chose laughing. It wasn't always easy, mind you, but I would let all my feelings out in a 'joking' way—like, 'Am I only of value if I am a baby machine? Ha, ha, ha.' She didn't give up and neither did I. And ultimately, I was glad. By the time

I did get pregnant, I hardly had to buy a thing and my mother-in-law is a wonderful friend and grandmother."

THE PREGNANT PAUSE

The day finally arrives when you can announce that, like Princess Diana, you have done your part to ensure the continuation of the bloodline. After the poorly concealed collective sigh from the relatives has died down, you soon find out that your body is not your own anymore. Not only are you poked and prodded by doctors, but complete strangers feel free to come up and touch your belly, while relatives move in closer, putting their ears to your protrusion while informing unborn Junior ("What do you mean you aren't calling him Junior? Isn't the family name good enough for you? He's going to be Junior the Fourth!") who's who in the family lineup.

Before you are even in your seventh month of pregnancy, you may already have been bombarded with applications for the "family school" ("Put Junior IV on a waiting list at birth; you can never apply too early"), three copies of Dr. Spock (except for your Butterfly sister-in-law, who gave you a copy of *The Harrad Experiment*), and daily telephone calls demanding that you confess everything you've been eating.

"I wanted to revel in every minute of my pregnancy," says Marty, "even the aches and pains. Every time I shared something with my mother, though, she went into her queen-of-the-mountain routine. You know, she had higher highs, lower lows, more violent morning sickness, more glowing skin, and more bizarre cravings. It was no fun. I felt as if I were always in a game of 'can you top this one?' Fortunately, I could communicate with my mother-in-law on a more equal level. She helped offset the upset feelings I would get after talking with my mother, who I really wanted to be there for just me."

Blair was not as lucky. She had a difficult labor and delivered her daughter by Caesarean section. When she joyfully carried her daughter through the door to her home, her husband's mother took one look at the baby and said, "Well, better luck next time. I knew you couldn't do anything right, anyway."

The family drama, at this point, is well underway. Just when you were looking forward to a little intermission, the stage whisper demands, "You're not stopping at one, are you?"

* * *

EVERYONE'S AN EXPERT
ON YOUR CHILD

More than 32 million children in this country have working mothers. Some work from necessity, some work from choice. All have to juggle myriad responsibilities and most admit that they carry a load of guilt, whether justified or not, around with them constantly. These two-career families, emotionally fragmented by needs, time, workloads, and guilt are vulnerable to criticism. And they get it.

Belding is a high-powered attorney; her husband, August, is a corporate executive. After the birth of their first child, she stayed home for two months and then went back to work. The daytime caretaker for their son was all right, but frequently unpunctual. As a result, schedules had to be shifted at a moment's notice. After the birth of their second child, Belding went into a depression at the end of her two-month leave of absence. Six months later, she still hadn't pulled out of it, and she had to return to work. Part of her irritability stemmed from lack of sleep. Even at eight months old, her baby was not sleeping through the night, so each night she would get up and sit with him.

When she turned to her family for support, she found little. Her sister constantly criticized her for "dropping children like an animal and then leaving them. Why bother to have them if you aren't going to stay home?" Her parents, who struggled to put her through law school, would say, "What's your problem? You can handle it. Don't waste your schooling." Her husband, though supportive, traveled extensively on business and was too often physically absent to offer a consistent hand.

Tamara Engel, a New York clinical social worker and co-founder of Parent Workshops in the Workplace (PWWP), is a specialist in family and marriage therapy. Her workshops focus on the complicated dynamics of the family childcare-provider relationship. She says that family conflicts centering around children, particularly those with two-paycheck marriages, are tricky because of the exposed and often dependent position of the working parents.

"The bind for most working people is that work is their most gratifying experience," says Engel. "Work is the nurturer. There is a great sense of competence, of validation, and of creativity. When those people have children, they certainly love their children, but on a deeper psychological level. The child and work are in competition—for some there really is no competition—although the parents may not admit it even to themselves. They may make decisions around childcare that aren't protective enough of their child, or they may find that they are totally dependent upon the childcare person. Turning the caretaker role over to a stranger is a situation whose traumatic nature is not emphasized often enough. What those mothers have to do is allow themselves to mourn the loss of that child—yes, the loss. If they don't, you wonder if they ever bonded in the first place. "What happened with the attorney is that she didn't allow herself the opportunity to mourn. She really didn't want the child to sleep through the night because that was their bonding time," says Engel. When family support systems are not there for them or are, in fact, a system of criticism and conflict, the trauma of the situation is magnified. "These people are defensive and defensive for good reasons," Engel continues. "What they are defensive against is the loss of the connection to the child," as much as against having their decisions questioned.

Parents may find themselves labeled "uncaring," "cold-hearted," "self-centered," or "no better than a mongrel." Very often these accusations will be made by a relative who considers herself a model mother. But take heart—all is not as perfect as it seems in the "model mother's" Candy Apple household either.

If the parents in the two-paycheck type of household are uncertain and vulnerable, the children in the Candy Apple household can feel equally uncertain. Overprotectiveness, extreme child-centeredness ("I do everything for my kid!" is a popular cry), and lack of differentiation between child and adult roles (the "we're buddies" syndrome) may produce children who lack boundaries or confidence and get under the skin of everyone else.

"My brother's kids drive me crazy!" says Al, father of three girls. "They have absolutely no discipline. They are always cracking jokes about used-car salesmen because that's my job, and if I say anything about it, my brother says I'm being overly sensitive and can't take a joke. They walk in and expect everyone to jump and get them things because that's how it is in their house, and you should hear the mouths on these kids—and they are only nine, twelve, and fourteen! My brother and I always got along, and we were raised in the same way. I just don't understand how we could have such different views on child rearing. And the thing is, he's always telling me that I'm too hard on my girls—right in front of them. They adore their laid-back Uncle Jack because he spoils them rotten."

How often have you heard the refrain, "I don't know how they could have turned out so differently; they were raised exactly the same way." That sentiment is 70 percent myth. Children may be raised in the same household and perhaps with the same values, but by parents with different levels of experience and at different stages of their own lives. The children, themselves, have different inherent personality traits and abilities. Then, as adults, they marry one of *them* (as in *us versus them*). The result is a completely different person from the one family members think they are "supposed to" be.

"My sister is too hard on her daughter and too easy on her son," says Andrea. "She slaps that girl around something awful, yet her son can do no wrong. I'm afraid that girl is going to run away from home, or fall in with a bad crowd for acceptance, or just commit suicide when she really gets pushed. I've tried to point that out to my sister, but we always wind up in a big fight. We weren't treated that way when we were being raised, so I don't understand why she acts like that."

Patty's family problem is different. Patty's husband travels frequently on business, so she is often left with their son, Brandon, for weeks on end. Although Brandon is only nine, he has been treated like an adult companion—a situation that grates on everyone else's nerves when he expects to be treated as an adult by the rest of the family. If he doesn't get his way, he gets belligerent and verbally abusive until his mother jumps in to protect him. "I've tried to tell her she's ruining him," says Martha, Patty's mother-in-law, "but she can't see it. This kid doesn't know whether he's a child or adult. I hate to say this about my own grandson, but he's a real pain in the behind to be around."

A CONFLICT OF STYLE

There is an old proverb that says, "Praise a child and you make love to its mother." The reverse is also true. Attack a child and you have a fight on your hands, because you are, in a very real sense, attacking the parent as well. Yet relatives feel free to impose their opinions and methods without much reservation.

Sometimes, as in the case of physical or emotional abuse, the family is in the *best* position to *intercede* and they *should*. To ignore abuse is tantamount to abusing the child yourself; some states, such as New Jersey, have laws that make not reporting a suspected abuse a crime. If you are faced with a situation involving child abuse, your duty is to protect the child first—not the family connection or your relative's feelings.

Sometimes, however, conflicts arise when one relative's definition of abuse represents merely a difference in parenting styles and philosophies, and one has to define the difference carefully. For example, if your sister allows her eight-year-old to stay up until 11 P.M. every night and her household copes with it, although you may not consider this healthy, it probably won't emotionally scar the child. If, however, she belittles the child continually, making statements to the child like "I wish you had never been born," or if the child seems particularly defensive about frequent "accidents," you should step in. Doing so, however, requires thought and tact in order to be effective.

"If the parent feels attacked, he or she is going to take a defensive stand," says Engel. "The question is, how can you respond empathically so the parent can open up? How do you teach empathy? That's the nuts and bolts of daily living. This is a very difficult situation, because your first impulse is to protect the child. Even in family therapy, say you have a mother who is kicking a child, the instinct is to run up and save the child. You do that, though, and you lose the mother.

"What you have to do is align yourself with the mother and say 'That child must make you feel so angry' while you get in the middle and separate them. If we could educate people to take the position to not just jump in and protect the child, but address the parent with empathy, the connection would be more effective. The parent then might be able to connect to the child in a more positive way. It is a difficult thing to do in a family situation, but it can be done."

If the cause of the conflict is a case of personality differences, grandparents indulging a child or discipline differences, you must decide how much of that actually affects your life and realize that you do not have to endorse a relative's views or actions. Tolerance is easier if you limit your exposure to those who drive you crazy while communicating what your bottom line is in your household. If you do not abide bad language in your house, you have a right to restrict it in your relatives and their offspring. Make it into a joke, if you must, but be prepared to accept the fact that they may balk and that it will not affect your existence if little Johnny's mother doesn't talk to you for a week, because you told little Johnny that you would not tolerate four-letter words in your home.

Of course, if little Johnny rules the roost, it may be a long time before you hear from his Mom. We discussed the Dictator personality earlier in the book, but we didn't talk about the Dictator in diapers.

THE CHILD AS DICTATOR

When Marvin was two, he began to read. By the time he was four, he had memorized the names of all the United States presidents and the dates of their terms in office. He was the only kid in his kindergarten class allowed to take BASIC computer programming with the sixth-grade students and write his own computer programs. By second grade, he had been invited to play his violin with the local symphony orchestra. And by the time Marvin was ten years old, few people could stand to be around him—particularly family members.

Marvin's father and mother are in awe of their wonder child. A mill supervisor and waitress, they revolve their conversations, schedules, vacations, meals, and social life around Marvin. He has no responsibilities at home, as his brother and sister do, and his wants and desires are always top priority.

Likewise when there are other family members around, Marvin's parents expect their son to be accorded the same kind of treatment they give him. Thus, his parents have a limited social life, because few adults want the company of a ten-year-old at adult dinners and gatherings. On the rare occasion when everyone gathers, there has been a great deal of friction.

"My brother expects me to kowtow to his ten-year-old kid like the king of Spain or something," says Marvin's Aunt Lily. "Give me a break! This kid comes in and demands to know how much money I make, how much my house is worth, and where I got such a cheap couch. Then he *tells* me to get him a Coke. Forget it. I tell him it's none of his business, and he can get the Coke because he knows where the glasses and refrigerator are. He stomps out and two minutes later, his mother comes in and gets his Coke for him.

"If we're at dinner, everyone is expected to shut up and listen when the little weasel opens his mouth. Every word is a pearl, according to my brother. Ha! Is he in for a rude awakening one of these days!"

Joan Howard, who worked in the educational field for gifted and talented children prior to becoming a therapist, says that cases like Marvin's are not that unusual. "Very often what you have are two young parents, and this little person walks all over them ruling the roost. Even the child's sleep and waking schedules are the ones parents revolve around rather than the other way around. The child has everyone snookered. The parents don't really know how to parent. They are afraid to set limits because the kid might throw a tantrum or not stop crying.

"It is a particularly common phenomenon with child prodigies. These parents are literally afraid of their kids and don't realize that they are children first. They don't know how to treat them. So the kid becomes the Dictator."

The key, again, in building a bridge to this branch of the family tree, is to attempt to educate, rather than attack, the parents. You are entitled to set limits in your own household and perhaps attempt to involve the child in an activity involving responsible action. This child is the one who is going to both suffer and cause suffering. He or she is a Dictator in the making and will be forced to perpetuate anxiously the Dictator myths unless some boundaries are learned.

Another aspect of the child Dictator may come to the forefront in remarriage. Whether a parent remarries following a divorce or death of a spouse, the child's happiness is usually foremost in the remaining parent's mind. Children understand this and many, to get attention or exact some subtle form of revenge, learn to manipulate the adults in charge. In many cases, the custodial parent will wake up to the situation and begin to act from a position of strength. In some cases, however, the manipulation can go on for years and involve whole branches of relatives.

Deanne's was such a case. A young, childless divorcée, Deanne fell in love and married Rod, a widower with a seven-year-old daughter. Whereas Rod and his family were reserved and undemonstrative, Deanne was exuberant, warm, and energetic. She felt sorry for little motherless Susan and blew into Rod's household like a breath of fresh air, mothering both father and daughter with her own special brand of love and humor.

"I didn't marry Rod because of Susan—she was just the icing on the cake," says Deanne quietly. "I always wanted children, so Susan was a bonus. I tried to be sensitive to her needs; I didn't want to force myself on her, so I didn't stop working at first. Rod had a housekeeper, but when Susan asked if I'd stay home, I quit my job. Despite the fact that Rod wouldn't let anyone touch his dead wife's things, everything was all right at first. Then a year into the marriage, I got pregnant and that's when the trouble with Susan began."

When Rod traveled on business and Deanne would serve Susan a favorite dinner, Susan would insist that she hated it and wanted something else. When Deanne refused, Susan would tell her father and other relatives that Deanne refused to make her a dinner she liked. They, in turn, believed Susan and reprimanded Deanne. In front of an audience Susan was a model daughter, but when the two were alone, Deanne could not get through to Susan on any level.

Then Deanne began to notice that Susan's teachers would give her a cold shoulder. Deanne didn't know what was going on until a Hebrew teacher took her aside one day and accused her of beating Susan, which is what the child had told them. Deanne was shocked, Rod was nonplused. Susan would also throw a fit if Rod and Deanne planned to go out to dinner alone and Rod would appeal to Deanne to include her. "She was actually angry that she did not go on the honeymoon with us," says Deanne. "Rod would think nothing previously of pulling her out of school to travel with him. Now she was being treated like a normal child and didn't like it."

By the time Deanne and Rod's baby was born, Susan had everyone dancing to her melody and Deanne was a basket case. "I went through a complete reversal," she says. "I went from being a conscientious, secure person to one who wouldn't go out of the house. Rod undermined me at every turn, even in front of his family. I would break down and cry in the middle of the day."

It wasn't until Susan began making up stories that got the police involved that Rod finally agreed to allow Deanne to take Susan and seek some professional help. What led to this turn of events were several kidnappings and subsequent murders of young teenagers in the area. Susan came in from school one day and announced that a strange man in a car had accosted her as she waited alone for the school bus that morning. She told of how she had to run away. When Deanne checked with the mother in front of whose house Susan waited for the bus with three other girls, the mother reported watching the girls as usual; Susan was not alone, and no stranger had attempted to accost them.

"We have been through years of counseling and therapy off and on now," says Deanne. "What I learned is that I must make changes within myself. When you marry a man with a child, the man tends to believe you are going to be a fairy godmother. But I wasn't in control and he undermined me every step of the way. We had to get together and be consistent. Rod didn't want to face Susan's problems—he felt so sorry for her, he would do anything she wanted. When children have that much control, they go crazy.

"Finally, the rules I set in the house were the ones we lived by, but Rod was responsible for Susan's discipline. And he handled his relatives as well. I also learned not to take the good things people do for you for granted. It takes only a moment to say 'You're a good mother for taking her to the doctor.' And I learned to cope by picking my battles instead of fighting over every little thing and to tell myself that I am a good person. I try to dissociate myself from the nasty things that were being said and keep my self-esteem intact."

CUSTODY AND CARE: LOVE ISN'T ALWAYS ENOUGH

There are few areas involving children that can become as volatile within the family framework as custody and the continuing relationships following a divorce. Since children are the bloodline, questions involving custody, adoption, and visitation rights cause battles involving not only the principals, but grandparents and aunts and uncles as well.

When Connie and Matthew, married nineteen years, sued each other for divorce, both declared that they wanted custody of the two children. There were allegations of infidelity on both sides, which were denied, but other than that, their reasons for divorcing were based upon years of incompatibility. Matthew had spent much of his marriage traveling extensively on business, while Connie had retired from the business world to stay home and raise the children. Both had property and business holdings that would have to be sold and divided.

Relatives on both sides lined up behind their respective offspring, and Matthew secretly threatened Connie that if she didn't give up the children, his brothers and friends were willing to swear that she had been to bed with them. Connie's main priority was to keep the children with her, and Matthew made use of that fact to get what he wanted from Connie. The issue was finally settled without a full-blown custody hearing when Connie agreed to give up her share of certain property holdings in exchange for the children.

Gary, on the other hand, was awarded custody of his three children when Michelle, his wife of sixteen years, left one day and didn't come home. Fearing that she had been abducted or worse, her father, sisters, and brother set up shifts to take care of the children, who ranged in age from eight to thirteen, while Gary coordinated a search with the police. Michelle called three days later from the Bahamas, where she had flown with a boyfriend; she said wanted out of the marriage but wanted the children. Gary refused, and despite a guilt campaign waged by Michelle's family, stuck to his decision. He fought for and was awarded sole custody; Michelle was awarded limited visiting rights.

Stephen Sepaniak is a New Jersey attorney specializing in family law and health and hospital law. Throughout this book, he offers his experience and insight in these areas. However, it is important to remember that he is not offering legal advice tailored to particular situations, and, since the law in these areas is ever changing and may vary from state to state, if you have a legal problem, you should consult an attorney in your area.

Growing up as one of seven children and fathering two has sensitized Mr. Sepaniak to the struggles of maintaining tenuous family relationships across vast gulfs of differences. He says that, in his experience, the courts are still predisposed to leave the children with the mother unless there are circumstances that would be destructive to the children. He often cautions fathers and their extended families that unless a father can prove not simply that he is a better parent but that his wife is an unfit one, it would be more prudent not to fight a battle that isn't going to be won.

Twenty years ago, a charge of "unfit" could be levied against a mother for a sexual indiscretion or being drunk in public. Today, the concept of being unfit has evolved and is limited to cases in which severe impediments exist to caring for a child due to choice of job, drug abuse, or mental illness.

"This kind of fight is a very painful situation for all concerned," says Sepaniak. "Not only do two people have to say unkind things about each other, but they have to put the children in the middle of it all. Everyone has to go through a psychiatric evaluation. The children are counseled and brought in and asked what their preferences are. In a full-blown custody case, all that happens and it is very wearing and hard on everyone."

Despite grandparents' encouraging their offspring to go for sole custody, the questions for the parent to consider include: Are you capable of handling sole custody; that is, do you have the flexibility to do it? Is there anything to prevent your getting sole custody? Do you have any skeletons in the closet; do you use drugs or are you an alcoholic? Are you a go-go dancer at a nightclub or do you have any job that would prevent you from being home to take care of the children?

"In 95 percent of the cases I am aware of, the children remain with the mother," says Sepaniak. "Or some sort of joint custody is set up with liberal visitation. If the other spouse is an addict or alcoholic, a monitoring system can be set up for visitation to make sure the person is not on drugs or drinking when they visit the children in a controlled setting."

There are those situations, however, where relatives (usually grandparents) will fight and win a custody battle, terminating the parents' rights and adopting the child themselves. Such was the case of the Bakers, whose daughter and son-in-law met in a mental institution, married, and produced a lovely little boy. During the stormy three-year marriage, there was a history of physical and emotional abuse, infidelity, threats, and violence. It was after a report of child neglect that the Bakers were given temporary custody of their grandchild. Three years later, their daughter and son-in-law filed for divorce, and the Bakers moved to cut off parental rights and permanently adopt the child they had been lovingly raising for five years.

"There's nothing like an adoption proceeding to bring forth all the paternal and maternal rights that were never felt when the baby was in your possession," says Sepaniak. "You can terminate a person's parental rights if parental responsibilities have been abandoned. Seeing the child and patting it on the head while you're passing through town doesn't constitute parenting or nurturing in any sense. If the child has not been supported, if the parent has not taken an active interest in how he or she is being raised, whether he or she has been to the doctor or goes to church, then parental rights have been abandoned.

"The touchstone in everything regarding the children is, 'What is in the child's best interests?' That is what people have to keep in mind."

* * *

TO ADOPT OR SURROGATE?
NOT IN THIS FAMILY!

While adoptions resulting from a divorce or death can carry an emotional wallop for all concerned, a different kind of family involvement arises when a childless couple decides to adopt a child to complete their ideal family. Usually a joyous situation for the couple, the adoption can exacerbate an extended-family relationship in which no one has ever successfully dealt with the us-versus-them conflict within the family.

Ken and Tanya found themselves regretfully having to lower their expectations for their families when they adopted a Korean child. While Tanya's side of the family took to little Lynn happily, Ken's family, with the exception of one sister, viewed Lynn as an outsider and treated her as such. "Sometimes it was overt, but most of the time it was little things," says Ken. "My parents would take their other three grandchildren to the circus and not invite Lynn. Or they would favor each of the grandchildren with a special overnight with Grandpa and Grandma, but not Lynn. It hurt, it really hurt.

"Lynn is like any other little girl and we love her as if we had given birth to her," he says. "My wife and I view adoption as similar to getting married. You aren't connected by blood to the person you marry, yet you fall in love and promise to share a whole life with that person and bond with them. Well, we fell in love with Lynn and that bond is growing deeper each day—just like a marriage. It is sad that my family has chosen to respond the way they have. I still love them, but we limit our time with them and spend a lot more time with my wife's relatives, or friends who accept the three of us with love."

For every baby put up for adoption, there are at least forty couples vying for the position of parents. A large number of those couples remain on waiting lists for years, while others are considered low priority, if considered at all, because of mixed religious faiths or because they are forty or older. Some couples who have been unable to conceive turn to a surrogate mother to bear their child.

Surrogate motherhood exploded across the headlines in 1987 when housewife Mary Beth Whitehead refused to honor her contract and give up the child she bore for William and Elizabeth Stern. The ensuing battle resulted in such contracts being declared illegal in the state of New Jersey. There are many states in which surrogacy is legal, however, and so long as women choose to bear babies for infertile couples, controversy will remain. Sometimes, despite noble intentions, the woman's decision causes upheaval in her extended family circle.

Caroline, a Midwest mother of three, set off a family war when she began a surrogate pregnancy. Her in-laws threatened to disown her husband and attempted to remove Caroline's children from her custody, declaring she was an unfit mother. Her husband's support helped Caroline bear up under her in-laws' harassment and accusations that she was a prostitute.

Support of the surrogate mother, particularly from a husband if there is one, or from family members, is of critical importance, says Dr. Nina Kellogg, a clinical psychologist and founder of the Surrogate Parent Program, established in Los Angeles in 1981. Working from the professional offices that serve as home base to surrogates and couples from all over the country desiring children, Kellogg is surrounded by albums, portraits, and framed letters from smiling families and ecstatic new parents. To dispel the myth that poor women are surrogates for rich couples, Kellogg doesn't consider accepting anyone into her program who is not already self-supporting, and who does not agree to monthly counseling sessions and group support meetings during their involvement, which can take up to two years.

"One of the questions I ask the woman is whether she has discussed her desire to be a surrogate with the members of her family—both immediate and extended," says Kellogg. "If she hasn't, she must do that before we go any further. It is important that the children already present in the family, as well as other family members, realize that this is not going to be their baby. That has to be said over and over again."

Dee was acting as a surrogate for a second time, because she had "such a good time being pregnant" and she wanted to share the joy of having a child with a couple who couldn't do so on their own. The twenty-six-year-old mother of two said that while her husband was very supportive, she had a difficult time with her parents.

"My father found out in a terrible way—on the answering machine," she says, tossing her long red hair. "I had called my mother to tell her I had decided to be a surrogate, and since the answering machine was on, it recorded the phone call. When my father got home from work, he played the tape—and hit the ceiling. At first, my mother felt the baby was going to be her grandchild, and my father was really angry. But I had them meet the couple I was bearing the child for, and by the end of the pregnancy, my mother gave the couple a baby shower."

The surrogates in Kellogg's program all share the philosophy that bearing a child for another couple is one of the greatest gifts of love and joy that can be given. According to a Gallup Poll for a *Newsweek* magazine survey, more than 60 percent of the public also shares that opinion. When it occurs in your own family, however, your philosophy can be put to the test.

As with any other decisions made by family members that may not mirror your own desires or beliefs, when it comes to decisions about children, all you can do is support the relatives whom you care about—whether or not you endorse their decisions. Tolerance of another's viewpoint may make for an interesting cycle of growth within the family circle.

Since children do carry the family banner as they sail into the future, it would be much more productive to contribute to calming the waters rather than lobbing explosives onto their decks. What better place to break the cycles of unrealistic expectations, noncommunication, and power games, than to invest time in showing the younger generation the positive relationship-skills of planned communication, adjusting expectation levels, tolerance, and humor.

Teaching these skills by example and building bridges between the silent navigators means more than just strengthening the family network; it links us with a future we might not otherwise touch.

9

Divorce, For Better or Worse

Just as one marries a whole family, the reverse is true when a divorce takes place. By it's very definition, divorce is a complete separation, a pulling apart. And if anything can ignite the dynamite to blow up the emotional bridges between relatives, it is divorce.

On the day that Ellen and Jonathan appeared in court for their divorce, they burst into tears and quietly held on to each other. They had married extremely young and had endured both their own immaturity as well as their families' intervention. But facing each other in the courtroom for this final step of separation reminded them that they really had tender feelings for each other.

"Just as I was about to suggest that we postpone the proceedings and opt for counseling," says Ellen's attorney, "Ellen's father stepped in to pull them apart. 'After all the money I've spent and the hell we've gone through over this, you are damn well getting divorced today,' he snarled."

Sometimes the explosions resulting from divorce may even cause injuries and bloodshed. Family conflicts over divorce proceedings often resemble a custom of some primitive societies called "blood vengeance." This custom grew up in the days when there was no strong public authority to punish acts of violence. When a person killed or seriously injured another, the dead or injured person's nearest relative considered it a sacred duty to take vengeance on the murderer or injurer. But the killing of the offending party usually imposed a duty on *his* nearest relative to seek revenge in turn.

Thus a whole series of killings often resulted from one initial act of violence.

Chris and Davis were high school sweethearts. They began a business together and, through hard work, built a successful service corporation over eight years. The success, however, went to Davis's head. He began running with an unsavory crowd, got involved in the South Florida drug scene, and became increasingly violent toward Chris and unstable at work. Needing to escape the physical as well as mental abuse, Chris filed for divorce. During the ensuing year, she and members of her family were nearly forced off the road by service trucks, her parents' home was burglarized several times, cruelly obscene calls with specific family information were made to her mother shortly after her father's death, and her brother's vehicle was found to have been tampered with, resulting in a near fatality. In addition, the day before the divorce was to go to trial, Chris's attorney was shot and killed in the driveway of his home. In each of these cases, although circumstantial evidence abounded, no charges could be brought against Davis.

Sometimes, as in Mort's case, family conflicts over divorce can just drive a person crazy. "In the course of two weeks, my wife's brothers—I know they did it; I can't prove it but I know they did it—sent eighteen pizzas, nine newspapers, twenty-three magazines including *Quilting World* and *Modern Secretary*, a load of white stone, exercise equipment (which was sent C.O.D.), and—the one that pushed me over the edge—I woke up one morning to find piles of cow manure covering both my outside doorsteps. I literally couldn't get out of the house!"

The good news today is that the divorce rate in this country is declining: only 4.8 per 1,000 couples in 1988, as opposed to 5.3 divorces per 1,000 in 1981. The bad news is, divorce is still the death of a relationship—indeed, of a very way of life—and there are no easy ways to face that death except to allow yourself a period of mourning. Illinois psychologist Dr. Michael Rosenzweig likens the trauma to the death of a loved one. In an article for *Redbook* magazine, Rosenzweig says that after the couple's decision to separate, the grieving process follows these stages: first, a period of denial; second, an angry phase in which indiscriminate anger may be expressed toward family, friends, and members of the opposite sex; and finally, an acceptance of the situation and the necessity to make decisions for restructuring one's social and personal life.

These stages also mean parallel stages of vulnerability. This adversity inspires extended-family members either to rally around and be supportive or to instigate small wars according to their own agendas. This is also a time when those family roles that were discussed earlier really explode across the big screen—at a time when the divorcing member is least able to duck.

DECISIONS SHOULD BE PRIVATE

When Helen was in the throes of deciding whether she should file for divorce from Perry, her husband of twelve years, she confided the situation to her sister, Alice. Alice, good little Pot-Stirrer that she is, alerted the family network. Soon the telephone began ringing off the hook with relatives (including an aunt four states away) relating stories concerning Helen's husband that they had saved for years. She heard what a louse he had always been, how her mother was sure several times during the marriage that he had been unfaithful, and how her father was hiring a private detective to follow Perry around and "get the goods on him." The telephone was ringing when Perry came home from work. It was Helen's sister who screamed, "It serves you right, you S.O.B. I never liked you or your hick family anyway!" Thus Perry found out that Helen was thinking of divorcing him.

In her book, *Crazy Time: Predictable Stages of Divorce,* author Abigail Trafford states that divorce is not only the death of a relationship, but "a war with your past and the confrontation with your dreams of how you wanted your life to turn out." The key word here is "your." Not "your family's," "the group's" or "everybody's," but the singular "your." Even at its best, a divorce in the family throws everyone into various stages of limbo and chaos, but the initial decision making should stay between the two people concerned. This is not to say that a divorce should be kept secret, an unlikely and unnecessary scenario, but families, being what they are, should not be consulted until the decision is made. Unless, that is, you want to stage a family feud that will complicate issues and tear you into emotional confetti.

"My ex-wife's mother knew about our divorce before I did," says Glen, an athletic man in his mid-forties. "Of course, that was typical of our relationship. My ex used to call her mother every day and discuss all of our private business with her including, if you can believe it, our sex life. She kept saying that she and her mother were buddies, best friends. I wanted to be her best friend, but everything I said or did went straight to her family. I felt like I was constantly on display. When her sister made some comment to me about the way I kissed—something she could have only gotten from my ex-wife, that was it!"

Sometimes people make mistakes when they marry—maybe a lot of mistakes. Hearing what a rotten monster a husband or wife is only heightens one's sense of failure and delivers a karate chop to an already crumbling sense of self-esteem.

"What drove me nuts during my divorce was when all my relatives felt they had to get their licks in," says Faye. "I mean, I knew my husband was a bastard. I just didn't want to talk about it twenty-four hours a day. And a funny thing happened; the more my family sided against him, I almost felt I had to defend him. Now that really threw me into a tailspin, because I was trying to make sensible decisions for my daughter and myself and would find that I was waffling on simple issues so as to protect him— not because I felt he needed protection, but because if he was as bad as they kept saying, I guess that made me a pretty stupid jerk for being married to him for so long. Does that make sense?"

Few things make complete sense during a divorce. One psychologist, who has counseled teenagers following a massive earthquake in California, says that what really upset the youngsters was that everything that was supposed to be still and solid was moving. That threw them into a panic and they began to regress. Divorces are like that, too. The relationship that was supposed to be solid breaks apart, moves, and those involved, faced with uncertain living arrangements, financial upheaval, and shattered confidence, can regress and fall back into old, familiar family roles and patterns.

OLD ROLES RESURFACE

"I was brought up being taken care of," says April. "I expected it and I wanted it. When I got married, my parents were opposed to my fiancé. I was from the Midwest, he was from New York, and we had very different upbringings. The one thing my husband had in common with my parents was that he took care of me too.

"My parents were very supportive during the divorce. Afterwards, they started taking care of me again," continues the former teacher and mother of one son. "They do help me financially, and I speak with them every day on the telephone. They are getting older now and I know they'd like to see me married again—taken care of—because they're worried about what will happen to me when they're gone. I'm not very good at taking care of myself. I'm forty years old—I should know how by now—but I don't."

Whether the old familiar caretaking roles are welcomed or not, they are generally put into motion in varying degrees as Mom and Dad or big brother or sister or some other older, stronger relative moves in to "take care" of the wounded, divorcing member. Of course, sometimes it's difficult to tell when caretaking ends and blood vengeance begins, particularly if, for ex-ample, you are the recipient of pornographic cards sent to your office or to your boss with your signature forged.

If growing up and separating from the fold is difficult under normal circumstances, the dependency during a divorce—however temporary—can return you to an adolescent mode of operation faster than you can throw a dart at your ex's photo. This dependency on, and involvement of, extended-family members is in no way limited to young couples divorcing.

"When the people who are getting divorced are older, the children are always a part of it," says attorney Sepaniak. "Whether the people involved are in their fifties or sixties and the children are adults, or whether the client involved is a bit younger, with teenagers, I've never seen the chil-dren just step back and say 'It's too bad about Mom and Dad getting divorced.' Somebody's always the good guy and somebody's always the dog and rarely do the kids stay out of it. I've had countless office conferences with clients who have been accompanied by their sons or daughters. The typical scene is Mom or Dad, sitting there worrying, while the son or daughter is sitting there with the looseleaf notebook with a list of ques-tions. You end up with the client being the son or daughter."

If emotional support is a powerful entanglement with extended-family members during a divorce, financial support involves an even tighter net-work of constricting bonds. In the case of Ellen and Jonathan at the be-ginning of this chapter, the dissolution of their marriage was engineered, in part, by the person writing the check. Fathers (or older brothers) paying for the daughter's (or sister's) divorce is not an unusual occurrence. Al-though in recent years, as women have become more financially indepen-dent and do not have to rely on a relative's assistance, the monetary involvement has decreased somewhat. Even without that aspect, the family cavalry charge to defend one of its own can still exacerbate or manipulate a stressful situation to its ultimate conclusion.

Colleen found herself in just such a situation. Her parents and family opposed her marriage to Henry. After five years and one child, when the relationship began developing some cracks, Colleen's family saw the op-portunity to dispose of the stranger they hadn't wanted in the first place. Colleen's father offered to pay for the divorce, since Colleen had quit her job to stay home and raise a family. He contacted an attorney and attended the initial meeting with her—to lend moral support. Her brother intro-duced her to two women from his office who had been "successfully" divorced and looked into the possibility of Colleen's getting a job there. Her mother appointed herself the official timekeeper, encouraging Colleen to "get the divorce out of the way by Christmas" so she could start the new year fresh and meet the nice man whom her mom had lined up for the New Year's Eve party.

Colleen did get divorced from her husband, but three years later, the couple began dating again. This time, her family threatened to disown her.

"It becomes very difficult in a case like this one for the client to separate his or her own interests from the axe that family members are grinding," says Sepaniak. "It is a difficult situation for all concerned because you end up walking a very fine line. The attorney knows who is paying the bills, but that person also thinks they are privy to certain information and, of course, they're not. They also feel they are entitled to some input and again, they are not, because they are not the client. They may be the financial source, but they are not the client, and that is difficult for some people to understand," he says. "So when they call up and ask how things are going, you can't really tell them. If they call with suggestions, you can't follow them. You can agree to discuss the suggestion with their son or daughter but you really can't just say 'Okay, fine.'

"There is only one client, and an attorney must act in that client's best interests," Sepaniak says. "Sons, daughters, fathers, and mothers—while their position is understood, it cannot be used to subvert an attorney's loyalties. Sometimes, if left to their own devices, a couple may separate and, then six months later, work out their problems. But when a family rushes in to get rid of a member they never liked in the first place, there is no opportunity for reconciliation."

Not only does the relative's influence affect the ultimate outcome, but perhaps the settlement as well. "We had a family fight right in the divorce attorney's office," says Rene. "I couldn't afford to pay for the whole thing myself, so my dad offered to help out. I accepted gratefully. So when I went to speak to the attorney, he and Mom came with me. My sister, who had also gone through a divorce, came to lend moral support. Well, the attorney asked me if I objected to letting my son have overnight visitations with his father. Before I could say anything, Dad exploded and said no way would my husband get our son overnight. Then Mom jumped in and said he couldn't separate a father and son, and they started having a fight. My sister jumped in and told Mom that she wouldn't feel the same if we were talking about a daughter instead of a son, and *they* started yelling at each other and dragging out old hurts. I'll tell you, by the time it was all over, going back to my husband didn't look so bad."

The only way to handle all the well-meaning relatives without losing your autonomy is through planned communication. Planned communication puts you in control of what you choose to communicate and when. Once the decision is made to separate, you can ask for the emotional support you need, but make clear to all involved that you really don't want to hear a laundry list of grievances against your spouse every time someone calls. Even if the divorce was initiated by your spouse, you are still in control of your own self-esteem and actions.

You know your own family. If borrowing money is going to carry the unspoken agreement that you will be required to meet their expectations regarding the divorce and settlement, discuss how much you are willing to listen to their suggestions, but make it clear that you will make the decisions. If that is unacceptable, look elsewhere for the money—or be prepared to fight for autonomy every step of the way. In any event, adjust your expectations of what your family members can and will provide during that stressful time. Now it is *their* turn to be made aware that they can support *you* while not endorsing every decision you make. And when your attorney returns only three of their twenty-two telephone calls, remind them that the key word in "your divorce" is "your." Attorneys have one client to represent. A divorce is not—despite what families may think—a class action suit.

PRENUPTIAL AGREEMENTS TAKE THE WORRY OUT OF BEING CLOSE

The pre- or antenuptial agreement has become a popular tool for contemporary couples who, due to divorce, death, or family disposition, realize that marriage may not be the "happily ever after" ending from the storybooks of their childhood. A desire to protect material assets for themselves and family members motivates many headed for the altar to stop off at an attorney's office first. Since the prenuptial agreement is a legal contract, anything can be included as long as it does not conflict with the laws of the state, but the agreement is used primarily as a means of simplifying the division of goods should the marriage dissolve for any reason.

It also relieves anxiety on the part of extended-family members, who wonder how they will fit into the new marriage arrangement and, more importantly, who will inherit Uncle Joe's diamond-studded stickpin and Grandmother's candelabra from the court of the Czar.

Scott and Rachel planned to marry soon after college graduation. Plans hummed along until three weeks before the wedding, when Scott's father sat him down and advised that Rachel sign a premarital agreement to protect Scott's interests in case the marriage didn't work out. Those interests included a good deal of money, trust funds, and investments in the family's numerous lucrative businesses. When Scott approached Rachel on the subject, her family went through the ceiling. After many bitter exchanges between family members and the couple themselves, the agreement was signed and the wedding continued, but the bitterness has soured the familial relationships.

Even the best intentions can fan the flames of a family argument if the desire to have an agreement is interpreted as a means of chipping away at the block of trust and aura of romance that is supposed to surround a marriage. And the more extended-family members involve themselves in the bride and groom's agreement, the hotter those flames burn. Such was the case with Rachel and Scott. Communications soon centered around "My attorney said . . ." and "My lawyer and my father said . . ." Rachel began to wonder, "If he wants me to agree to *that*, what kind of person is he really? And what happened to romance? I feel as though I am negotiating a business deal instead of planning a wedding!"

Rachel's mother, Analise, who is a first-generation American, unlike Scott's family, which claims relatives on the Mayflower, was appalled. "The invitations were out, relatives had made travel arrangements to attend the wedding, the caterer had already been paid, as had the band—everything was ready and this bomb was dropped. Suddenly it was as if we weren't good enough for his family, he didn't trust my daughter, or he wasn't going to try hard enough to make the marriage work and was already planning for the divorce," says Analise. "I was in tears, Rachel was in tears. We went through with the wedding anyway, but I don't even want to see that boy's family for awhile. It just makes me angry."

The fact that marriage is "supposed to" be a romantic liaison does not preclude the fact that couples may feel the need to protect themselves financially through a prenuptial agreement.

Darby is a writer who was working on her sixth novel and her fourth husband. Jim had also been married before. They, too, agreed to sign a prenuptial agreement but they added their own flair. Aside from protecting a complicated network of financial interests, Jim wanted to be assured that he could play golf every Sunday for the duration of the marriage and that Darby would agree to travel with him twice a year. Darby insisted that the agreement include specific, uninterrupted periods of writing time each day, and every Tuesday evening off to do as she pleased—no questions asked. When she wanted to include a provision for sexual intercourse at least twice a week, Jim balked. They decided to work that one out on a weekly basis.

The prenuptial agreement, like the decision to divorce, should ideally remain between the two people involved. Rarely does this happen, since the ultimate beneficiaries of the agreement are extended-family members. Not only do they coach the bride or groom, they will also attend the agreement meetings and demand that their ideas be acted upon—a situation that can drive both their relatives and the attorney crazy.

Terry and William had both raised families and been alone for awhile when they fell in love and decided to get married. Both in their early sixties, they had collectively six adult children, eight grandchildren, three homes, numerous antiques, works of art, and family heirlooms. The children on both sides advised that the pair sign a prenuptial agreement to protect inheritances. They gladly complied.

"Typically what happens is that a family member attends the conference with the attorney," says Sepaniak. "Or the client sits there reciting, 'Well, my son said . . . My daughter said . . . My father said . . .' and it is very apparent that they are really worried about this. The next thing you know, you have three clients, not one. You are trying to please three people, not one. That isn't to say that the suggestions they're making aren't legitimate or valid concerns, but it just intensifies the mix. The couple starts out with a focus, and then they begin hearing from multiple directions and try to please everyone. This gets very difficult for all concerned."

Even if the agreement has been struck, a divorce occurs, and the financial settlement is a foregone conclusion, the emotional division of family members when one relative divorces can cause other problems.

REVIEWING, REDEFINING, AND RENEGOTIATING RELATIONSHIPS

If you had asked a child to define the term *family* fifteen or twenty years ago, chances are you would have gotten the traditional answer involving a father, mother, sisters, brothers, and grandparents. The celebration of such holidays as Mother's Day, Father's Day, and even the newer Grandparent's Day reinforced those ideas. But today it is a different ballgame.

Consciousness raising begins in nursery school with books like *Free to Be a Family* by Marlo Thomas and *Families* by Meredith Tax, which illustrate the various modes of single parent, grandparent-caretaker, and blended family situations, which all qualify for that ubiquitous term. They end up by getting the point across that "families are who you live with and who you love." But what happens if a divorce occurs? Does this mean families are not forever?

And what happens with those warm, fuzzy holidays? A child of divorce may need a generous allowance when holiday time comes, because he or she may wind up spending a fortune on presents and cards for several sets of stepmothers, stepgrandmothers, stepfathers, stepgrandfathers, stepaunts . . .

All those labels represent relationships that need to be reassessed and, very often, renegotiated during the divorce process. It can be both exasperating and alienating, depending upon which definition of family your particular extended family adheres to.

Shirley's father always taught his five offspring that "once a family, always a family." As a result, when Shirley and her husband of fifteen years got divorced, the separation may have been legal, but as far as Shirley's family was concerned, that was no reason not to include Dennis in family functions and celebrations. After all, he was the father of three children—the family bloodline. This did not sit well with Shirley and it was awkward at first for Dennis, but they had seen this mentality at work previously when Shirley's brother Roy got divorced, so they attempted to "keep up their end" of the relationship. Although they grew accustomed to the situation, it took on a different aura when Shirley began dating again and eventually brought a prospective husband to the family gatherings as well. He was not happy with Shirley's ex-husband in tow.

The "family is forever" philosophy is directly opposed to the other method of dealing with divorce, which resembles the poker game rule that states "once you're out, you're always out." Or in family parlance, "once you're out, you're dead meat." This presents divorcing members and their children with a different kind of pressure.

When Mindy got divorced, not only did family pictures that included her ex-husband disappear from the piano top, where family portraits are displayed, but her father would leave the room if her sons brought up their father's name. When her oldest graduated from the eighth grade, her parents refused to attend the ceremony if her ex-husband was going to be present. And if, by chance, they showed up in the same place during a holiday celebration, Mindy's parents and sister would leave.

Both the "once family, always family" and "once out, you're dead" philosophies represent the two extremes of the spectrum. Most people's views lie somewhere in-between, with extended-family members feeling torn when a daughter-in-law they have grown very fond of is being divorced, or fearing the loss of ties to grandchildren, or even step-grandchildren.

Carol Kurtz, family therapist, counsels that these relationships need to be renegotiated in a sensitive manner. Perhaps the interpersonal bridges can remain intact if the former daughter-in-law visits the parents at a time when their son is not present. It is also very important for grandparents to take the initiative to stay in contact with their grandchildren, even, and maybe especially, if a remarriage occurs.

In any event, the "supposed to's" of family life will need to be shed as expectations are adjusted. It may not be possible to have all the family members, including ex-spouses, attend weddings, graduations, and birthday parties without fighting. Perhaps this means doing away with the traditional receiving line at a formal event or celebrating Mother's Day on two days instead of one, or even a week ahead of time.

As with other family situations, divorce presents the extended family with the challenge of supporting a person, if not their actions. We do not have to endorse a relative's action in order to tolerate it, but the emotional support we lend during a stressful time will go a long way toward keeping the family bonds strong without choking the good out of our relationships.

10

When Sex
Becomes the Issue

Sex. Just saying the word pricks up our interest. It has caused wars, changed countries, and has been the prime motivation behind some of the most heinous crimes and the most beautiful artistic creations. Sex sells everything from magazines to bath towels, and there are even some people who, no matter what book they select, will look at the table of contents and turn first to the chapter on sex. And believe it or not, according to the book *100% American*, by Daniel Evan Weiss, 47 percent of American men enjoy sex more than money!

If our families are the silent navigators of who we are, sex is one of the navigational tools, because it goes to the very core of our existence. Our sexual identity, like our self-image, is born within the family framework and can be either nurtured or twisted depending upon the emotional health of the family. If everyone in the family, including those members by marriage, behaves in a compatible way, then all is right with the world. But families, being the checkered patchworks that they are, replete with varying hues of difference in attitudes, morals, and customs, find that sexual issues are highly explosive and potentially divisive. There are few areas in which the same-versus-different viewpoint is more crystalized than in our approach to sexual situations.

"My brother's wife acts like a prostitute on the prowl around any of the male members of the family, and my brother seems oblivious to it," says Eileen angrily. "They have been married for five years and she hasn't changed. She puts her hands all over my husband and other brother, even my father! I tried to tell my husband how I felt and he said that Terry is just a warm person, that it was all in my imagination. But my mother and other sister-in-law feel the same way. I really try not to overreact, but between her tight-fitting clothes, her sitting on the men's laps or patting their behinds as they walk by, and her pressing herself up against my brother in front of anyone who happens to be around . . . I mean really, some things are really meant for the bedroom, not as entertainment for a crowd. I have two children, and my twelve-year-old son is beginning to notice Terry's behavior. It's too much! The only problem is I don't want to alienate my brother. I love him, but I don't know how much more I can take of his wife!"

While some family frictions involving sexual issues may be relatively easy to resolve through communication of feelings, views, and interpretations, others appear to be tragically stymied.

Henry is a twenty-eight-year-old AIDS victim. Although he always thought that his family had accepted his gay lifestyle ("They just didn't refer to it," he says), the AIDS diagnosis altered his ideas. "I went to visit my aunt, uncle, and their three children for the holidays and was greeted by a huge sign on the front door saying 'AIDS Freaks Unwelcome Here.' I still can't believe it," he says, tears welling in his eyes. "Not only am I looking at losing my life but I'm already losing the people who matter the most in the world to me."

AN OPEN OR CLOSED SUBJECT

"My father is seventy-five years old and, according to him, he and my mother still make love every day," says Anthony. "He is a very strong-minded man, very open, and a mentor to all of his grandchildren. As a matter of fact, he has taken it upon himself to give each of them a sexual education when they are about seven or eight, whether the parents want him to or not. He is not ashamed of his sex life, and in this day and age of disease and mixed messages about sex everywhere you turn, he feels the children should know all about sex at an early age, be able to ask questions within the family, and feel comfortable with the subject. In a sense, I guess it's an asset, but my wife grew up in a family where they didn't even hug and kiss out in the open. And they never discussed boy-girl relationships, so she was a little shocked at my father's practices."

Everyone laughs at those sitcoms where the parent is attempting to explain the birds and the bees in a very embarrassed manner to an inquisitive youngster. Despite the "sexual revolution" of the 1960s, our level of comfort in discussing sexual issues is based on the manner in which we were raised. There are some homes in which everything from the sexual act, reproduction, and a woman's menses are discussed at the dinner table, and yet others where the children receive the same kind of information either from the media or school because the parents are too embarrassed or reserved to speak about such subjects out loud. Not only is the factual information passed down through the generations in this manner, but so is the value system attached to it. What is appropriate and what is inappropriate? What should you feel comfortable with and what is "wrong"? What is moral and what immoral? What is normal and what should be viewed as abnormal and a reason to seek help?

Given the variety of approaches parents use to pass on those attitudes and information, it is necessary to examine carefully a situation in which we perceive something to be wrong. It is critical to understand the difference between privacy and secrecy. If one were to rely solely on *Webster's*, the two words could almost be used interchangeably. In the world of relationships and sex, however, Carol Kurtz defines privacy as "allowing you to keep to yourself things that are personal and you don't feel you should or need to share. Secrecy, on the other hand, is something that has an impact on the relationship. If you have an affair, you keep it secret because you know on some level, it can be destructive to the relationship. In a sense, the secret itself is destructive because you can't have an intimate relationship if you have secrets."

Marie and her brother wish that their father would keep his activities more secret. Their parents have been married for thirty-three years and have worked together in business for most of that time. Mother just likes to collapse on the weekends, while Dad, who is an avid sailor, likes to spend his time on the water. Since Mother doesn't like sailing, Dad invites attractive young women to accompany him on his weekend jaunts. "I just don't think it's right," said Marie. "I can see that it bothers Mom, but she doesn't do anything about it, and it's begun to affect the way I feel about my father. It's true that he's a very outgoing, good-looking man, but I just don't think this is right."

Marie obviously doesn't endorse her father's behavior, but unless her mother chooses to act upon the situation, all she can do is show a little tolerance or remove herself from the vicinity. But what if a relative chooses to share a relationship with you whether you want to know about it or not? Every time Jean's sister and husband of three years are around, Jean finds herself becoming uncomfortable. "Young love and hand-holding in public is one thing, but these two stand around and kiss and press up against each other, even out in public!" she says. "I have tried to tease them and said such things as 'Would you two like to be alone?' or 'Gee, am I cramping your style?' but they don't seem to get the point. It's almost as if they are trying to prove something and it just gets very wearing."

Sometimes our relatives *are* trying to prove something—to send us the message that they are active, desirable, and attractive. After all, they have years of other impressions to erase from our minds—like the times they had Oreo cookies smeared all over their childish faces or the times when we saw them at their worst, sick and running for the bathroom, defeated after a test or game, or rejected by others. No wonder they are trying to "show us." Planned communication revolving around validating their worth, but then telling them what you need, is effective in this case. "I know you and John are very much in love, and how could he help loving you? You're sexy and wonderful. But you know, I begin to get uncomfortable when you press up against each other around me. I really need you either to tone it down, or to let me know when you would like to be alone." Calm and rational communication should help the situation.

LIFESTYLE COLLISIONS

Clashes in lifestyle choices have caused conflicts between the generations for years, such as when those who openly choose to live together without marrying find that their living arrangements are unacceptable to other family members. Not all the conflicts are cross-generational, however.

Karen would love for her sister Kay to visit, but sleeping arrangements present a dilemma. Kay is living with Jack, her third boyfriend since her divorce. Although Karen's two children like Jack, they know their aunt isn't married and Karen would rather her sister and Jack sleep in separate rooms in her house. This has heated up the family hotline.

"At twelve and nine years old, my children are not babies nor unaware," says Karen. "They adore their aunt and are at very impressionable ages. In view of today's problems and diseases, we are trying to instill old-fashioned morals. Besides, Jack is the third of Kay's boyfriends. What if she breaks up with him and moves in with someone else? Should I sleep them together as well? It's pretty clear-cut in my mind, but you wouldn't believe the fuss it's causing in the rest of the family—stemming from Kay herself."

Your home is your castle, and you have the right to dictate the moral standards within it, but before you communicate those standards, you must identify the conflict and decide just what the issue is. Sometimes the real issue is not what it seems.

Kathey knew that her living with Jed made her parents unhappy, but after two unsuccessful marriages, she did not want to jump into another before she was certain of her feelings. Her living arrangements were a constant source of bickering, however, as her mother would lay guilt trips on her. When Kathey turned thirty-six, Jed planned an elaborately elegant evening of dining and dancing for her. Upon being told of the impending plans, Kathey's mother threw a fit over the telephone, stating that she had planned a little birthday dinner with cake and Kathey's siblings and uncle for the same evening. "She wanted me to make a choice between Jed or the family, saying that I was turning my back on the family just because I was living with this guy, this person who wasn't really family," says Kathey. "I suggested that we have the party the following day, but she got really angry and hung up on me. This isn't the first time she's made an either/or demand concerning Jed, but I keep hoping she'll change. I was so upset, I couldn't really relax and enjoy my birthday evening with Jed, so I guess she got her way after all."

The issue here is not necessarily Kathey's living arrangements, but a power struggle of us versus them, with a little bit of the family "supposed to's" thrown in for good measure. Another time at which the "supposed to's" surface to cause family conflicts around sexual issues is when senior citizen members of the family begin dating and having intimate relationships.

"I can't believe it," says Judith, mother of three. "My own sixty-three-year-old father is acting like a teenager. He has been a widower for six years and now he's dating this woman who's in her forties. The change in him is ridiculous! It's as if he has discovered the sexual revolution single-handedly. He stays over at her place frequently, goes around humming current rock tunes . . . Honestly, I just don't want to deal with this. How do I know what he's doing? He's very open about telling all of us what he is doing, including how great it is to discover that sex can be so much fun. He keeps implying that my mother was not 'fun,' as he puts it."

There was a radio commercial not too long ago in which an adult male was discussing his mother's upcoming vacation. He painted a picture of her tamely playing cards with her lady friends by the pool in a sedate hotel, taking her white gloves off only to attend crochet class and sip another lemonade. He went into shock when his wife informed him that Mom was going to an all-adult Club Med where, according to her, she could dance all night and run barefoot along the shore.

What contrasting images! One is of the image of what that son thought his mother was supposed to be, and the other image is of an energetic, vibrant woman, who just happens to have a grown son and grandchildren. Divorce and widowhood do not just happen to the young, who decide eventually to get on with life, but to senior citizens as well, who are living longer, healthier, and more active lives. Just like the old joke about the kid who, finding out about where babies come from, disgustedly asks, "You mean my parents had to do that—twice?" many of us don't like to think of our parents as sexual beings. They are parents, that's it, not real people. Thinking of them in a different context means we have to change not only our image of what they are supposed to be, but perhaps our relationship with them as well. That can be scary, because it may very well mean a change of roles.

The mother of three children feels that she has lost her father if he is out dating "like a teenager" rather than staying home to provide the sure and steady hand of assistance when *she* needs help, as he's *supposed to*. Although she focuses on the sexual issue, her real conflict is coming from the fact that her father is not meeting her expectations, and she does not endorse his actions.

There are conflicts within the family that *are* sexual in nature, however, and the only way to approach these is by some sort of confrontation.

ALL IN THE FAMILY

More than 150,000 children were the reported victims of sexual abuse in 1986, the most current statistics available from the National Center for Child Abuse and Neglect when this book went to press. That figure, however, is misleading. Not only does that number represent a 300 percent rise in sexual abuse of children since 1980, with experts predicting a continuing rise each year, but for every reported case, an estimated five more cases go unreported.

What makes those numbers even more horrifying is that in more than half of all those cases, the abusers were "loving" fathers, mothers, grandfathers, uncles, aunts, brothers, sisters, and cousins. In theory, everyone agrees that sexually abusing a child is wrong. In actuality, when suspicions of incest arise in our own families, it is frightening to face.

Some years ago, it was my privilege to be a founding member of the Child Abuse Parent Education (CAPE) program in Morris County, New Jersey, which eventually served as a prototype for similar programs throughout the country. CAPE was a two-pronged program: On the one hand, we made a speakers' bureau available to social and civic clubs, as well as government institutions; on the other, CAPE representatives went into high schools and taught juniors and seniors a consecutive three-day course encompassing everything from defining and recognizing child abuse and children's legal rights and options, to making life choices and parenting skills.

We learned early how to gauge the teens' reactions to the material we were presenting. Some shotgun-blasted us with very specific questions, and some would not lift their heads to meet our eyes. Both obliquely conveyed personal situations with which they were all too familiar. More intense were the ones who approached us after class, having built up a trust and their courage for three days to ask in a small, quiet voice, "I'm sorry, I don't want to bother you, but . . . could I ask you something?" In three years of presenting the CAPE material on almost a weekly basis, I cannot ever recall *not* being approached by a child afterward who either sought additional information on sexual abuse or recounted a horror story and needed direction to a counselor. In most cases, someone else in the family, very often the mother or father, knew what was going on but either could not or would not deal with it.

One who came forward was Anne, a wispy sixteen-year-old who told me of a weekend when she was fourteen. Her parents went on an overnight trip, leaving her sixteen-year-old sister in charge. Her sister invited a boyfriend over, and when Anne and her sister got into a big fight, her sister held Anne down while the boyfriend raped her. Anne tearfully related that when she finally got up the courage to tell her mother a week later (her sister and boyfriend had threatened her with other attacks), she got into trouble for making up lies against her mother's favorite child.

Was this a case of incest? Technically no, but it is clearly a case of sexual abuse, and the sister was just as guilty as the boyfriend. Anne's case is unusual. More common are those situations in which a father is abusing one or more children in the family, or an uncle or grandfather has targeted a particular child.

It is very threatening to our concept of family and the image we hold of our relatives to confront the possibility that a younger member of the family may be suffering sexual abuse. It taints us as well for being related to the abuser. Foremost in the minds of many is the thought, What if I accuse Uncle Ned and I'm wrong? He and Aunt Martha . . . and maybe others . . . might not speak to me again. But what if you accuse Uncle Ned and you are right? You will literally be saving a child's life—a child who desperately needs an advocate.

In a particularly moving letter to advice columnist Ann Landers, a man recently recounted the times he and his cousins had been molested by their grandfather. The man went on to relate that he, himself, had in turn molested his two young daughters and a son before he was caught and punished. His letter ended with a plea to parents and other relatives to protect the children in their families and said that if abuse occurs, parents should take action against the offender and keep him or her away from the children forever.

Once an accusation of sexual abuse is made, it *will* change your relationship with the accused relative forever, so I encourage you to gather your evidence. Talk with the young person and gain his or her trust. Pay attention to the nonverbal signs of the relationship, and then make yourself known as someone whom that young person can count upon to believe him or her. Perhaps your relationship to the accused *will* change, but with a good foundation and concern on your part, it is a risk well-worth taking. As a member of the family, you are in the best position to do something about a destructive and horrifying situation.

FLIRTING WITH TROUBLE

A more common situation with sexual overtones is one in which a family member flirts to varying degrees with others. In many ways, this is almost more difficult to deal with because, unlike a case of sexual abuse, which is obviously wrong, flirting within the family spans the spectrum from innuendo to actually touching someone else inappropriately. And then, as was pointed out earlier, there are different opinions as to what is appropriate. Is one pat on the bottom inappropriate? Is holding on to someone too long inappropriate? Are the long and lingering looks being exchanged more appropriate to lovers than in-laws?

Due to the fear of sexually transmitted diseases, our society is once again encouraging people to engage in prolonged and sexually innocent courtship rituals. Everywhere we turn these days there is another magazine article on the art of flirting. "Have fun with it!" cheers one. "Practice on everyone you meet," says another, and still another actually states that "Flirting with a married person is safer." While flirting can be a fun game in the appropriate arena, flirting within the extended family is an explosion waiting to happen.

Eileen, the woman at the beginning of this chapter, whose sister-in-law was getting too friendly with the male members of the family, was getting ready to explode. Kurtz says that the flirt needs to be confronted head on. Some planned communication is called for here as you let the offender know how it makes you feel when you see it happening. You might try saying, "It embarrasses me when I see you acting like a flirt," or "It hurts me when you flirt with my husband because I think you and I have a special relationship, and when you act that way it makes me angry with you." And then finish up with the second part of that communication: what you need from them. "I need you to stop doing that. It feels inappropriate to me."

If the person protests, as he or she very likely will, "I'm not doing anything"

or "It's all in your imagination!" then you need to reiterate your interpretation. "I know you don't believe you're doing anything but I have to
tell you my feelings. It feels to me like you're flirting, so I am asking you
to stop . . . stop flirting so we can keep our relationship."

"It takes a lot of guts to do this," says Kurtz, "but the relationship is
going to be damaged anyway. If that other family member is flirting with
your wife, husband, son, daughter, or sibling and you don't say anything,
the relationship is going to be damaged. Family members say to themselves,
'If I rock the boat and say something, I'm going to hurt someone's feelings. It will hurt our relationship and they will not speak to me, or they
will abandon me.' That is a risk that will have to be taken, if there is truly
a problem going on."

Again, one must proceed with caution in making accusations, making
sure to identify the real issue. Then, if you are satisfied that it is an uncomfortable or inappropriate situation, recognize that the only effective
way to "make it go away" is a confrontation.

HOMOSEXUALITY IN THE FAMILY

"Everyone knew Aunt Marlene was gay, but nobody ever talked about it."

"My brother Bobby is a homosexual and our dad refuses to talk to him
when he comes into the house. I love him and he loves his family so he
keeps coming around and pretending that everything is okay, but it hurts
me to see him suffer because of our father's rejection."

"I have one son who's homosexual and one who is straight. Although
the two get along all right, my straight son won't let his children spend
the night at their uncle's apartment. I've tried to talk to him about it, but
he is adamant that the children will be under a bad influence."

In the same-versus-different mentality of families, there is only one situation where seeking out sameness definitely makes one different: homosexuality. How secure we are in our own identities determines how we deal
with others in the family who may be different in any respect, but particularly in relation to sexual preferences. Often, a family's acceptance of
such differences also depends upon how they find out about them.

For example, one son, who chose a cousin's wedding to come out of the
closest and flaunt his relationship before the entire family, shocked his
parents and alienated many others, including his brother. What might
have been discussed and accepted in private was made a public spectacle,
thereby putting his family members on the spot. Of course the focus was
his homosexuality, but the real issue was his using his alternate lifestyle as

a club to take a whack at his family in public. Only a few family members speak to him a year later.

Fears that homosexuality may be "contagious" or that prejudice would be extended toward the homosexual's family prevent some from acknowledging their familial relationships. "I'm married with two children. My sister, who is an executive, is gay and has lived with the same woman for the last eight years," says one woman. "When I went to visit her last summer, she and her partner took me out to dinner at a lovely restaurant. The waiter assigned to our table obviously knew them well, and I began to feel very uncomfortable. I felt as though he had accepted me as gay too. For all I knew, other people thought I was gay as well. I know it sounds crazy, but I began to think about flirting with the guy at the next table just to prove that I wasn't. I am very conscious of those feelings when I am out with my sister now."

Our expectations for our family members usually include various aspects of the American Dream—a spouse, children, a house, a good job, a station wagon, a dog, and so on. Homosexuality is viewed by some as having no place in the American Dream; it is feared by many and denounced as immoral or evil by others. Since the issue of sex is integral to our identities, when a relative is gay, the "gayness" may become their sole identity in the eyes of their family, and this is what causes major conflicts.

"We had to throw out everything that we had ever hoped and dreamed for our son," says one mother. "His father still cannot speak with him for long periods of time without getting upset. He is a wonderful, talented man. I know I should look at those qualities instead—and maybe eventually I will—but right now I can only think 'gay' and it colors everything."

One young woman consciously chose a gay lifestyle due to influences in her early life. She was physically abused by her father and sexually abused by her step-grandfather for a period of about seven years. Because of the abuse, she felt safer and more nurtured in the company of women with whom she felt she could bond. She led a very open gay lifestyle with a long-term partner who, in fact, had two children. When the children visited, the women would co-parent. The few relatives who ostracized her were sadly, but simply, written off. "If you lie about who you are, then there's a secret, and you can't have a relationship with a secret in the way anyway," she says.

If there is one thing we would like to have from our family members, it is approval. Those who walk a path that veers from the normally accepted one, however, realize that not everyone is going to approve. But whether or not approval or endorsement is given, tolerance and acceptance can be—once our expectations are adjusted to what *is* rather than what is "supposed to" be.

Unfortunately, AIDS has complicated the acceptance of homosexuality in recent years, which "makes it seem as though the 1960s never happened," as one therapist commented.

THE TRAGEDY OF AIDS

It is 2 P.M. in the therapist's office and Tommy, a twenty-seven-year-old homosexual, is sitting on the small couch, alternately running his pale hands through his dark hair and clenching and unclenching them. Although he was pursuing an acting career in New York, his hospital stays have been increasing in frequency to the point where all he can do is return to his parents' home in between treatments.

"Today is my grandmother's eighty-fifth birthday, and we are giving her a huge family party," he says excitedly. "A big limo is going to be sent for her to take her to the restaurant. She'll complain a lot about everything, but I know she'll appreciate it, and as long as I don't have to sit next to her, I'll probably have a pretty good time.

"No, she doesn't know I have AIDS. Most of the family thinks I have cancer or leukemia. My parents and sister are the only ones who know, and I'll just make sure I don't kiss anyone there today. It was really a family decision—meaning my parents and myself—not to tell anyone. Why tag myself and let them put a label on me? Besides, if there' a cure in a year or so, there's no need to go through all that.

"Mom and Dad didn't even want to tell my twenty-two-year-old sister, but I felt close enough to her so I told her. We ran out of excuses not to tell her, is what really happened. That's why it's so hard to hold onto the secret—once you know, you have to release it. You need support. My sister is supportive, but now she says she feels suffocated because she can't talk to anyone. And she's developing a lot of phobias. If I invited her to a party, for example, she would have a difficult time going, particularly if gay people were there.

"My family makes decisions that revolve around me without even consulting me. It's a weird feeling, but I have really seen my parents' love through all of this. My father sends everyone to therapy but he won't go himself. He feels he can live with it. Never mind that we have to live with him and his attitudes. I used to fight about things like that with him, to try to make him see my point of view. I finally realized that I wasn't going to change him or teach him. He's the father and that's how he views himself. My sister hasn't learned that yet.

"My mother should join a support group. It's very hard on her. Facing this life-and-death situation has put an urgency to my thoughts. I've put a heavy burden on my parents. To do that to someone who loves you makes you feel very guilty, but I'm so grateful for their love and acceptance. I'm not so sure the rest of the family would be that loving. It's difficult to live with the feeling that I'm contaminated—that I have become the disease. AIDS is the only disease where that happens—that's why I told the rest of the family I had cancer. With cancer, you're a victim. With AIDS, you *are* the disease."

If I were to quote some statistics on AIDS here, no doubt they would be outdated quickly. We are all aware now that AIDS is not just a disease of homosexuals and hemophiliacs, but that large segments of the heterosexual population are also at risk.

Because it is a sexually transmitted disease, however, and a large proportion of the victims in Europe and North America are still homosexual, the disclosure of AIDS in a family is a shocking discovery that impels members to pass judgment on aspects of the victim's life, which had previously been private. Some are angry that they were not told about the disease at the onset and threaten lawsuits. Others simply cut off relations with the afflicted member or go in the opposite direction and look to the victim and his immediate family for help in dealing with their own feelings.

Although the body of AIDS law is in the process of evolving and may vary from state to state, in New Jersey, generally speaking, an AIDS victim is not required to inform anyone that he or she has tested positive for the virus, other than the state health department. According to Stephen Sepaniak, whose practice includes a number of hospitals and medical organizations, "There is a lot of anxiety about that, because relatives say that the person may be promiscuous and he or she could infect the spouse or even other members of the family. The legal answer is that the patient's hospital records are confidential. One's spouse, children, mother, brother, or lover are not entitled to them.

"The moral issue regarding disclosure, which had been previously left up to the patient, has undergone some rethinking, however," says Sepaniak. "The patient will be counseled to inform anyone whom he or she has put or is currently putting at risk by exchanging bodily fluids that the AIDS virus is present. If the patient refuses to disclose this information, the physician may be ethically bound to inform the party who is in danger of becoming infected."

Gray areas exist, however, because medical and legal experts are not in complete agreement at this time, and practices may vary from state to state. As with any new disease or legal situation, a definitive course of action will become the rule only after legislation is passed.

Counseling as a means of support is essential, according to the experts, not only for the victim but for the family members as well. This was something that Carina, a nurse and mother of six, realized when she got a telephone call from her twenty-five-year-old son Charlie who said "Mom, I have AIDS." Those were words that turned the family's life upside down, as Carina found a mixed reaction among relatives and friends.

"Some would be tremendously supportive and I would find bags of groceries on my front step, while others would say 'How can you go into that house?' " Since her son's death in June 1985, Carina has founded the Charlie Club, a support group in Madison, New Jersey, for families of AIDS sufferers, has served on state task forces on AIDS, has written newspaper columns, and is a popular lecturer on the subject.

"Anyone going through this needs support," says Carina. "There are lots of support groups out there now, and many of them meet at churches in the evening because people are afraid of the stigma attached to the disease. Just knowing that someone out there cares, and may be going through the same emotions and practical obstacles, can help a person cope tremendously."

To keep the bridges open in a family situation, one must first get all the factual information available. This will outline the limits and risk of exposure. Once the facts are in place, then comes the difficult part of changing one's expectations both for that relative and for the relationship. As relatives revise their expectations, however, they must remember that the victim and his or her family have far more drastic expectations to revise and cannot be counted upon to be the "strong ones." On the contrary, this is an ideal opportunity to strengthen the family network and bond through compassion and practical assistance.

11

Sibling Rivalries, Again and Again

Brothers and sisters hold a unique place in the family chain and are, perhaps surprisingly, some of the most powerful in the roster of our silent navigators. They are our contemporaries growing up and share a common gene pool and family history. When everyone else has passed on, they will still be around to remember you as the child you once were—something that is rarely shared even with our spouses. You may be a big hotshot executive now, but they'll always remember you as the three-year-old who, wearing nothing but a grin and yellow socks, had to be chased two blocks before your embarrassed mother caught up with you!

Given those kinds of memories, they are also the ones who possess the knowledge of our weaknesses, as well as our strengths, and know how to use that knowledge to their best advantage. Who else can push your buttons more quickly and send your blood pressure racing to the stratosphere?

Margo was always considered the "smart one" who won awards, whereas Annette was the "pretty one" who got all the boys and attention. Today, although they are both in their fifties, their rivalry not only still permeates all their family relationships but has been assumed by their children. This was evident at Margo's recent birthday party when Annette "accidentally" dropped her wine glass into her sister's elaborately designed cake. Later, Annette's daughter made a show of presenting her mother with a blouse identical to the one Margo was wearing, thus continuing the rivalry into the next generation.

Rick and Lucy argue all the time. Both widowed and only three years apart in age, they still attempt to boss each other around and vie for family attention. Although their parents are long dead, other family members are now the recipients of this ongoing rivalry as the two octogenarians even try to outdo each other with gifts for grandnieces and grandnephews. When they traveled to Europe together to visit their parents' homeland, they were asked to leave the bus because of their constant and loud bickering. "Getting old doesn't mean you know how to get along!" insists Lucy.

LouAnn and Nancy would agree with that. These sisters haven't spoken to each other in nine years. Their children don't really know their cousins, and neither family has attended a family event at which the other has appeared during that time. Family information is passed on through a sister who lives in another state. This is a particularly bizarre arrangement considering that both LouAnn and Nancy live on the same residential street. They have regulated their lives so stringently, however, that they rarely come or go at the same time. Their neighbors would be shocked to discover that these two are sisters.

Most people, when asked to reflect on their childhood, give a brief description of the roles their parents played, but then give detailed memories of their brothers and sisters. Sometimes, the overall tone of the memory is determined by the sibling relationship, not the relationship with the parents.

"I had a happy childhood," says one man. "Our family was pretty close and my brothers and I shared a lot of activities. I remember one time when . . ."

"I had an okay childhood," says another. "I was one of five children and you should have heard us fight. It used to drive my parents crazy!"

"I didn't really have much of a childhood," says one woman. "I was the oldest of four and both my parents worked, so I was responsible for my sister and brothers as far back as I can remember."

At its best, the sibling relationship is one of the most intimate friendships in existence. With whom else do you share the secret that your bed broke because you were both doing the forbidden jumping act on it, instead of the story that you told your parents of the dog's chewing through one of the legs? At its worst, the rivalry among siblings can be like that of the most formidable of enemies or the coldest of nations divided by a wall with no Checkpoint Charlie as a means of egress.

Do you cringe at the memory of being called "Chubbs," "Pest," or "Toad Face"? Chances are, those were the kinds of names bestowed upon you by a brother or sister. And chances are just as strong that to this day, you are still trying to outgrow them. One very thin woman told me that both her mother and sister were model-thin and she was the chubby one of the family. When her sister started calling her "Chunky," her parents laughed. So did she, to hide the hurt, but eventually she found herself trying every diet that came down the pike in order to shed that chubby image. "Every time I look at the dessert menu in a restaurant or reach for a cookie or piece of candy, I can hear my sister's voice calling me Chunky and I'm afraid to go back to that," she says.

Our sibling relationships have affected everything from our self-esteem and confidence to our negotiating techniques. Dr. Eric Berne, in his book *Games People Play*, maintains that raising children consists primarily in teaching them what games to play, and that parents rarely impress upon their children the consequences of those games.

In the early years of sibling rivalry, few follow the advice that the solving of children's squabbles should be put back in the laps of the children. Rather, parents succumb to the pitfall of mediating, demonstrating loyalty to one child over another, and even setting up a competitive atmosphere that stretches well into adulthood. Parents are easy to blame for our shortcomings, adult frustrations, and behavior patterns, but in the case of our sibling relationships, parents *are* the primary course setters. Their handling or manipulation of sibling identities and rivalries early on creates the views that we tend to live with for a lifetime.

This game playing and relationship making exists in blended families as well, depending upon the ages of the children when the families are combined. Although they don't share a common gene pool, they are involved in constructing a new family history.

At some point, we should be able to take responsibility for a good relationship ourselves. We should be able to put aside Mommy and Daddy's methods of dealing with us and forge a successful adult relationship with that brother or sister who always seemed to be brighter, better looking, and more favored. What keeps it from happening?

ACTING ACCORDING TO SCRIPT

"When I was growing up, my younger brother was always the sick one," says Todd, a thirty-six-year-old jeweler. "He had a muscle disease, and my parents didn't know if he would make it or not. As a result, a lot of our family life centered around how Tim was feeling. I was supposed to be the strong one who could handle anything, and my sister was the clown of the family who could take my parents' minds off their problems. They didn't seem to recognize that I sometimes felt like I was floundering and my sister wasn't always happy. Even today, although Tim is an adult and well, my parents still help support him and he expects that from all of us. He thinks nothing of borrowing a few bucks here and there or asking for favors. I almost cringe when I hear his voice on the phone because I know I'm going to be hit on for something. He never calls just to see how I am or how the family is doing. And it drives me nuts that my parents don't seem to see his selfishness, just as they seem to take it for granted that I built this business all on my own with no help from anyone. It just hurts not to be recognized."

If someone asked you to describe your brother or sister, what would you say? Without even thinking about it, you may come back with, "Oh, she is the beauty of the family," or "She is the smart one," or "He is the jock" or "the sensitive one," "the funny one," "the successful one," "the sickly one," or "the real troublemaker." Where did these labels come from? I've never yet heard of a case where an obstetrician in the delivery room turned to the new mother and said "Aha! I see by the stamp on the baby's rump that you have a Grade A Troublemaker, Mrs. Jones." Rather, these identities tend to come about in one of two ways.

First, just as the roles discussed earlier in this book are taken on by members according to what's needed in the family at a certain time, these identities are often distributed in much the same fashion. If parents are particularly in need of an athlete, brilliant child, or beauty, they will tend to bestow that label on the next child that comes along—whether it's deserved or not.

"My dad was a real jock, football trophies and everything," says Hayden. "Unfortunately, I was undersized and had little interest in football, but he was determined he was going to have another jock in the family. He tried every sport imaginable on me. I did all right, but mostly to please him. The pressure was off when my younger brother came along. The screwy thing about it was my younger brother was really more the athlete, and I enjoyed music. To this day, the first words out of my dad's mouth when he sees me usually revolve around what games are on television and the sports pages. It makes me crazy, but he's deaf on the subject, and I know I can't change him."

The second way in which the labels are assigned is that a child, at some point early in life, demonstrates some fulfillment of the assigned label, and so he or she is stuck with it for life. In *The Prince of Tides* by Pat Conroy, Tom Wingo examines the dynamics of his Southern family:

I tried to think of all our roles. One member of the family, by a process of artificial but deadly selection, is nominated to be the lunatic, and all neurosis, wildness, and displaced suffering settles like dust in the eaves and porches of that tenderest, most vulnerable psyche.

Luke had been offered the role of strength and simplicity. He had suffered under the terrible burden of being the least intellectual child.

My designation in the family was normality. I was the balanced child drafted into the ranks for leadership, for coolness under fire, stability. "Solid as a rock," my mother would describe me to her friends, and I thought the description was perfect.

The myth that exists here is that you can have only one of each kind in a family, and that every label is static. For example, if a daughter is pretty, she becomes the beauty—a title her sisters, despite development to the contrary, cannot aspire to. If a child is a good student, he or she becomes the family scholar and is treated with a certain amount of gravity. Never mind that the scholar also has a good sense of humor and the "family clown" is making nearly straight A's. This fallacy of thought goes hand in hand with the myth that there is only so much power to go around—that if one member becomes stronger, the others must then be weaker.

Is it any wonder then that as we go hurtling toward adulthood, we treat our siblings in the same manner as did our parents? It is a learned behavior, with an added twist—resentment. We resent that we are not recognized for some of those traits identified with our sibling. It is a resentment we sometimes perpetuate when we slide right into our assigned roles among family members—no matter how old or independent or successful we may be outside the family circle. And we resent it when someone steps outside an assigned role, the result may be a major conflict!

"My sister was always thought to be the successful one," says Megan, a petite brunette. "She always got the better grades in school, and when she married, she and her husband had more money, because my husband went into the military. Well, twenty years, a passel of children, and several careers later, I finally got my master's degree. She never congratulated me, said 'Drop dead,' nor asked questions—nothing. We invited her and her husband out to dinner to celebrate my graduation, and do you know, she ignored the topic the entire evening until her husband made some comment, teasing me, and then she jumped in. Well, I exploded. I told her she was being ugly, and she left the table hysterical, which was her usual way of dealing with things.

"I was just as happy not to speak to her, but my husband believes in confrontation, so he kept encouraging me to go after her. Well, I did confront her and told her how hurt I was. She got hysterical again and finally apologized and said it was because I had done something she always wanted to do—and me, of all people—her little sister. She just couldn't handle the fact that I didn't fit her mold any more."

Breaking out of the assigned role was also a continuing struggle for Curtis, the youngest of four and the only boy. His oldest sister, as chief sibling, manipulated the others and demanded a certain amount of attention. "When one of our other sisters would come to town, Jen would get offended if Karen didn't stay with her because she's the oldest," says Curtis. "Three days into the visit, Karen would call and say that Jen was driving her crazy, to please come and get her out of there. It has become somewhat of a ritual."

But the real conflict reached a crescendo when Curtis, at an unusually young age, became a successful financial consultant on Wall Street and his parents and other relatives began turning to him for advice. "His sisters, particularly his oldest sister, just couldn't handle it," says Curtis's wife. "I guess what happened was, they never expected him to grow up. Jen feels displaced, and she's taken it out on us in different ways. For example, we were having lunch at a downtown eatery one Sunday, really engrossed in conversation with this interesting old man at the next table—he was an old drama coach—and having a lovely time. Suddenly, Jen comes up, all red in the face, and accuses us in a loud voice of seeing her and snubbing her. She was angry that we didn't say hello first. Can you imagine? We *didn't* see her, but you'll never convince her of that. She's the type to keep a scorecard; you know, 'On September 27, you snubbed me in the restaurant, on November 16, you didn't call when you were supposed to . . .' Then, if you really have an argument over something, she pulls out this little mental list and begins rattling off all these supposed insults!"

Do these people who drive their siblings crazy act the same way toward their friends? Probably not. I heard it said over and over again, "I look at my brother [or sister] and they seem to have friends who value them. They go out of their way to be nice. Why do they act so badly to members of the family?"

First of all, friends will not usually put up with the same aggravations that family members will endure (family is the place where they usually have to take you in). Second, they are not fulfilling those scripted roles. I bet you've done it yourself. No matter how old or accomplished you envision yourself to be, you tend to revert to old childhood roles when you get around your family. Try to break out or bring it to your parents' attention and you get the classic line, "Well, I don't know why he could act that way. After all, we raised you all exactly the same." Sound familiar? This is another myth of family life: A common childhood and upbringing should bring about harmony.

* * *

SHARED MEMORIES—ARE THEY REALLY SHARED?

There is an old adage that says, "Where you stand depends upon where you sit." Nothing could be more true, especially for siblings. Just because brothers and sisters are raised in the same house doesn't necessarily mean that they will grow in parallel fashion. The order of their birth, the parental life stages relevant to each child, and innate personality differences among siblings all contribute to exploding the myth that siblings are "supposed to" know instinctively each other's thought and needs. As a matter of fact, those very same parents who lament that you were all raised exactly the same, are the first to tell their friends how completely different each of their children is.

In college journalism classes, a popular topic of debate is whether or not there is truly such a thing as objective reporting, given each reporter's human tendency to absorb information through the filter of his or her background and experiences. Debating the reality of true objectivity is a favorite exercise, which demonstrates that several people can witness the same event simultaneously and walk away with very different impressions (ask any police officer attempting to gather eyewitness accounts at the scene of a crime).

This was poignantly revealed to me when one of my sisters and I were sharing a memory and were startled at the different perceptions that influenced our lives. The particular incident occurred during a time when our mother, an award-winning artist of international stature, had been informed of a particular tour available for professionals of her caliber. Since it would take her away from home to roam around the globe for three months, she turned it down. But somewhat wistfully reflecting upon the opportunity, she sat at the kitchen table, staring out into space, and commented, "If I didn't have children, I could do it."

At fourteen, I overheard the comment and felt anger. I took the comment as an aspersion (as most fourteen-year-olds are wont to do about anything their parents say) and resolved never to say such a rotten thing when I was a parent.

My middle sister, who was nine years old at the time, heard the comment and thought, "Oh, I don't ever want to be sad like that. I'm never going to have children until I have done all I want to do in the world." At this writing, she holds several pilot's licenses and scuba diving certifications, can sail a boat with the best of them, and as my son says, "she's the adventurer of the family." And no, she doesn't have children . . . yet.

Finally, our youngest sister, who was only five at the time, heard the same comment and thought, "She doesn't love me."

One shared memory, but three different realities. Combine that with inherent personality differences—such as those presented in the often-used Myers-Briggs Type Indicator, which classifies personalities as extraverted or introverted, sensing or intuitive, thinking or feeling, and judging or perceiving—and you have the ideal recipe for misunderstandings, downright hostility, and division.

"I can't believe this silly incident started a whole family argument," says Janie, shaking her head. "I was talking with my sister and she was all upset about something that I thought was off the wall, so I said, 'Are you crazy?!' and laughed. Well, she told her husband that I told her she was mentally ill. He called me back and screamed at me that I was never to say anything that hateful about his wife again.

"I was floored! Her problem is that she has no sense of humor. She takes everything too literally. She feels that I take everything too lightly. But I've had to deal with a lot more crises than she has. You either laugh or crack up. That's my philosophy," says Janie.

Sometimes marriage breaks up "that old gang of yours" when a sibling marries someone who either doesn't care for you or who grates on your nerves. And how, you ask, could that brother or sister be attracted to someone so "alien" in nature to your family, anyway?

"In the twenty years that I've been married, my brother has never once visited me," says Marie sadly. "There's always been an excuse—too short a vacation period, his wife's family commitments—lots of excuses. I have always had the feeling, though, that it was just that his wife didn't like me. My brother and I used to be close growing up, but now we hardly talk. I finally got up my courage and asked him if I had done anything that I could apologize for, and he said nothing that he knew of. He said not to worry, that one of these days, he'd just drop in and surprise us. I said, 'Yeah, and I'll be in a wheelchair by that time.'

"My brother and his family do live in a different state, but it's not that far away. Certainly not twenty years away. As I've gotten older, I realize that family gets more important. My dad is ill, and when he's gone, my brother is all I'll have left. Maybe there are just some people you meet in life that you don't care to spend a lot of time with—the chemistry isn't there. My brother has turned into one of those, but because he's family, I feel we should be in touch. It's just so sad that we tend to focus on the differences in people, instead of trying to find the common ground."

How true. We do tend to focus on the differences, of which there are many, and view them in a negative way instead of as a means of growth for ourselves and our relationships. Different lifestyles, different interests, and different types of spouses tend to generate clashes among adult siblings in much the same manner as sibling children will fight over which cereal to buy, which television program to watch, and even the air that they are breathing (I distinctly remember fighting over that one on a long car trip, before my father's hand snaked over the back of the front seat like a robotic club in search of impact).

Sibling rivalry is, by definition however, a competition at any age. Like charity, it begins at home. But unlike charity, the more you engage in the competition game, the more imprisoned you become, and the crazier.

THE COMPETITIVE EDGE

"I guess I come from a very competitive family," admits Gail, an entrepreneur who recently opened her own boutique. "My mother was a strong woman and I always felt I was in competition with my sister and brother—particularly my sister. We are only two years apart in age and we even competed for the same boyfriends. She went to the same college I selected and got involved in even more activities than I did. Then she married one of my old boyfriends. I know every dollar she makes, how much her car costs, and where she's going on vacation. At family gatherings, she knocks herself out preparing special dishes. I have to admit that I play the game, too, because my parents look at what she's doing and at what I'm doing, and I don't like to feel I am disappointing them.

"I got really angry, though, when she had a daughter and named her Elise. She knew I wanted to name my daughter that—not that I have a daughter yet, but she knew it was my favorite girl's name, and she stole it from me! We don't have to compete much with our brother because he is in a different category anyway, having the 'male advantage.' In my parents' eyes, the sun rises and sets on his head. All this competition gets very tiring. I'd like to just say 'Stuff it,' but then I'd feel like I was falling behind. Does that make sense?"

Comedians Tommy and Dick Smothers built a whole show business career around the concept that "Mom always liked you best!" In Woody Allen's hit movie *Hannah and Her Sisters*, sibling rivalry was the motivating force behind everything from rebellion to infidelity ("Do I make love better than my sister?" one character asks her brother-in-law, with whom she is having an affair). Although audiences laughed, the laughter was probably tinged with discomfort, because adult sibling rivalry is aggravating and the source of many family feuds.

Every child wants to be the shining star on his or her parents' horizon. It is a natural desire that sits like an idling engine, ready to roar forward with the application of a little gentle pressure. Usually, however, the pressure is all but gentle and it is applied by the parents themselves.

"My husband's parents breed the rivalry," says Betty. "It's very insidious. They are constantly comparing one to another. It is almost a way of manipulating the children, so that whatever you're talking about, whatever your accomplishment, they constantly bring up the others in that context to detract from your achievement."

More hated than the "teacher's pet" is the "parent's pet." It is a position that is rarely asked for, and although enjoyed, many realize the inequities and spend the rest of their lives trying to make up for it with siblings.

"I was the favored one, I admit it," says Arlene. "My mother got me contact lenses when I was thirteen; my sister had to wait until she was seventeen. I got my way much more often, and my parents always made a big deal out of what I did in school. Now as adults, my sister and I are very distant. If I tell her what I'm doing, she acts as though I'm comparing our lifestyles. If I dress fashionably for a family gathering, she makes snide comments about my frivolous spending habits. I can't win. I'd like to have her for a friend, but I don't think it will happen."

As authors Adele Faber and Elaine Mazlish found in compiling their popular book *Siblings Without Rivalry*, it isn't always necessary to compare siblings outright in order to breed competition. Just mentioning a sibling in the wake of an accomplishment is catalyst enough. Even those misguided parents who attempt to stifle competition by treating all offspring equally, no matter what the cost, breed contempt.

"I'll never forget that my parents did not come to my high school graduation," says Craig, a successful physician who grew up in a privileged environment. "I was at boarding school and my two brothers were at home. I had a lacrosse game, graduation, and awards banquet all in the same week, and my parents felt that if they attended all those events for me, my brothers, who had nothing going on, would be jealous. So they just stayed away. In their minds, they treated us all the same. In my mind, I was royally snubbed, not to mention hurt."

The competition may have started back when we were kids, but it rages all through adulthood for many. You don't have to be in constant contact (as a matter of fact, most prefer not to be!) but the issues with brag value are as varied as the personalities. What are some of the favorites?

- *Homes.* "Ha! You call that a bathroom? Our bathroom is bigger than your kitchen and back porch put together!"

  "Hey, I know you're cramped for space—I really don't know why you wanted the whole family over there squashed together, when they could have breathing space over at my home—but if you'd like, I can bring a tent to set up outside. At least the kids can escape from underfoot."

"Of course I don't mind having Dad's birthday party over here, but do we have to include the kids? After all, my home is filled with expensive antiques and things, and I know your kids aren't used to having to be careful around things like that."

- *Incomes.* "Yes, Jerry just got another raise—the second one this year. So how are you doing?"

"Listen, do you know the name of a good financial counselor? I just got a $100,000 bonus and don't want to have it just sitting in a savings account. I realize you don't have to worry about those kinds of things, but . . ."

"Boy, am I having problems. I can't believe I have to shell out another forty grand in taxes in addition to what was subtracted from my paycheck." (Usually told to a sibling who is making under $40,000 a year.)

- *Schools.* "Yeah, when I was at the Yale Club on Saturday . . ."

"Of course, since you went to a state university, you wouldn't realize the importance of networking, but . . ."

"Well, you could have gone to college instead of going to work, so sure you're having problems now. It's your own fault."

- *Children.* "Yes, Johnny just got accepted into the Gifted and Talented Program at school and will get his black belt in karate next month, after he finishes with the town's traveling soccer team. Have you talked to the school counselor about your Susie's learning disability yet?"

"I feel sorry for you. My Bobby would never think of hanging around with the kinds of kids your Sam hangs around with. No wonder you look so terrible lately."

"Yes, little Anton was invited to play his violin with the symphony orchestra. They are even talking about a television special, but it doesn't faze him. You know what a poised child he is."

- *Vacations.* "I know, I can't stand this weather either. I don't know if I'll make it another week until we can leave for Hawaii. Of course I'll think of you stuck here."

"Well, we will be going to the Virgin Islands for Christmas; then in February, we have to go to a company conference in Paris. Then we'll do our usual Easter break in Aspen, and then I'll have to think about summer vacation. All this packing and unpacking can drive you crazy!"

"I know it's hard for you to get away, so I will go keep Mom and Dad company at the lake house again this summer."

There are many more variations, but the common feeling upon hearing these "loving" comments is the desire to drop-kick a sibling into the next century. As easy as it is to get sucked into the competitive race, one woman found that her conflicts with her siblings have arisen because she has tried to break out of the cycle.

"Every year it's the same thing," says Marchia. "The family gets together for Thanksgiving at my parents' home. Many of us come a long distance and we need to stay overnight. Then the fights begin because my parents can't sleep all five of their grown children plus grandchildren. One sister will whine that she deserves to sleep at my parents' rather than the motel because she's pregnant. Then another complains that it's more expensive for her and her three children to sleep at a motel than it is for my brother and his wife, who are coming halfway across the country for dinner. My husband and I find that—to avoid going nuts over all the bickering that continues for three days—we are the last to arrive and the first to leave, and we always stay at the motel. But even this has been criticized.

"Now my sisters are engaged in a battle to see who can be the best daughter to Mommy, since our father died two years ago. They knock themselves out arranging their schedules to take her places, buy her things, and bring her over to their homes. This in itself isn't bad, but what I see happening is that each one is trying to outdo the other in attempting to make Mom dependent upon her—to show how much better a daughter she is. I have tried to do things to help Mom become more independent, but that's been seen as not caring. It drives me crazy and it hurts sometimes, but I am not going to play their game."

While competitive patterns are learned early, sibling rivalry does not observe rigid boundaries. Actually, real rivalry not only crosses generational lines but is often accentuated by the arrival of new generations.

RIVALRY CROSSES THE LINE

"My husband's family has always been competitive," says Lou. "To the point that before his brother took a vacation, he would check to see where we were going first and then try to outdo us. His wife and I got pregnant at approximately the same time—she a little earlier than I. It should not have been a surprise then that after we announced we were pregnant, they went and had an ultrasound done so they could find out the sex of their baby before we did. They even called us on the phone that night and said, 'Well, at least we beat you on knowing. We are going to have a girl.' I didn't want to know the sex of our baby until it was born. Turned out to be a boy and we were delighted. Jack's brother, though, was pissed off. Really, he acted as though we were sharing bad news instead of good. His reaction was, 'Oh well, I'll beat you next time.' That's so sick in this day and age!''

Not only do the siblings compete themselves, they compete for their children. Gift giving seems to be a big stumbling block because it is viewed as an expression of thoughtfulness, esteem, and one-upmanship. Siblings fight if:

The gifts given to their children are not equal in value to the ones given to the sibling's children. ("She's such a cheapskate. She doesn't even bother to think about what she's giving, and I always spend a lot of time and thought on a gift!")

The gifts given are more expensive. ("They're always trying to show off how much money they have. What does this kid need with a pocket television, anyway?")

The gift is late. ("She's never been on time with anything in her life, and I always make sure my gifts get there on time. It doesn't bother me, of course, but it really disappoints the kids!")

The gift is early. ("They are always afraid I'm not going to buy something of equal value for them, so they always send their present early—and usually with the price tag left on it!")

The child is overlooked and no gift is given. ("That's it! After all the time and money I've spent on this family, and he doesn't even have the courtesy to send my son a two-dollar puzzle!")

Then there are those sibling rivalries that cross generational lines when a sibling changes roles. John, for example, was the patriarchal figure in his family ever since his father died when he was a teenager. He was the favorite uncle and godfather and, since he was unmarried, had plenty of time to devote to his brother's and sister's families. Then at the age of forty-four John fell in love, married, and was a father himself a year later. "That was the day my brother and sister started giving me the cold shoulder," he says angrily. "My sister actually said that now I wouldn't have time for her and her family, so forget it. I can't believe such small-minded selfishness! As if I was supposed to sacrifice my life for them!"

All right, you have had enough. In fact, you have had more than enough and you are going to give that little, selfish, small-minded, kowtowing, sniveling, bossy, self-centered, and thoughtless brother or sister a piece of your mind—if you have any left. *Building* a bridge to this person? "Maybe *tie him* to a bridge during a lightning storm," you say. The stage is set for battle, the skirmish begins, and then what happens? They go and tell Mom or Dad!

THE GET-ALONG GANG

What are the three familiar parental refrains from childhood? Along with "Tie your shoes" and "Eat your vegetables," it's "Stop fighting!" If you continued to fight, what happened? Mom or Dad stepped in to mediate, swat, punish, or preserve their nerves.

The parental refrain does not change all that much when the children grow up. Now it's "How is your job?" "You're looking too thin" or "too fat," and "Stop fighting!" The players, however, have changed a great deal. Years of secrets and experiences (drug experimentation, abortions, financial cheating) can be wielded as weapons. The accusations become ever more inflammatory (the "you always" and "you never" accusations), and the hurts are more devastating and even life-changing. (One man purposefully neglected to pass along some financial information to his brother, resulting in great monetary gain for himself and financial hardship for the brother. They haven't spoken in four years.)

Parents, approaching a point at which they are thinking of a time when they will no longer be around, thrust themselves into the squabbles of their adult offspring in an attempt to bring about peace. Or they may be dragged into the arguments by those offspring who are still resorting to earlier, childish behavior patterns: the I'm-gonna-tell-on-you syndrome. This intrusion, however well meant, instead of bridging a gap and drawing siblings closer together, actually pushes them further apart. It also makes sibling bridge-building more difficult in the future. Emotions are treated as problems to be rooted out, stifled.

"I can't say anything against my sister," says one woman. "Even though my mother knows what a selfish brat she still is at thirty-five, she won't acknowledge that I may be right. She just wants us to get along."

"Getting along" becomes the goal; disagreement and conflict are seen as bad and undesirable. What happens when natural conflicts arise? We can refuse to recognize a problem and deal with it internally, causing a rise in blood pressure. Or we can recognize it and then refuse to deal with the people involved by cutting them off. This avoidance technique is practiced every day. If you listen carefully, you can hear telephones being slammed down in siblings' ears across the nation with the resonance of a metroliner hurtling from coast to coast.

Neither of these methods strengthens the connections between family members. What it does promote are ulcers and guilt feelings because we are not "supposed to" have bad feelings towards our siblings. We are "supposed to" love our siblings—it makes Mom and Dad happy. We are "supposed to" get along.

I said, in chapter one, the Chinese character for crisis is composed of the characters for danger and opportunity. I would like to take this idea a step further. Rather than view all conflict as bad, particularly among siblings, I feel that conflict presents the opportunity for either chaos or growth. Which path we take depends upon how we handle the conflict. If we rigidly adhere to the "supposed to's" of sibling relationships, we will never break out of our childhood patterns.

So how do we take the path of construction and growth, rather than chaos, in dealing with our brothers and sisters? First, give them away. That's right, start fresh. Of course, you can't really give them away—although I know a man who has not maintained contact with his sisters for years. Several have remarried and he doesn't even know their new last names! But more realistically, give away the images of those siblings that were dictated by your parents. Look at them as people (I know this can be hard) rather than as your brothers and sisters. What is it in them that their friends see and you don't? Throw away the idea that your brother is the funny one of the family and your sister is the beauty. Those were assigned roles. What are they like outside the family circle?

Second, recognize that, for all the reasons discussed in this chapter, there *will* be conflicts. Conflict is acceptable, if you approach it in a positive manner. Rather than engaging in warfare like enemy submarines sent out to seek and destroy, ask yourself what can you *get* from your particular argument—perhaps a new view of yourself, or a new perception of your sister or brother.

Benjamin Franklin, that founding father who had something to say about everything, promoted the idea, "Blessed is he who expects nothing, because he'll never be disappointed." That could be applied to our adult sibling relationships as well. We need to accept our brothers and sisters for what they are, rather than the vision of what we would like them to be, what they are "supposed to" be. Are those arguments petty power plays? If so, realize that they are caught up in the family myth, and get on with your own life.

Lisa, a thirty-two-year-old music teacher and mother of two, found that in laying the foundation for a strong bridge with her family, she was empowered by the construction. "When I couldn't take it anymore, I wrote a fourteen-page letter to the entire family, with copies for each of my brothers and my sister," says Lisa. "I told them I wasn't going to play the competition game anymore, and that I expected to be treated with the same respect I show for them. I love them, but I don't always like them and what they do, and I finally realized that it was okay. I didn't have to feel guilty if I got angry with one of them.

"My parents got hysterical. They took the letter to mean that I didn't want to be part of the family anymore. I had to assure them that I would always be part of the family, but not a part of the petty bickering. Suddenly, I realized," says Lisa "that I was in control of my options for the first time in my life!"

In order for your resolutions to work, you must communicate your new attitudes. Whereas one particularly secure and outspoken woman feels comfortable with verbal confrontations, other people use letters so they "don't forget anything" in their nervous assumption of this new role. And one woman, who hasn't yet been able to confront her relatives at all, vents her frustrations in a journal. "I write down all the things I should have said, but didn't think of at the time. I cuss and call them nasty names and even devise what I think are fitting punishments," she says. "I get all my bad feelings out and then I'm able to let the pettiness wash over me."

Finally, if your sibling relationships are still not satisfactory despite all of your good intentions and construction, develop your surrogate sibling chain. Perhaps in a friend you will find the closeness you were "supposed to" have with a sister. Friendship won't substitute for familial ties, but when conflicts do arise, you will be able to place less importance on jealousies, competition, and family roles if you are assured that you are a person of value to others. Sometimes, that's the hug we need.

Part III

THE MOST
COMMON
DIVIDERS:
MONEY

12

Money Is
Thicker than
Blood

All kinds of people are fascinated by money: those who have it, those who want it, those who have lost it, those who have found it, those who manipulate it, and those who give it away. It is the subject of numerous proverbs and warnings: "Money is the root of all evil"; "A fool and his money are soon parted"; "Money isn't everything"; "Money is power"; "Money talks."

In family circles, a commonly accepted favorite adage is "Blood is thicker than water," but, too often, people unfortunately learn the wisdom in the up-and-coming adage, "Money is thicker than blood." As a cause of family feuds, it stands as one of the prime stumbling blocks to the building of good relationships.

One of the most warmly embraced myths is that you can always trust your family members to do the right thing. You are "supposed to" trust them. After all, your interests are supposed to be their interests, and this in turn is supposed to ensure the continuance of the family line. When it comes to money, however, human greed sometimes bubbles up like a powerful acid dissolving the tethers of kinship. Others view those tethers as personal lines of credit to a source of financial assistance with no governmental regulations and few oral obligations.

Bruce and Marie, both immature in money matters, just couldn't seem to make it financially. Bruce finally turned to his older and more successful brother Peter for help. It was a pattern that was repeated over a period of seven years, during which Bruce had two more children, moved away, was struck by illnesses, and continued his irresponsible spending. Each time he got into trouble, he'd weep on the phone to his brother who, suffering pangs of guilt over the disparity in their circumstances, would write Bruce another check—after all, he didn't want his nephews and niece to suffer. Finally, the arrangement came to a blow-up when a bank official, with whom Peter did business professionally, told Peter that his credit rating was bad because of a loan he had cosigned for his brother. Bruce had not made payments in five months and neglected to tell Peter.

Some money feuds begin when one party feels that the other relatives have not contributed their "fair share." Margaret, although less financially comfortable than her four siblings, took in and supported her elderly father during the last six years of his life. Her repeated requests for financial assistance during those years produced only token contributions. Upon her father's death, she found that his estate, such as it was, had been divided equally. Margaret produced receipts for her father's expenses and demanded that the others "pay up." When they refused, Margaret took the matter to her lawyer. Margaret and her relatives are still on cool terms.

Still other family conflicts arise when one member acts independently. Eighty-year-old Irene, widowed three times, moved in with her spinster sister Mathilda, age seventy-four. The two lived a fairly independent life in their cluttered little apartment in New York until senility began to set in. More than once, relatives were sought to give assistance when the fun-loving pair indulged in such entertaining antics as dropping water balloons on the heads of passersby. When the two died within six months of each other, no one knew who would "clean up" their little estate. Since neither had left a will, one of Irene's middle-age daughters, unsophisticated but good-hearted, decided that the simplest thing to do was donate all of the ladies' trunks of clothes and bags of memorabilia to the local convent for their white elephant sale. After all, they thought, the apartment was mostly just filled with junk. Unfortunately, when several of the more worldly-wise members of the family attended the sale to lend support, they were horri-fied to find that the two sisters' apartment had actually been a treasure trove of period clothing in perfect condition, first-edition books, American primitive antiques, and valuable original art, which had been jammed be-tween books and clothes. Battles over lost sentimental, as well as mone-tarily valuable, items went on for years.

The family relationship presents a two-edged sword piercing the dollar sign. On the one side is kindly Uncle Mo, who generously empties his pockets to help a relative in trouble; on the other, is sneaky Sammy, the relative who just sold the house out from under his mother in order to invest in the stock market. And at the point of the sword is the mother, father, brother, or sister who declines to press charges against the offending relative because of that wonderful family tie, which allowed them to be taken to the cleaners in the first place!

* * *

MONEY AS AN IDENTITY

Part of the great American Dream is to have wealth—whatever the personal definition for wealth may be. For some, it is simply to have a bit more than one's father. For others, it is the accumulation of vast storehouses of material possessions. But something happens in a family when one branch achieves the American Dream in terms of dollars, while other branches are still swaying in the breeze. The specter of silent "supposed to's" materializes: "You are *supposed to* share the wealth"—whether in terms of loans, vacation homes, or gifts. "You are *supposed to* continue living in a manner suited to the rest of the family." (Notice that these two restrictions contradict each other.) This means no country clubs, fancy vacations, or purchases that can inspire jealousy in other family members; unless, of course, you plan to live by the first "supposed to" and share it all. "You are *supposed to* remember the great Puritan work ethic." This means that even when you've made it, you should not indulge yourself with cleaning services or lawn help as long as there is a breath in your body and a free hour in which to do those chores.

Arthur worked hard all his life. He worked hard and was lucky. Trying to pass a little of life's riches on to his brother, he loaned Mike money to get a business started and then even worked for him for free. The business took off, and now Mike is a successful developer, while Arthur is retired. But Mike always charges Arthur for the long distance phone calls he makes while visiting.

Theo is a millionaire several times over. He drives his relatives crazy, however, with his thrift. He has been known to scoop up teabags that have only been used once and save them in a baggie stashed in his pocket, all the while delivering lectures on waste. He wears his clothing until there are holes for natural air-conditioning, and whines that he cannot afford hotel rates when he goes to visit relatives.

Shelly and Eric take just the opposite tack. They are the wealthiest couple in the family and they flaunt it. Although young family members love the lavish gifts, older members are critical of the pair's lifestyle, selfishness, and ever-constant bragging. Shelly and Eric have adopted the attitude that because they are the richest, they are the most important and therefore demand homage.

Since financial success is a measuring stick of worth today, it can be a sticky family situation no matter what size your stick happens to be. "I had a rich aunt, my mother's older sister, to whom my mother always paid a certain amount of homage," recalls Leona. "I was a kid who loved to sing, and one day when I was thirteen, my mother took me over to my aunt's. I had even gotten a permanent for the occasion. My mom asked me to sing for her, so there I was, really wailing away in the middle of a song, and this aunt said in a loud voice, 'Where did she get that awful perm?' I was shut down. I didn't sing again until college. My mom brushed off the incident because she didn't want to offend her sister, who was loaning her money. But I never forgot it."

Unlike Leona, Julia is the one who achieved the American Dream in her family. One of eight children from a blue-collar Irish Catholic household, she is now a mother of two and wife of a doctor. Instead of being able to spend time enjoying a closer relationship with her extended-family members, she has found that her husband's hard-earned success serves to drive them further apart.

"Our lifestyles are different and so are the lifestyles of my children," Julia says. "Because I have hired help for the housecleaning, one of my brothers always asks, 'Do you have a new slave yet?' Because my kids went to summer camp with their friends, a sister said, 'What's the matter with you—can't you take care of your own children?' And when we bought a cabin in the mountains so Greg could get away from the phones once in a while, everyone else decided it was going to be a great retreat for them all. When we told them that they should wait to be invited, they got mad.

"I have one older brother who has been very successful, but until last year he kept it very quiet. He lived very, very modestly—I don't think even his children knew how much money they had. Then he bought a new house and everyone realized that he had done all right for himself. It causes some jealousies," says Julia.

Just as irritating as those who have been successful are those family members who are at the bottom of the financial heap and embrace that identity with gusto. Their self-deprecatory remarks serve to remind everyone else just how tough they have it and how guilty everyone else should feel because of it.

"I have one brother I love but can't stand being around," says Leslie. "He never misses an opportunity to tell us how poor he is—if not directly, then indirectly. For example, if we are talking about going on vacation, he'll sit there with sad eyes and say, 'Gee, I guess I'll never get to see California, so take lots of pictures for me.' I just want to scream. Whenever he's around, everyone else walks on eggshells to downplay anything they might be doing or buying—even if it is just a new shirt!"

Building a bridge over the money gap is easier if you separate the person from the dollar sign and focus on the real issue that's causing the problem. Is the issue that your brother-in-law makes more money than you do, or is it that he is an insufferable ass whom you've never liked anyway? Does the conflict center on your sibling's whine about money, or is it really a rivalry situation; and if it weren't money, would it be something else causing the fractured feelings? Are you really dealing with dollar signs, or it is actually a Dictator trying to exert control, a Pot-Stirrer playing with others' weaknesses, or a Scapegoat shouldering misplaced blame? Once you have identified the *real* issue, then you can attack it by laying your bridge-building supports.

Disparities in income are at least out in the open. A more insidious and dangerous family money situation is one in which things look straightforward on the surface—and then explode.

MONEY AS A TIME BOMB

Bob invested money through his brother-in-law Stuart, as did most of his wife's family members, despite Stuart's tendencies toward pompous bragging. After all, as Bob says, "Why go to an outsider when a family member will always look out for your best interests?" Most of the transactions were unremarkable until October of 1987. Upon Stuart's recommendations, Bob had been trading, and making large profits, on margin. In early September, however, with college tuition and some medical bills staring him in the face, Bob instructed Stuart to settle up his accounts. He wanted out of what he considered a roller-coaster method of acquiring cash. Stuart told Bob he would do it.

In late September, Bob asked Stuart again to pull him out of the market. Stuart said he would take care of it. On Black Monday, October 19, 1987, when the market crashed, Bob breathed a self-satisfied sigh that he had gotten out just in time. Then the hysterical phone call from Stuart threw him into a tailspin. Since Bob was family—and Stuart felt that he had been panicking needlessly—Stuart had decided to surprise Bob by letting his stocks rise a little longer, without telling him. Unfortunately, Stuart waited too long. Not only did he plunge his brother-in-law into financial ruin, but his actions divided the family so drastically, that it will take great feats of engineering to bridge those gaps.

Nowhere does the myth that you can always trust family members burn as brightly as in financial investments and loans. While it may be irritating to have to deal with a braggart, it can be financially devastating when a relative is given powers over our money decisions. And nowhere does this hurt more and become more divisive than in a parent–child relationship. As one elderly man, working as a bag boy in a Miami Beach grocery store, told me, "I'm here because I trusted my goddam son with my life savings. I was trying to do something nice for him while I was still alive, and he blew the whole thing. Just look at me." He waved his arm in the direction of grumpy shoppers nudging each other through the lines. "Isn't this a nice way to spend my supposed golden years?" he demanded.

Lawrence couldn't even get a job as a bag boy. The seventy-six-year-old retiree decided to transfer the title of his home to his son, so his son could get the tax write-off. After eighteen months, however, Lawrence's son decided he would rather take advantage of the healthy real estate prices on Florida's Gold Coast and sold the house during his father's trip to visit his sister. When Lawrence returned from Michigan, his son informed him that he would have to move to a nursing home. His son magnanimously offered to foot the bills.

That's terrible, you say. What can be done to that rotten slug who dares call himself a son? Nothing. Lawrence willingly signed over his house in good faith and fatherly love. The legal contract stands. "People often start things in motion during their lifetimes with the idea that they can trust their family to always do the right thing," says attorney Sepaniak. "They find out too often that it is just not the case."

THE LOAN BOMB

Just as common a situation, though one that leaves a more debatable paper trail, is the family loan. The word *loan* in family parlance can mean a number of things to a number of different people, and therein lies the source of friction. To some highly principled individuals, it means exactly what wordsmiths intend it to mean, money that is lent on a temporary basis. It is usually lent with love and sometimes repayable with interest. These situations appear to be in the minority, however.

More often a family loan is viewed as:

1. A private source of income with a fuzzy repayment schedule.
2. A nasty situation, which is continually brought up by either the lender or the borrower.
3. A gift—a definition usually unknown to the lender. This can make the Great Divide look like a crack in the sidewalk.

Sally had been married to a successful professional man for thirty years when their marriage broke up. Although she collected alimony, it was not enough to support her in her accustomed fashion, so she began to borrow from family members. Eventually her sister wouldn't speak to her, and although her brother continued to lend her sums, his wife was at her wit's end. "I'm tired of these handouts," she says. "Sally is fifty-five years old and I know we'll never see a penny of this money. It's about time she learned to cut back or do without."

That seems like logical advice and certainly, if you were a bank's loan officer, you would be quick to point that out to a prospective client. But the loan officer does not have to deal with the guilt inherent in the disparity of incomes within a family, or sister Sally's sad eyes as she recounts all those wonderful family memories.

Dinah is also finding that a family loan is separating her from her sister, even though she is just an observer. "When my husband and I got married, we worked hard and paid for everything ourselves," says Dinah. "But when my sister got married recently, she and her fiancé borrowed money from my brother for the wedding, from my aunt for the honeymoon, and from an uncle for the down payment on their house. Then, as a wedding gift, my brother said to just negate about half the loan—which amounted to probably $4,000 to $5,000. When I asked her about repayment, she just laughed and said that by the time she can afford to pay back all the relatives, the aunt and uncle will probably be dead, so all she has to worry about is our brother! Can you imagine? I'm having difficulty speaking to her civilly."

While some relatives make an avocation out of borrowing money that you know will never be repaid—unless someone takes a vacuum cleaner to the inside of their skulls and replaces the contents with common sense—others are embarrassed at having to borrow and thus settle on a the-best-defense-is-a-good-offense theme.

"Even though my husband's sister and her husband were always touted as being the successful ones in the family, they had to come to us to borrow about $5,000 to get through a rough period," says Elaine. "We loaned them the money and said, 'Just pay it back whenever you can.' We never brought the subject up, but they did, every time we saw them or talked with them. We kept telling them that they could just take it easy, but that seemed to make them madder, and they began making comments about what spendthrifts we were. I couldn't believe it. We loaned them money and we were made to feel guilty. Four years later we received a check in the mail for the entire amount, no interest. But I was never so glad as to have that episode over!"

Having to ask a family member for a loan is a ticklish situation. Still more dangerous is having a loan dangled before you in time of need, perhaps even unasked for. If you give in to temptation, realize that the repayment schedule may have some invisible clauses.

* * *

MONEY AS A POWERFUL STRING

There are certain times in all our lives when we are more financially vulnerable than others. These include the time we go to college, marry, have children, purchase a home, divorce, or start a business. Unless you are one of the very lucky few, whose family background is such that you do not have to worry for a moment about a large outpouring of cash, the offer of monetary assistance from within the family can be very attractive. Sometimes it is an absolute necessity. But beware of the strings attached when accepting family help.

"My husband and I accepted a loan from my grandfather to buy our first house," says Pat. "I offered to draw up an agreement and repayment schedule, but he said he would be insulted by something like that, so I backed off and accepted gratefully. What a mistake! For the next seven years, our lives were miserable. I was expected to save every receipt of anything I spent for my grandfather's review once a year, and he would question me if we had a party. After all, he asked, how could I spend so much on a party instead of putting the money back towards repayment?

"My husband was in graduate school at the time; I was supporting us but didn't really make enough to be able to take out a loan from the bank, or I would have done it in a minute," she continues. "What I thought was a loving gesture at one time, I began to view as making me an indentured servant."

Myrna's parents used money as a string to manipulate where their children went to school—and how far. "There were four of us in my family, two boys and two girls," she says. "When I graduated from college—the family college, by the way, not the one I had wanted to attend—I wanted to go to grad school. My parents' attitude was 'You graduated from college, now get a job. Let's not go crazy with this graduate school business.' But it's funny how they agreed quickly to my younger brother's going to law school—which he eventually flunked. It took a lot of years before I could afford it on my own, but I did go to graduate school and am glad I did it on my own. My brother has never heard the end of his law school fiasco."

In chapter 9, I discussed how relatives who lend money for divorces expect to be a part of the decision-making process. Another situation in which the lender expects to be a part of the decision-making process is the start-up of a business. "Just consider me a silent partner," says brother George or Uncle Jack, with a twinkle in his eye. Yet, how many relatives do you know who are truly silent?

"Mistake, mistake, mistake," says Barry shaking his head. "I was tired of working for someone else and decided to take the risk and start my own business. The mistake was that I accepted some money from my brother, who was supposed to be a silent partner. Forget it. He called me every day to find out where I was locating, what inventory I was purchasing, why I had spent so much on cosmetic improvements, when I was opening, and what I was going to run in the ads. I paid him off as quickly as I could. It took less than a year, thank God, and he didn't want to take the money. He said he decided he liked being partners. I just put my foot down though, because he was driving me crazy! I couldn't have gone on like that without strangling him."

Dealing with relatives in business requires tact and firmness as well as realistic expectations. When one is dealing with an ailing parent, however, the expectation that all the offspring will want to help seems to be realistic—until they prove otherwise.

THE "FAIR SHARE" PAYMENT CONFLICT

Estelle raised six children on a farm, and even through widowhood remained an independent person. When she was felled at age seventy-two by a series of medical problems, five of her children declared that they could not help with her care. Her daughter Alise took her mother in to live with her family of five, cared for her, and took over the medical expenses. Despite pleas to her brothers and sisters, she received little aid.

Upon Estelle's death, Alise found that her mother had designated her older brother, the only boy of the family, as executor of the estate, which included the 260-acre farm and a number of family heirlooms. Without consulting anyone, her brother auctioned off the farm and its contents, including the heirlooms and sentimental items. He then divided the money and told Alise, "Here. Now are you satisfied?" The handling of the estate resulted in family battles raging from Maine to Illinois over the last ten years. And Alise was never compensated for her mother's medical care.

More and more offspring are finding themselves in a position today of financially supporting a parent (the emotional ramifications of supporting dependent parents will be dealt with in chapter 16). As people tend to live longer (though they are not necessarily healthier), senior members discover they cannot afford to maintain an independent residence, and families are, once again, expanding to include Grandma or Grandpa.

Just as one expects to support one's offspring for a period of time (although some kids never take the hint and move out), there is the expectation that the offspring will support the parent, if necessary. Reality, however, sets in when the need arises and brothers and sisters all claim that they are too far away, that their children are too young, or that they never got along with Mom anyway. The child who does welcome Mom or Dad may find him- or herself burdened with numerous medical expenses beyond the level covered by insurance or Social Security. Then the call goes out for financial help. "Sure, we'll help," they say, and they do, for the first few months. Then the excuses, both legitimate and contrived, begin.

"I finally decided it just wasn't worth the hassle," says Carmen. "I felt like I was trying to collect child support from errant fathers when I would call my brothers. My husband wasn't thrilled, but family is important to us. Poor Mom thought everyone was helping because that's what I wanted her to think, but it was hurting us financially. When she died, her little estate was divided equally. My share didn't begin to cover what we had spent, but do you think my brothers offered to give me some of theirs? Are you kidding?"

Hard feelings also develop among family members when the caretaker not only does not get some financial assistance but discovers upon the parent's or sibling's death that those expenses are not recoverable.

"If I didn't think my sisters were contributing their fair share to my parents' support, there is no action I could bring to compel them to do that," says attorney Sepaniak. "As far as personal expenses like clothing, food, and medicine—those are made out of love and affection for the parent, and there's no recourse for that.

"Often, the only action that can be taken is one that people are usually not willing to take," he adds. "If you have a heavy outlay of monthly expenses, you can ask the parent to carry those expenses as a loan, which can then be presented as a lien against the estate upon the death of the parent. It's very awkward, and it's hard to imagine a child going to a parent and saying, 'Look Mom, I love you but it's costing me $400 a month over your Social Security check to keep you here, so why don't we annualize it and call it a loan of $4,800 a year?'

"It's not a practical solution," Sepaniak continues. "It's a legal one, but not necessarily a practical family one. If, on the other hand, you put money into a parent's home and can prove it, and the home is to be divided equally among children, you may be able to press a claim for the improvements or maintenance over the years with the proper records."

Sheilah envisions just such a situation in the near future. Her seventy-four-year-old mother is still living in the home that her deceased father built with his own hands. Although it is in a remote area and her mother doesn't drive, "there is a tremendous emotional investment in that house. The problem now is that things are starting to fall apart," she says. "We recently had to replace a bathroom to the tune of almost $7,000. My brother took care of the bill and I have to make my contribution, but some of our siblings I know are not going to be able to help pay for the things that are going wrong. Yet Mom always says, 'Don't worry. Everything is going to be divided equally among you.' "

Sometimes "equally" is not really equal, but it all comes down to that document that can inspire boundless love as well as unbridled hatred and greed: the will.

MONEY AND WILLS—
THE LAST WORD

Raymond's elderly, widowed father decided to marry his nurse, a woman less than half his age. Upon his death eighteen months later, Raymond and his brother found out that their father had rewritten his will to leave everything to his new wife. "He loved us," says Raymond. "We had a good relationship, but he thought that woman would do the right thing by us. She told us not to expect a penny."

Emil also left a will of sorts, a handwritten one, which was found by one of his children the day after his funeral. When the son presented it to his mother for opening, she ripped it into little pieces and said, "I get everything anyway. What do we need this for?" There have been hard feelings ever since.

Rosalie's brother Joshua didn't even wait for the reading of the will. He had never gotten along with his father and hadn't seen him in two years. He declined to go to the funeral, but when the family returned, they found that Josh had cleared out all the things from the family home that he felt were his. These included paintings and portraits taken right off the wall, pieces of furniture, photographs, books, and other memorabilia. "He must have just backed a van up to the door," says Rosalie. "Forget trying to get hold of him, too, because Josh is the type that covers his tracks. That stuff is just gone!"

Sometimes the real test of a family's strength of character comes about when a deceased's will is read. Whether members observe the old adage "Do not speak ill of the dead" depends upon what goodies the dead left them. Sibling rivalries rush to the foreground in dividing up goods that may or may not have been included in the will, and the true spirit of "us versus them" sounds its horn as family members by marriage get into the act. The splits that occur at this time can last for years.

"When Mom died, we all reverted to our old roles," says Majorie. "Even though I had been Mom's financial advisor during the last ten years of her life, my brother was named the executor because he has the penis. His wife insisted on being present when everything was divided among the five children. My sisters and I didn't want any problems, so we bent over backwards trying to be fair to each other, but my brother had an ace up his sleeve.

"He had found a picture of our grandmother that we had been looking for like crazy. His wife literally bartered with that photo for two of my first-choice items. When I balked, my brother said that, as executor, he could auction everything off, so I agreed. The real kick in the teeth came when his wife sold off all the things they took from the inheritance without telling us. I mean, if she had wanted those things of my mother's—that's one thing. But she could have given us the opportunity to have first crack at them. I haven't been able to feel the same way toward them since."

High-stakes wills that are contested, such as the Johnson and Johnson family's, usually make newspaper headlines. People delight in being voyeurs of other families' feuds. It is an affirmation that their own family is not necessarily the craziest around. No matter what the stakes, there is nothing to stop a relative from contesting another's will. For this reason, particularly because of the higher percentage of blended families and more complicated estates, the question arises, Is there such a thing as an airtight will?

"Yes, you can draft a will that is basically airtight, but you cannot control a family member who has been excluded from the will, attacking the will at a later date, claiming the will is invalid," says Sepaniak. With younger people, it is not a problem if all the appropriate steps are taken to exclude people specifically so that they cannot claim they were forgotten. With older people, however, if competency could even be an issue, extra care must be taken in drafting the will.

"In some cases, if you have someone who is getting on in years, someone in a nursing home, or someone who is in and out of the hospital—where you talk to them one day and they're drifting away, or you can only talk to them in the morning, because they get hazy by afternoon—then it could be helpful to have a doctor see them in fairly close proximity to the date of the will's being signed. This is so that, at a later date if necessary, the doctor may be able to testify that yes, he saw Mrs. X. on that day and she was alert, not under the influence of any medicine that could affect her judgment, and otherwise competent," he suggests.

Also, particularly when you are dealing with a situation where a new will might be contested by a new spouse or close friend with whom the testator is living at a time when he or she is particularly vulnerable, it is important to ensure that all medical records are up to date and in order.

Very often, it is not merely the will that presents the stumbling block in families, but the disposal of items not mentioned in the will. Who gets Mother's pearls, for example, or the bed that you all remember crawling into every Sunday morning as children? There are two ways to head off disaster in this area. The first is for the testator to draft a letter, one copy of which can be kept with the will at the attorney's office, declaring just who gets the pearls, the bracelet, the mink coat, the car, and the hand-made lace tablecloths. Unless you are meticulous, however, you will still see relatives fighting over the books and items not mentioned like a passel of dogs fighting over the last bone.

Pat had an alternative suggestion for her mother "I came across a little book in the stationery store called *The Household Inventory*," she says. "It is good to fill out anyway, because in case of fire or theft, most people don't really know what they have in their jewelry boxes, closets, or shelves. Then I suggested to her that next to each item, she place the initials of the person who she thinks would like to have the item, or who she would like to leave that item to. That way, there won't be any guessing and bickering."

Whether dealing with wills, loans, investments, or simply identities, we need to adjust our expectation levels of our family members realistically *down*. Unfortunately, they cannot always be trusted to do the right thing concerning money, or at least the right thing according to our individual perceptions. If you are going to give in to the myth, then do so with your eyes wide open and a signed document in your hand.

Some families believe in the myth so strongly, however, that they figure that just being a family isn't quite enough. So they decide to be a business as well. For some it works. For many others, it does not.

13

Family Businesses—
Friends or Foes?

Nine out of every ten companies in the country today, of which there are approximately 13 million, are owned and controlled by a single family. Family businesses account for 40 percent of the country's gross national product and 160 firms of the legendary Fortune 500 are family owned or controlled.

It is the fulfillment of part of the American Dream, that sign above the door that says "X and Sons" (or "X and Daughters"), but that dream may tarnish as family jealousies, rivalries, and tensions sweep across it like a bitter wind.

How can a child, particularly an adult child, separate successfully from a parent if the parent is also the boss and in control of all the finances, and therefore of the child's future? Where does a family member go to let off steam about the boss, who is also his or her parent, sibling, or other relative? What happens to the business and family relationships when there's a difference of opinion or ultimately a parting of the ways? How does one separate the business relationship from the true family relationship after hours?

Bridges between family members in business together must not only have great tensile strength but be flexible enough to accommodate a variety of uses and abuses. No circus high-wire act is more fraught with danger than the family business, and the more family members involved, the more potentially treacherous the tightrope. "And half the problems are caused by spouses," says Kerry who, with his father and brothers, runs an equip-

138

ment and party-rental business. "I'm in the process of getting a divorce, and a big part of the problem was my wife's jealousy of the time I spent with my relatives."

Since family businesses represent an estimated 90 percent of all businesses in the country today, that makes the family business, hotbed of tension or not, an important factor in the United States economy. It has only been in the last decade, however, that family businesses have been recognized as special entities with specific challenges and stresses. Even the prestigious Wharton School of Business, among other institutions, has recognized the importance of the family business, with specialized seminars and workshops to enhance their organization, operation, and succession. Innovative centers, such as the Edward Lowe Center for Entrepreneurial Management, attract experts and business families from across the country to attend intensive three- to five-day programs designed to improve the family's dynamics while analyzing their company's problems and future direction.

But before we can get to bridge building, we must take a look at the problems and stresses that produce the feuds, that divide the family, and that can topple the company that Jack built.

THE PATRIARCHAL BUSINESS: OR, DAD, THE INESCAPABLE BOSS

When Winnie graduated from high school, she was told that she was joining the family contracting business, just as her two brothers did. Her father, "Big Jack," who started the business, was fond of telling everyone that his word was his bond; he demanded a high degree of loyalty and obedience from his three grown children, both at the office and out of it. Jack told his sons when they should begin looking for wives and with whom to settle down; he vociferously approved or disapproved of Winnie's dates and eventually filled her life in the office with tension when she married a man against Jack's wishes.

Many family fights erupted in the office, spilling over into their personal lives, and finally, Winnie's older brother quit the business and moved across the country. Winnie was thinking of doing likewise when the IRS came knocking at her door. It seems that Jack, realizing he was in financial difficulty, had transferred his assets to his wife's name, leaving Winnie listed as the responsible officer of the company. In order to pay the company's debts, the IRS confiscated Winnie's house and a good portion of her savings. Her husband, sick of living under Big Jack's shadow, filed for divorce. "My life was in a shambles, thanks to my father," she says, "but where could I go? Where could I run? He is still my father, and my mother, who cried through the whole thing, is still my mother, so here I am. I'm thinking of leaving, but I'd rather wait until I can help them build up the business again. I can't just leave them desperate, can I?"

During that infamous development period known as adolescence, parents and children engage in the age-old battle of psychic separation and individuation. Most American children achieve a good measure of independence and a separate identity by the time they reach their late teens or early twenties (only to look up and wonder why Mom and Dad have suddenly turned gray). Their identities are reinforced by outsiders— instructors, employers, and co-workers. But what if your instructor, employer and co-worker is the person from whom you would normally try to separate?

Although more women today are starting businesses than ever before, the vast majority of family businesses were founded and are run by a man, the father, sometimes known as "the great man," "the chief," or even in extreme situations, "God" (as on the Post-it notes that announce, "From the desk of God"—chances are, that was conceived in a family business!). The personality of the chief, in most cases, is quite naturally a Dictator. This is not to say that every family business has a Dictator who causes major upheavals and feuds; some manage to keep everyone in line with a gentler touch. But a very high percentage do have to face this unique stress in the workplace.

Not only does this present separation problems, but company founders are also known to have sometimes unreasonably high expectations of the offspring they bring into the business. They really don't ask for much; they just want their sons and daughters to be perfect—like them!

"I am not allowed to make mistakes," says Frank. "It's as simple as that. I am an example to the rest of the company. If I goof up, my father takes it as a personal affront to his abilities. In other words, I am an extension of him—not my own person. Sure we have fights, but although he seems to think nothing of screaming at me in front of other employees, I just can't yell back at him. I was raised to show him the utmost respect, and I just can't do that to him in front of people. So I take it and then go out and kick a tree or something. One of these times I'll probably break my foot."

To criticize or question the boss in a family business means questioning Dad, and it takes an enlightened and secure father to be able to handle professional criticism from one of his offspring. Some, with the best of intentions, send their sons or daughters to all the right schools, the right seminars, and management programs, and then find that their sons or daughters come back and begin to do what they were trained to do— manage the company, and maybe even Dad.

"I have to give my father a lot of credit. He built the business the hard way," says Alan. "Then he sent me to school to learn the modern way to make it thrive and continue. The problem is, every time I try to suggest something, he shoots it down as 'fancy-shmancy'—his term—or too 'highfalutin.' This causes battle after battle. I don't know why he bothered to send me to school, because he really doesn't want to change his methods. It is going to be done *his* way and that's that."

Some patriarchs will actually let their second generation make decisions and handle negotiations, but then go over their heads to "do it themselves." This should not be a surprise for those who have had any dealings with a Dictator personality anyway. Remember, at the root of such a person's actions is a feeling of insecurity; a loss of power means loss of identity and control.

"My father and uncle started the business and my mother works in it as well," says Sharon, a real estate appraiser. "My father feels the need to do everything, however. He makes a good pretense at giving away responsibility, but then he takes it back. For example, I will deal with some client and have the situation nearly completed, and then he will come in and turn everything around. He may not even know anything about that particular situation, but he undermines my authority with outsiders, constantly. Or he has my mother step in.

"I have to walk on eggshells when I talk with him—much more so than if I were working for an outside employer, which I did for several years after college. I love my family, but when we have a disagreement at work, it becomes a major argument within the family."

Not only are the parent-child conflicts exacerbated by the blurring of roles and the patriarch's determination to keep the power in his lap, but daughters may find that they have a particular hurdle to clear.

"My father and I are the only family members in the business," says Serena. "He started the publishing firm, and my brother was never interested in joining it, but I love it! The problem is that Dad still sees me as his 'little girl.' This is despite the fact that I have worked long and hard in the business and that we are starting a new publication, which he told me I would head up. He does not confide anything about the company to me and I am not even allowed to attend the financial or legal meetings concerning what is supposed to be my publication.

"When the family gets together, he talks to my brother and my *husband*—who isn't even remotely connected with the company—about the business aspects of the company, even though I've told him that I feel it's necessary for me to have that kind of information. Yet he points to me as his example to others that he's a feminist. I can't stand it!"

Some daughters who have worked alongside the men of the family find that while their labor is appreciated, their management skills and opinions are not.

"You don't know how many times I've decided that I was going to quit," says Dierdre, a cog in the family retail chain. "Oh, it's all very demo-cratic—the two girls own equal shares of stock in the company and put in at least equal time. Do you know how much time retailing takes away from the family, especially at holiday times? I think my sister and I have 'earned our wings,' so to speak, but my father will ignore our suggestions and listen to our two brothers instead. He just about pats our heads and says, 'Don't worry, honey. It will all work out.' I get so mad, I could spit. Then when I blow my top, he looks at me sweetly and says, 'You know, honey, you haven't changed since you were six years old.' I *have* changed. He just doesn't want to see or admit it."

Mothers who head family businesses come in for their share of grief as well, whether they find themselves in the managerial position by accident or by design.

OUT OF THE KITCHEN AND INTO THE BOARDROOM

Marie assumed the leadership of a family restaurant when her husband passed away. Although she had been comfortable running the food preparation side of the business, she felt she was floundering on the business side. As a result, she relied on her three sons and two nephews, which was fine, except that her three daughters had previously been handling much of the business and making decisions. To settle arguments among siblings, she reverted to her old standby, "That's the way it is because I am the mother."

"I have one sister who left to start her own catering business," says Rachel, Marie's eldest daughter. "It was less painful for her that way. Me? I'm going to hang in there and try to make Mom see that we have to try and separate the business from the family, but it's tough. It is a day-to-day battle."

Another day-to-day adjustment was necessary for Stevie when his mother Gloria purchased the video store in which he had worked for two and a half years.

"It was my eighteen-year-old, Stevie, who told me the business was for sale," says Gloria, an interior designer by profession. "I looked into it and it seemed like a good investment. We have gone through a number of conflicts and adjustments because, at first, I would say to him 'Tell me about the computer, tell me about the billing,' because he was the one who was familiar with the operation. Then I began to change things, and he resented Mom invading his territory. I instituted a dress code, and if I sent an employee home for not having a tie on, the kid would complain to Stevie, who would then come to me and tell me how much I was embarrassing him in front of his friends. I'd have to tell him that I was trying to run a business.

"Of course, there were times when I have left the store literally in tears because of the things he has said to embarrass *me* in front of his friends. The anger and frustration do spill over into the family life. Either of us could be so angry by the time we got home that we just couldn't speak to each other. I think it's driving my husband crazy."

Lots of people go crazy trying to sort out the different relationships inherent in family businesses. Part of the problem is that many tend to treat family businesses like a family, rather than a business. While the camaraderie of common roots and personal knowledge of one's partners can contribute to making the family business one of tremendous purpose and strength, those very same attributes can also undermine that strength as members struggle to remain separate as well.

AND THE FAMILY AND THE BUSINESS SHALL BECOME ONE

"I am in a family business with my brother and sister. We are spread out in three different locations, so we often have to use a conference call in order to communicate. I have been in the middle of conference calls when my brother will say something or have an attitude on, and I'll get angry, and then my sister will get mad at both of us and hang up! This doesn't solve anything, but it's the way we related as kids, and even though we're all in our forties now, I guess we haven't changed."

"My whole life is the family business. It has been my identity from the time I was a kid. In this town, the restaurant name is our family name. People meet me and think of eating. That's fun sometimes, there's a small amount of fame in that, but I feel as though I am living in a cocoon and that I'll never get to leave. It causes friction sometimes because there's a certain struggle to be separate—but it's nearly impossible."

"I feel as though I have never grown up. Don't get me wrong—I love my mother, father, sisters, and brother—but I feel sometimes that I will be tied to them forever, trying to please Mom and Dad forever. This really causes some problems in my marriage and with my children too, because I find I want them to please my mother and father as well. I don't know—maybe I should quit the business, but that would be like quitting my family, and I can't do that."

We have looked at using the five bridge-building supports in other chapters to deal with various roles family members take on. Can they also work within the family business structure?

It's true that you'll have to look a little more conscientiously to keep the humor in your work life, but the other bridge supports, coupled with specialized information cables, are particularly important when dealing with a family business. Whether you are the "boss" or "employee," planned communication, adjusting expectation levels, awareness of the difference between tolerance and endorsement, and even surrogate families play a significant role in successfully keeping both the business and family going when the edges begin to blur.

"I consider myself part of the sandwich generation," says Fred, who is president of a heating oil and diesel fuel company. "My father started the business, and I saw my role as the one who should expand it. Now I have a twenty-three-year-old son who has just entered the business. I feel I have had three stages of my professional life: learning the business, making it grow, and now I'm into passing it on and planning for an orderly transition.

"It's strange, though; I'll be sitting at my desk trying to explain something to my son and suddenly, I'm transported back—I'm using the same words and expressions my father used to me! It is critical to have an open communication for this whole thing to work. I am still in constant contact with my father, and I've told my son that sometimes it may be difficult to separate Dad–The Boss from just plain Dad, and to let me know when it's happening. It's frightfully easy to slip into the family role. You have to make a conscious effort to step back from it, but I think it's worth it. I know it is."

One of the more famous examples of how the family and business identities can blur and cause problems is the royal family of England. In an exclusive interview prior to his marriage to Lady Diana, Prince Charles rather abashedly told a television reporter that when he was very young, he really wanted to be a train conductor, but that as he got older he came to the realization that he was "sort of stuck" with his role in the monarchy. This man, who was born into the family business of being royal, is still working for his mother—another situation which has filled thousands of inches of tabloid space—and wondering when he will be allowed to fill the top position.

One person who has helped bridge the gaps in family business relationships by educating hundreds about the unique relationships that exist in the family business framework is Dr. Peter Davis, founder of the Wharton School of Business, Family Business Program. Davis is the first one to acknowledge the powerful streams of development and the kinds of interactions that occur in family business settings, which contribute to friction and feuds.

"Most people develop in two ways, professionally and personally," Davis tells participants from across the country in Wharton's seminars. "On the professional side, a person gets out of college and gets into the business world. I call this 'reality shock,' because all of a sudden, people find themselves doing dog work and learning the ropes from the bottom up.

"Next is the socialization and growth stage, where they have to prove themselves in the company, show that they're competent. They continue to move up and take on more responsibility and make an impact until they are finally ready to negotiate with the old man for the ultimate seat of power.

"On the personal side, however, you have the person who says, 'Hey, I'm thirty years old and I'm still in the nest! Who am I anyway? I live my whole life in relationship to someone else.' You are still in competition with siblings," adds Davis, "and the ultimate scorecard is 'Have I proved anything to the old man?' or 'Have I gained his approval yet?'

"Sometimes what happens is that the personal development process overwhelms the professional development one, and what you get is people who are acting up and at each others' throats and are not producing for the company."

Can the challenge be met? You bet! Davis emphasizes that people in family businesses need support, not only from family members but particularly from those who are not family members but who serve as mentors and guides (finding them is finding a surrogate family). He also feels that family members need to be given work tasks where they can develop some autonomy, perhaps without the direct control of and constant contact with Dad- or Mom–The Boss. If a company has a branch office or even just a different division, younger family members should be sent there, with the understanding that though they may not handle situations exactly as their elders would, they have to become competent through their own experience. By throwing away the "they are *supposed to* do it just like me" myth, the leader of a family business will actually be creating a healthier company as well as healthier relationships with offspring and or siblings.

Finally, family members need to maintain that emotional bond to the family. It is one of the most inspirational motivations in perpetuating the family business.

But what happens if the family business becomes part of your life through marriage? Just as when you marry a person, you marry the whole family, the same is true with family businesses. You marry both the family and the business for better or worse. And sometimes it's worse than others.

WHEN YOU MARRY
A FAMILY BUSINESS

Maryann grew up in the farm area of New Jersey, one of six children from a broken and then recombined home. But she had big dreams. "You know when you're traveling toward the Lincoln Tunnel on Route 3," she says, "and you get to the top of a hill and all of a sudden the whole New York skyline appears right in front of you? Well, I'd look at that skyline and say to myself, 'Someday, I'm gonna be there.' "

She met Mario at a party when she was eighteen years old. He was handsome, smooth, and interested. Though they hit it off, she didn't see him again for two years. When she did, he was engaged to another girl, but he broke off the relationship, and he and Maryann became inseparable.

"He told me he was in a family business, but nothing illegal," says Maryann, shaking her head. "Of course, I believed him. Why shouldn't I? I had no other friends—he was my best and only friend. I moved in with him and everything was wonderful. He took me to meet his family and I fell in love with them, too. His father was so warm and Italian. When he told his mother he was going to marry me, she said in a sad voice, 'So you found someone as stupid as me.' I didn't understand it then and I really didn't try, because they were part of my fantasy too."

Maryann was never alone. When she shopped, one or two of Mario's "friends" tagged along. "He didn't want me to get lost or have to carry packages, he told me." She didn't see her family, but that was all right, because they didn't really get along. Even though Mario sometimes disappeared for days "on family business," Maryann was content to plan meals, family gatherings, and activities for his return. "He was my world," she says. "I gave up everything for him. I really felt he loved me and took care of me. How could you do anything but love someone you learned so much from? Looking back now, I was so stupid, so naive. I didn't question anything and nobody told me anything. I just lived in this incredibly small, protected world."

Then Mario's father was found assassinated, gangland-style, and suddenly the "family business" was spread across the headlines. To top if off, Mario had to assume his father's position as head of the family organization. "Everything fell apart and I grew up fast," says Maryann. "Friends turned out not to be friends; you couldn't trust anyone really. We were constantly on the move so the authorities couldn't ask too many questions.

Then Mario felt he had to leave the area for six months in order to avoid prosecution. Again, I was told nothing. I would be contacted and picked up to meet him in hotels for a few hours' visit during those months, but mostly I had to keep on the move. Fortunately, since I really did know nothing about the business, I couldn't spill any information, but the constant fear was a nightmare."

Mario was finally captured by the authorities, brought to trial, and is serving time in a federal prison. Although Maryann obtained a divorce decree, she went into self-imposed exile for more than a year to eliminate any possible retaliation from other "family" members or their enemies. Today, she manages a small business, lives alone and frugally, and looks back very infrequently. "I had the best," she says. "Trips, jewelry, furs, cars, you name it. I had it and lost it. This time, I'm making it on my own—and it's better because it will be all mine."

Although blood family members have difficulty sorting out and separating the family from the business relationships, an "outsider" who marries into the family may see the differences, but he or she may never convince the others to act on that revelation.

When Janet married Nick, she knew she was marrying into a family retail business. As a matter of fact, that was part of the attraction. An only child, she loved the emotional warmth and close ties among her husband's four siblings and their mother, father, and uncle at the helm. Eleven years into the marriage, however, she has a different view of the family business arrangement. "We have no social life unless it's with the family," she says. "Dinner discussions usually erupt into an argument about the business. And Nick is constantly in competition with his brothers and cousins. Although our son is only ten, Nick is already grooming him to enter the business someday. Although I have created a life for myself outside the business, nobody, not even my husband, considers it important. It's what I do 'to keep busy,' according to his family. Not that I want to work in the family business—I already see too much of them! I get this urge every once in a while to just run away from home."

Sandra found that her family's business worked against her in an unexpected way. Sandra married Richard during their senior year of college. When they graduated, Richard went to work for Sandra's Dad and with her brother in the family printing business. He proved to be a creative and dynamic employee who inspired the company's expansion into several new areas and added substantially to the company's profits. He was placed in a position of tremendous authority where he exercised his expertise in marketing to make the company a household name in a limited regional area. Things were not as well tended at home, however, and after fifteen years and two children, Sandra decided to divorce the philandering Richard. During a very acrimonious divorce proceeding, Sandra's father and brother decided to side against Sandra and with Richard, who had made it clear that he would leave the company if he didn't have their support. That action split the family along irreparable lines.

Because family members also work together, being married to a family business is "like living in the smallest town imaginable," as one woman says. "There's no need to use a telephone—just tell a relative and soon everybody knows your business whether you want them to or not. There's just no privacy and you have to accept that or go crazy trying."

Naturally protective feelings toward one's spouse can also play havoc with the family relationship, particularly if the spouse is also a competitive person. "My wife just wouldn't let up," says Daniel, who is a second-generation member of a family jewelry business with branches in three states. "She either feels that I'm letting my brother walk all over me, or that my father is favoring a cousin over me, or that I should just go in and tell off my father and his sister—the company founders. I wind up arguing at work with family members, and then arguing at home *about* family members. Sometimes it just gets to be too much!"

All these family issues just come rushing up to meet you when you marry a family business: sibling rivalry, family secrets, psychic separation from parents, money issues, and control issues. And the resolution is far more complex than within a simple family framework, because of your partner's emotional investment in the family business and ties to the family method of operation (the "us-versus-them" concept all over again).

Building a bridge means more than simple communication skills. Constant *constructive* communication is necessary, in which everyone remembers to express both their feelings and their needs.

You may finally determine that you need your spouse to make a break from the family business. Beware: Consider this option realistically. There is a very real risk that such an ultimatum will be the death knell for your marriage because you will be asking your spouse not only to walk away from his or her family but from a livelihood as well. To reject either the family or the family business can be very traumatic; when you require your spouse to reject both, you may find that *you* are the branch that is broken off from the family tree, and that few will look down to watch you fall.

"I put my foot down and said, 'It's either them or me!' " says Gabriella. "After much crying, fighting, and pleading, my husband stuck by his family. And I married someone else who does *not* belong to a family business. I just wasn't equipped to handle the constant bickering, backbiting, and trauma that had become part of our every waking hour. I loved my husband, but I felt as though I was being strangled. For me, it became a matter of survival to get out."

WHAT DO YOU MEAN—CHANGE?

One of the very real challenges, both professionally and personally, to those involved in a family business is the issue of growth: growth of the company, the succession within a family dynasty at the head of the company, the growth of the individuals—particularly the relatives—within the company. Marital and family fights, affecting the business, erupt over these issues, and resolving them takes a most intense form of bridge building.

Lewis and his sister and brother, with whom he started a lucrative five-and-ten business, fought over methods of change in the company for years. Finally, Lewis paid the ultimate price. "I remember being drawn into these family conflicts as a teenager," says his daughter Tracie, herself a businesswoman. "He would want to do something and my aunt and uncle would not. He could see that the growth of stores like K-Mart was going to affect their business, but the company was supporting three families and my aunt and uncle didn't want to change or let go. My father felt that if he quit the business, it would go down the tubes, because he was the key partner. I saw him go through the protective role, the martyr role, and a number of depressions."

A family-wide meeting was scheduled to discuss these issues of change and succession. Not only did the three principal partners attend, but also Lewis's other two siblings and their offspring, who wanted no part of running the business, but wanted to show support for their favorite relative's point of view.

"I didn't attend that meeting because I had small children at home, and besides, I had attended others and they always wound up the same way—a huge, screaming fight," says Tracie. "But my mother went to this one." During the course of the meeting, it did indeed develop into a huge fight. In the midst of an impassioned speech, Lewis, clutching his chest, told the others that he couldn't catch his breath. The rest of the relatives, including a cardiologist nephew, passed off Lewis's claim as theatrics designed to upstage the others. Lewis collapsed on the floor.

"At that point, they began to take things seriously," says Tracie softly, "but he was dead by the time the rescue squad arrived. He gave it all for the damned company. Was it worth it? Are you kidding?"

Out of all the family businesses begun, only 35 percent remain family owned and run, because of issues surrounding succession and change. This statistic would come as no surprise to researchers at the University of Western Ontario, who published a study of more than 300 managers from major corporations to determine the greatest causes of stress on the job. Their results revealed that the three top stress-inducing situations were poor management-employee relations (with an emphasis on poor communication and lack of planning), blurred organizational structure, and uncertainty of promotion or recognition.

Given the context of the family business, the control, change, and succession issues take on a bitter flavor, as relatives react to difficult situations as people whose colleagues are "supposed to" be looking out for the family's best interests. These changes may be in the best interests of one member, but may or may not be in the best interests of the company.

For example, suppose brothers Jack and Joe start and run a successful service business. They proceed on their merry way until sons Leon, Greg, and Joe Jr. all line up to take over. Joe Sr., who would rather be marlin fishing in Hawaii, thinks the way around this hurdle is merely to sign his 50 percent of the company over to his only son Joe Jr., thereby solving everything.

Jack, who isn't ready to hand over the company reins, and who has always thought that Joe Jr. didn't have the brains of a slug, is not happy at the prospect of now being partners with his brother's son instead of his brother, and a big fight erupts. Leon and Greg are also not happy with their cousin's ascension to power, and not only has the family infighting soon spread to other branches, but the thriving company has started sliding downhill. This is due partly to inattention, and partly to vindictive ploys on the part of all involved to leave their "enemies" with a losing situation.

PLANNING THE POSITIVE TRANSITION

The Mennen Company is an internationally recognized American company in its fourth generation of family ownership, founded in the late 1800s by Gehard Mennen, whose first product was a corn remedy sold out of his Newark, New Jersey, drug store. More than 100 years later, his great-grandson, G. Jeff Mennen, is at the helm of the corporation, which produces a broad range of health and beauty aids as well as paper art products. The company has weathered the storms of family squabbles and buyouts, as well as the additional stress of government opposition during World War II because of its German name, but it has survived by careful design rather than luck, a design that is wholeheartedly perpetuated.

An avowed proponent of family businesses, Mennen feels that it takes someone with a tremendous vision to start a company, and someone else has to believe in and maintain that vision in order to keep that company going. Who are the people in the best position to understand that vision, intent, and desire better than anyone else? The family of the founder, of course. The vision can dim, however, when it collides with the reality of individual personalities struggling to assert themselves.

"In our company, we haven't had one generation that wanted to let go of the reins one day before they stopped breathing," says Mennen. "And I am sure that when my time comes, I'm not going to want to let go of them either. This is a very emotional issue for a number of reasons.

"First, even addressing this issue is a loss of power and an admission of mortality. If I'm willing to give up the reins, it means I'm admitting that I will have decreased usefulness—that I can't go on forever, running things. The second concern is the loss of identity. When someone has been a respected leader of a company, there's a certain aura about them, and that person, normally speaking, is scared to death of giving up that aura."

In order to keep the bridges open for an orderly transition of leadership, prepare the company head for the emotional changes, and avoid some of the fighting, which occurs over ownership and succession, experts insist upon treating the family business *as* a business—complete with all the legal documentation and provisions for succession.

Attorney Stephen Sepaniak, who has designed the framework for numerous family businesses, says that the biggest mistake family members make when forming a business is thinking that they don't need all the structure that "strangers" need. "They actually need it more," he says. "Especially in family businesses, ensure that everything is in writing. The most important thing you need is a buy-sell agreement. What if someone wants to get out? How are the shares valued and how will the business be valued? What are the buyout terms? It has to be handled in a very structured way so that if there's a problem, everyone knows exactly where they stand and what to expect.

"In addition, in many cases, it should be set up as a closely held corporation with all kinds of restrictions on the stock. This would prevent one relative just giving their stock to a spouse," Sepaniak adds.

A very common catalyst for family business feuds today centers around just such a situation: Father starts the company and makes each child an officer, so that they can run the company someday. Someday is continually put off until the kids are in their forties and Dad, who is eighty years old, marries a thirty-five-year-old woman. Dad dies, leaving everything to his new wife, and the children find they are working for their new stepmother, who may not know the first thing about the business. In some situations, Sepaniak recommends a system of stock options that can be exercised every few years, so the changing of the guard is a gradual process and the kids get an opportunity to run the company, just as they were promised. But obviously, the circumstances of a particular case may warrant a different approach.

To overcome the emotional resistance to such subjects, Mennen found an indirect approach more useful. "If you are the younger generation and you have to talk to the older generation about this problem—don't make a frontal attack! The older generation has all the weapons and all you've got is a slingshot. You aren't going to win that battle," he says. An alternative is to approach the challenge in much the same way a sand crab approaches the object of his desire—sideways."

Try to find a respected friend within the business from the older generation, preferably one who has been in similar circumstances, and sit down and have a friendly talk about what they are planning to do with the company. You can do it in a nonconfrontational manner, which allows the feeling of power or strength to remain with the acknowledged company leader. They then feel less threatened when younger family members approach, saying, "Look, we have to talk about where this company is going to be twenty years from now."

"If you are a member of the older generation, sit down and talk with the younger generation about how great it is to be in a family business and about the great things that can come their way because of the family business," suggests Mennen. "If the family has the vision and the company has the product, then the family and the company can stay together and grow together."

What happens, however, if the family does not share the vision? Unfortunately, many learn their lessons the hard way, through family treachery and financial ruin. And some, learning their lessons, pick up the pieces and recombine them, not only moving the company into a period of dynamic growth, but creating a surrogate family system to educate others about how to avoid the pitfalls and rebuild trust.

TAKING THAT ONE STEP BEYOND

Edward Lowe could easily be called a Renaissance man, but the appellation comes at the price of much personal struggle. Son of a tavernkeeper and jack-of-all-trades, Lowe spent his Depression-era youth helping his father do odd jobs, such as distributing clay granules used to absorb oil and grease spills. Years later, a neighbor asked Lowe if he knew of anything that she could use in her cardboard cat box that wouldn't be tracked all over the house, like the then-used sand or ashes. Lowe thought of the clay granules. Within weeks, his neighbor's cat-owner friends were pestering Lowe for clay granules and an industry was born. Filling brown paper bags with the granules, Lowe hand-wrote "Kitty Litter" across the bags, and began to peddle them to pet shops, grocers, and feed stores. A family business—and a whole industry—were born.

Today, the sixty-nine-year-old Lowe, who is often mistaken for the singer Kenny Rogers, holds eighteen patents and more than twenty trademarks; he controls more than 40 percent of the catbox-filler market. Operating from a 4,300-acre farm in his hometown of Cassopolis, Michigan, he points proudly to the fact that in front of each of his many plants, clay mines, and office facilities throughout the Midwest and the South, there are three signs that display his deepest beliefs: Quality, Pride, and Family. While all three ideals are hard won, it is the last that motivates this entrepreneur, who has emerged from the battlefield of family friction and greed to try to help others before they find themselves in similar situations.

Lowe married a woman from his hometown and had four children. "One of the problems, and I realize it now, was that my kids didn't really have to work," says Lowe. "I bought them everything, paid for college, clothes, cars—they never even held real jobs." In spite of their lack of business preparation, when they expressed an interest in various facets of the growing business, Lowe gladly accommodated them. Soon his son and three daughters, and their spouses, all headed various divisions or subsidiary companies in Lowe's industries.

As the corporation grew and prospered through meticulous planning, invention, and follow-through, Lowe's began to attract a number of take-over offers from other corporate giants. Ed Lowe, however, stuck to his principle that "Lowe's would never be sold." He had expanded to include among his many interests and businesses: a feline-research industry, a horse-breeding farm, environmental research, land reclamation, and historical restorations. For Lowe, the preservation of the past co-exists with the commitment of his energies and attention firmly to the future. Most important, he was surrounded by his family all working together. Or so he thought.

"They told me they didn't understand all my dreams and didn't have to share all my dreams," says Lowe, but they were very concerned about their "inheritance," and they found the corporate buyout offers that kept coming their way very attractive. The four children attempted to remove Lowe as chairman of the company as incompetent. What they hadn't counted upon was the determination of that Depression-era child who had single-handedly created a new industry.

Still struggling to maintain a relationship despite his children's defection, Lowe offered each of them continued employment, a cash settlement, and a 1-million-dollar line of credit. They opted for a simple cash settlement of $2.5 million each—a $10-million move that strained the then sixty-four-year-old Lowe both financially and personally. Divorced from his first wife and alienated by his children, Lowe remarried and threw his energies into creating a surrogate family out of his many employees—

providing them with numerous opportunities for education, advancement, and fun. ("Ed doesn't allow weekend meetings or even late Friday meetings, because he says it's more important that people be home to do things with their families," says one employee.) He established two specific enterprises designed to assist other family businesses in successfully building bridges across the unique challenges that must be conquered.

The Center For Entrepreneurial Management sponsors workshops and seminars that address the issues of succession planning, relations with nonfamily members, making family roles compatible with boss-employee roles, and maximizing the full potential of the family business, among others. "I am now a big believer in going back to the apprenticeship method," says Lowe. "It is also important to provide each kid with a mentor. You have to find out what it is that the child really wants to do in the company."

The jewel in the Lowe Foundation crown is the One Step Beyond Program. Through One Step Beyond, families involved in a family business spend three to five days at the Big Rock Valley Farm in Cassopolis, receive personal and business-profile counseling by a group of professionals to determine the family's goals and the best methods for reaching those goals. Family members then engage in an innovative and startling *Outward-Bound*-type outdoor exercise designed to reinspire trust and good communication. This is called the Ropes Course.

Set deep in the woods, it looks, at first glance, like a picnic ground for the hyperathletic. The course has wooden balance beams, trees with wooden beams extending to the ground at forty-five–degree angles, and even "log tightropes" twenty-five and ninety feet from the ground. Throughout the two or three days, an individually tailored program sets tasks for family members that cannot be accomplished without group input or support and trust.

Ed Lowe's eyes still fill with tears when he talks about his children and his grandchildren, whom he rarely sees. He maintains that being estranged from one's family is worse than if they were dead, because of the tantalizing hope of possible contact. He cautions other family businesses, however, to take a lesson from his experience. "I've tried everything I could think of to try to get back together with my children," he says. Although his new wife Darlene, a professional businesswoman who does share Lowe's vision, has children from a previous marriage who try to cocoon Lowe in family feelings, "it's not the same," he says. "I keep hoping that someday . . ."

Those involved in family businesses today have a wealth of resources with which to strengthen their interpersonal bridges—educational plans, legal frameworks, and their own credibility. By utilizing these and the other bridge-building skills, family businesses can continue to grow as the heartbeat of American progress.

Part IV

The Most Common Dividers: Values

14

A Question
of Religion

It has been said that more wars have started in the name of religion than anything else. While it may not be the primary cause of family feuds, it certainly ranks in the top five as reasons for family frictions and the crumbling of relationships.

Religion is usually the embodiment of one's ideals, values, and identity. For some, it represents a rich heritage as well as a framework for life. Parents raise their children in a particular religion because it is part of the value system they wish to pass on. No matter what religion they follow— Protestant, Catholic, Jewish, Muslim, or any other, or any of their various sects—people like their religious symbols, rituals, and traditions to remain the same like a security blanket in an ever-changing and volatile environment. To reject, attack, or attempt to modify those religious beliefs and practices within the extended family is viewed as tantamount to rejection of the family and its very identity. And is it any wonder? Religion is one of those tools used by our silent navigators to distinguish between themselves and others.

Bob grew up in a conventionally Protestant household. He and his sister went to Sunday school and sang in the church choir, but they took a low-key approach to their religious beliefs. During college and after marriage, Bob aggressively and successfully pursued material wealth. Then his young son went through a debilitating illness. Bob saw "the error of his ways" and embraced an evangelical sect wholeheartedly. The rest of the family can understand Bob's transformation, but they are driven crazy by his nonstop praising the Lord and his missionary zeal to convert them. It has gotten to the point that they sometimes leave him out of family gatherings because of it.

Kelly was raised in a strict Irish Catholic household. When she began dating Adam, who is Jewish, after graduation from college, her parents didn't interfere. When the pair announced their intentions to marry, Kelly's entire family, with few exceptions, turned against them. As the pair sought counseling prior to their marriage, they were thrown out first from a priest's office and then a rabbi's. They finally married in the temple when Kelly converted—a move that made her a family outcast. Not only did her family not attend the wedding, but fifteen years later, they still call Adam "the barbarian" and treat their Jewish grandchildren differently from their Catholic ones.

Marinda found herself in traction in the hospital, as a result of recurrent back problems aggravated by a spill that occurred when she took her children sledding. Immobile as she was, she welcomed company, particularly that of her favorite cousin Scott, who called and said he had a surprise for her. She had not seen Scott in two years and had no idea just how big the surprise was to be, however. Scott entered the semiprivate hospital room, splashing a liquid into the air and warding away "evil spirits" that might surround Marinda. She was surprised enough at his shaved head, peculiar clothing, and dramatic entrance, but she became bewildered as he immediately and calmly went about setting up crystals and photographs around her bed. When he began to strip his clothes off and chant, spraying her from an atomizer, Marinda's elderly roommate became alarmed and summoned the nurse. It took two security guards to remove Scott, who kept shouting that they were poisoning his cousin with their chemicals, and that he and the Great Healer were going to take care of her.

Even those who say they are not religious, or who were raised in households where religion involved mainly holiday celebrations, often find resistance if they choose to part from the "family religion" either on their own or through marriage. Later, they may experience some pangs of conscience or a change of heart when holidays approach, as ingrained childhood memories dredge up shared traditions of the past. Paul and Rachel Cowan, authors of *Mixed Blessings*, call holidays one of the "time bombs" of an interfaith marriage, because they are times when cultural and religious feelings that have been suppressed rise to the surface and can cause an explosion.

Holidays are potentially explosive for anyone who has changed religions, however, whether by marriage or on their own. They highlight the traditions of one's roots, which, though they are not religious beliefs in the strict sense, are nonetheless difficult to separate in the eyes of the family.

"I couldn't understand it," says one young woman. "My parents have never even been particularly religious, but they hit the ceiling when I told them that I found the way to salvation and had become a Jehovah's Witness. I was told to expect that kind of thing, but I didn't believe it of my parents. They looked at me as though I were a stranger."

A person's choice of a religious sect other than the one in which he or she was raised is often perceived, not merely as separation from the family or a search for compatible beliefs and self-realization, but a rejection of the parents' values and heritage. The stricter the "parent religion" or the adopted religion, the greater the perceived rejection. This ultimate rejection is what gives rise to feuds, some of which affect other facets of the family relationship as well.

We are dealing here with a whole set of "supposed to's," which have been mythologically emblazoned on tablets and handed down through the family chain just as surely as if they were passed on to us genetically.

It is important, in dealing with frictions over religion, to step back and take a hard look at everyone's motives. Is an "errant" relative sincerely pursuing his or her own heart's belief? Is the "rebellion" just that, a method of seeking revenge on parents or siblings? Is the behavior an attention-seeking device? If you object to a relative's behavior with regard to religion, you must ask yourself, "What's my problem with it?" Isn't it just the tiniest bit controlling to think that a loved one should believe, think, or practice exactly the same way as you do? Remember, we may have come out of the same family tree, but we are not clones of each other.

Keeping motives in mind, let's take a look at religious frictions and try to find ways to build bridges across those breaks in communication.

CHANGING THAT OLD-TIME RELIGION

Mickey (Woody Allen) is a man searching for structure in his life in the movie *Hannah and Her Sisters*. Specifically, he is looking for a religion. He tries Catholicism. "No, it doesn't work for me," he laments. He stops by the fence to watch Hari Krishnas beat their drums and dance. "I know you believe in reincarnation. Will I come back as a moose or aardvark or something?" he asks. Finally, he tells his puzzled Jewish parents who demand to know what's wrong with their own religion, "I need something to believe in. If I can't believe in God, then life isn't worth living."

Mickey never really finds religious peace. Some people do and some don't, but the process of looking can threaten the rest of the family members, who feel insulted either because their own choices are being questioned, or because they feel rejected by association or out of ignorance of the tenets of a newfound faith, or because they feel jealous that someone has the courage to break from family tradition—something that they did not do despite desires to the contrary.

Such was the case when Lisa, who after many years of dissatisfaction with the Catholic Church (the family religion), became a Baptist. Full of happiness and warm feelings, she called her parents to tell them; they, in turn, alternately sputtered and screamed into the telephone. "Mom and Dad accused me of turning on them because my original baptism wasn't good enough for me, and they told me that now I wouldn't be able to dance, drink, or have any fun—a cardinal sin in an Italian household!" she says. "For years I went out of my way to show them I hadn't changed except for the direction of my beliefs, but I took barb after barb. It's a good thing I could pray for patience, because I needed it! I think they were all afraid I would try to convert them, so they would insult me first. It's better now, but it has taken more than fourteen years for it to be a non-issue."

Babs found the issue of religion was complicated by a move from the North to a small town in the South where the church is also a means of socializing. "When I told my mother that I enjoy going to the Bible study groups, she told me she thought those kinds of things were just for weak people," says Babs. "I finally asked her if she ever read the Bible. She said yes, of course. Well, I hadn't, I told her; with all the problems my family has encountered, I have found some strength and peace in those words. I think it takes a strong person to admit that he or she is not all-powerful."

Allen's parents sat shivah for him (the traditional Jewish seven-day mourning period after someone dies) when he told them he had joined the group Jews for Jesus. "How do you tell your family that, in your heart, you think the beliefs your people have held for more than two thousand years are wrong?" he says softly. "Not only am I dead to my parents and anyone of the older generation, but my sister calls me to tell me that it's my fault that my father has been so sick with his ulcers, and if he dies, it will be on my head. I really love my father and I don't want to hurt my parents, but I have to do what's in my heart."

One of the freedoms our country was founded upon was the freedom to worship, or not worship, as we please, but that doesn't necessarily carry any weight with family members. Everyone knows that the law of the land is different from the "law of the family." Most of the time it evolves out of a sincere concern for the family's well-being; sometimes, it evolves out of fear. Whatever the reason for friction in your household, it can usually be categorized under one of the following:

I'm a failure as a parent. On the contrary, the parent who thinks this way has done a superb job of raising independent-thinking offspring who feel secure enough to separate from the family line and grow individually. (Plan to communicate this!)

You are falling under the influence of a cult. If a relative is no longer a minor, there is nothing that can be done to prevent them from making their own decisions (tolerance versus endorsement). There are cults, however, and then there are cults. Aunt Natty, who attends Mass every morning, may view the Lutherans as a cult, whereas brother Ted, who is into New Wave music, thinks the Krishnas are making a sensible fashion statement and those who sell carnations on the street corner are modern-day apostles. (Use education as a cable strengthener, then adjust expectation levels downward.)

You are being disloyal to your heritage. A change of religion is rarely an intentional slap in the face to one's heritage, but rather an act of conscience. What family members usually react to most vociferously is the rejection of cultural traditions, foods, and holidays. Each of us has to be true to him- or herself, however, and each may come to the conclusion that some aspects of one's heritage can still be incorporated at a later date when the level of confidence is higher. Family pressure rarely speeds the process along. (Planned communication includes assurances of love; then adjust expectation levels. Also, a sense of humor helps. New converts tend to be off-putting with their humorless attitudes.)

What will our friends think? The immediate reaction here is usually, "Who cares what they think?"; obviously some family members do. One father, who related how his son went through a phase of Rastafarianism (a Caribbean religion whose adherents worship the former emperor of Ethiopia, Haile Selassie, as a great leader and servant of Jah, or God), said he was embarrassed by his son's dreadlocks and unkempt appearance, but didn't banish him from the family, which was his first thought. On the contrary, he went out of his way to include his son in gatherings where the son would have to defend his newfound point of view (tolerance versus endorsement, plus a sense of humor). "My son decided that perhaps he had made a mistake. I'm glad I didn't lose him," says the father. "I guess it was just something he had to go through before he decided what he really believed in."

We will lose you. What's really being said here is, "I'm afraid you will become so different and so close to your church family that you will reject us; we won't have anything in common to talk about anymore." Janelle's sister decided to pursue the teachings of a small Middle Eastern religion. Janelle, who is married to a Protestant minister, was surprised and saddened. "My parents could not believe it, but we are all trying to keep a low profile. We feel sorry for her, that she's chosen to give up so many things that she always seemed to enjoy, but it is her life," says Janelle (tolerance versus endorsement). "When she comes for dinner now, we make sure there are adequate vegetables for her to make a meal, and we don't inhibit ourselves from enjoying the music and dance that we all have always participated in. If she can deal with being around us, the way we are, then we can deal with being around her—and we've learned something about another culture in the process. My parents are secretly hoping that she'll eventually 'grow out of it.' "

"Growing out of it" is a hope that helps many a family cope successfully with relatives who choose a separate religious path. As a tolerance-versus-endorsement coping mechanism, this is a very viable strategy, because people do tend to "try on" different beliefs at various stages of their lives. The danger in rejecting a family member at any stage is that the division will be there long after that particular stage has passed.

Not only is tolerance appreciated whether you endorse a relative's choice of religious practices or not, but a surrogate family is already built into your coping system—the members of your own religion. There you will find support, and perhaps the similar experiences of others, to help you adjust your expectation levels.

Coping with a relative's change of religion can be a real challenge, as can be accepting a new family member by marriage. But dealing with a new family member who may cause your relative to change religions is difficult, if not impossible, for some to bridge sanely.

MARRYING OUTSIDE THE FAITH

Much has been written recently concerning interfaith marriages, and with good reason. Research statistics now show that whereas only 6 percent of Americans had spouses of different faiths in 1957, those percentages have now skyrocketed to 25 percent for Protestants, 40 percent for Jews, and nearly 45 percent for Catholics. This is the melting-pot theory of America in full bubble, but it creates some volatile emotions among family and clergy.

While Protestant ministers tend to agree that marriage between people of different Protestant sects produces little friction, marriages between Protestants and Catholics produce a great deal ("Those people kneel before graven images!" one woman says), and marriage between a Protestant or Catholic and a Jew produce the most. This high level of friction most often occurs because the non-Jewish member, either bowing to pressure or for the sake of simplicity, converts to Judaism. How does the family react?

"Neither side attended the wedding," says Ellie. "Neither of us was raised in that religious a household, so we opted to get married by a Protestant minister in a small ceremony rather than by a priest or rabbi. We have tried to bridge this difference over the two years we've been married but haven't really gotten past the cordial stage."

Withholding one's endorsement of a union by not attending the ceremony seems to be the most popular method of attempting to control the couple's direction. If a couple can get past that hurdle, they may have to face more than their share of prejudice within the family unit.

"We were at Thanksgiving dinner with all my relatives when my uncle, who had had a bit to drink, asked my husband how the Jews described the 'why' of suffering," says Tina. "My mother decided she didn't like the answer and called him an ignorant Jew. It was a nightmare from then on, with everyone getting into the act."

Extended families provide the biggest single source of friction to interfaith couples. Even if a couple decides that it will go the "dual faith" route and incorporate both religions into the union, every holiday and major decision becomes a debate for the family chorus. "But that's one of the realities of a mixed marriage," says one religious counselor. "We often recommend that the couple ask themselves all the hard questions prior to marriage—those questions concerning holidays, children, and religious celebrations. They have to be able to take the heat, not only from their own beliefs and traditions, but from their relatives as well."

Louisa, an Italian Catholic who married a Jew, concurs. "First of all, most of all, and beyond all, be sure you're in love. Don't be fooled by good looks, good potential, or a nice figure," she warns. "Make sure, when you're getting into something this complicated, that you really can count on each other, because there are many things lurking in the dark that can jump out at you!"

Helen, a Protestant, also married a Jew. Her family is upset that he does not allow Helen to celebrate Christmas, have a tree, or attend church with her relatives. "He's like a dictator about it!" sputters one sister. "Helen has slipped us little Christmas presents on the side without his knowing it, so I know she must be miserable. I just think it's so unfair!"

Of course, Helen made the choice and Helen must live with her choices or change them. Perhaps she is trying to please both sides of the family, but the strategy doesn't seem to be calming the waters. For all the reasons discussed in the previous section, there are no easy answers to the "mixed marriage" situation. Some couples do try to accommodate both sides of the family with varying degrees of success by celebrating all holidays or emphasizing nonthreatening ones such as Thanksgiving.

Decisions over child-rearing also fan the flames of friction since, as discussed in chapter 8, children carry on the family bloodline. "My family had no problem with my marrying outside my faith," says Jan, "but when little Peter came along, that's when the trouble started. Since we don't believe in infant baptism, my parents went into shock. My younger brother told me that Mom and Dad performed a baptism on him the last time they babysat. It made me so angry that I haven't been able to speak to them about it yet. When I cool down, I guess I will."

Letting go and respecting another's choice—whether we agree with it or not—is difficult in the family context. But if the bottom line is that you want to remain a family, if that is an important priority in your life (and it must be, because you're reading this book), then some accommodations and compromises must be made along the way. Name-calling is not communication and only serves to sever relationships, not build them. Adjusting our expectations by throwing away the myth that our offspring, sibling, or other relative is "supposed to" believe and practice the same faith as we do takes a certain amount of courage—the courage to view differences as opportunities for growth.

What if the conflict isn't necessarily one of "difference," but of "degree"? Some families go right up the proverbial wall when cousin Tish starts blaming everything from the camera jamming to your tripping over the toddler's toy on Satan.

TOO MUCH, OR NOT ENOUGH, RELIGION

One of the most frequent sources of family friction concerning religion is the relative whom others perceive as either having "too much" or "not enough" religion. It's all right, most people would say, for relatives to have their beliefs, so long as they don't try to force them down your throat, embarrass you, use their faith as an excuse for unkind actions, or act hypocritically and stand in judgment of other family members.

"My sister thinks she's such a big Christian, but she's got to be the most unchristian person in the family," says Kate emphatically. "She was always the one in the family who needed a little extra help financially, and even when she married, she married a real loser. Fifteen years later they got divorced and her three kids were all either in trouble or doing drugs. My husband and I took them all to live with us for nearly a year," says Kate. "We were glad to help her try to get on her feet. The teenagers got jobs and we spent a lot of time with them. Then all of a sudden, she joined this charismatic church and discovered that we weren't the kind of people she should be hanging around with anymore. But it's all right for my seventy-four-year-old parents to continue to help support her, because she's working in a Christian bookstore—on commission. Christianity begins at home, too, and so far all I hear is talk."

So, you have a Catholic relative that's more Catholic than the pope? Or maybe an Evangelical who gives thousands each year to the church, but can't spare money to get your parents an anniversary card? Maybe your Jewish father-in-law will eat nonkosher foods at restaurants, but insists on keeping kosher in your home to keep you on your toes? You are not alone. But religion is only partly the issue; what we are really talking about is either control or attention.

Maxine thought she had a pretty good handle on her sister's devout prayerfulness. She took a relaxed attitude as Letitia spent most of Thanksgiving giving sermonettes to whoever happened to be standing closest to her. Maxine even threw in a few praise-the-Lords herself. She listened intently as Letitia explained about the phenomenon of speaking in tongues and was polite when Letitia emphasized that it was necessary for all people to give away a high percentage of their income to the church. On the flight home, Letitia not only thoroughly blessed all the passengers attempting to settle themselves into the seats around Maxine, but she blessed the surprised flight attendants, and then walked right into the cockpit of the airplane and prayed that the pilots would have a safe journey. "By the time she got off the plane, she had gotten what she wanted—all the attention of everyone within earshot," says Maxine. "And all I wanted to do was sink under my seat. Remind me never to travel with her!"

Religion is often used as an excuse for hostile actions. The brother who tells his sister, who fell while ice skating with a group of children, that the fall was her fault "because God was punishing her," is no more Christian than the Spanish Inquisition executioners. The family member who deliberately snubs the rest of the family in the name of "religious purity" is working with a hidden agenda of hostility and revenge, not the love of God. And while we can cluck our tongues in sympathy at the "preacher's kid" syndrome, in which the child of a minister is always expected to be more perfect than the next person, few realize that it's not just the preacher's kids who are afflicted. Very often those expectations, or "supposed to's," also affect the offspring of those who are active members, deacons, elders, or followers of a particular church or sect. Again, the issue is control and the rebellion is an act against that control, not necessarily against the religion.

"My parents cared more about the church than they did about my brothers and me," says Winston, a fortyish professional. "At least, that's how I felt growing up. It seemed our week revolved around Sunday, which I grew to hate. As soon as I could, I purposefully took a job that required me to work on Sundays so I wouldn't have to go to church with my parents. Nobody questioned my father's authority, but I felt that he couldn't argue with a job. I admit I got in trouble in high school and college—nothing serious, just pranks mostly, like running naked through the girls' dorm at the Christian college I was sent to—just to get a little attention. It was really stupid, though, because he was convinced the devil was working through me. It took me many years of distancing myself from my father before I could see the situation for what it was. The church was important to him; therefore it became the way I could get at him."

Although one's interpretation of another's degree of involvement is as subjective as one's interpretation of a cult, in some instances it becomes apparent to all concerned that a family member has gone off the deep end.

THE TRUE FANATIC

From all corners of the country, the words are hauntingly similar: "You can't speak to her about anything except religion. It is her total world. Even her husband and children come in second or third, at least!"

"I just can't deal with him anymore. I love my brother—or at least the brother I used to have. But this person is so rigid. You can't talk with him about anything but religion; religion *his* way, that is."

"I have seen that woman forget that she has children at home who are expecting to eat, as she goes running around the community doing 'good deeds' for other people. I have tried to talk to her, but I just can't reach her."

We tend to marvel at the church member who is always there for others: chairing committees, paying visits to the sick, or doing telephone counseling, whatever the time of day or night. Often that person receives a lot of praise for his or her selfless acts . . . but what of the family at home? Individuals who spend all their time in the service of the church but neglect their home and family have a real problem. They are the true *fanatics*, or, in more contemporary terms, they are *addicts*—yes, addicts.

Addictive personalities will be covered in greater detail in chapter 15, but because religion is considered a whole value system unto itself, the religious addict will be discussed here. Even the word *fanatic* has a revealing origin. From *fanum,* the Latin word for "temple," a fanatic is defined as "one who is possessed of the enthusiasm or madness of the temple, engendered by over-indulgence in religious rites" *(Brewer's Dictionary of Phrase and Fable).* Just as religion is sometimes used as a blind to hide other motives and actions, the religious fanatic has found an approved outlet for his or her needs or obsessions. Under the guise of devotion, the fanatic pares the world down to one thing, religion; he or she uses religion as an excuse to withdraw from reality.

In order to understand fanaticism, Carol Kurtz, who frequently uses her early arts background for family therapy analogies, recommends that you try to imagine an old-fashioned wagon wheel with the individual at the center of the wheel and the spokes representing the ways in which the individual relates to the world (see diagram below). If that individual were to focus on just one of those spokes, or become obsessed with one of those spokes, such as with religion, then the wheel begins to roll off-kilter. Pretty soon, the only avenue open to reach that individual is the one that has been left open, the obsession itself.

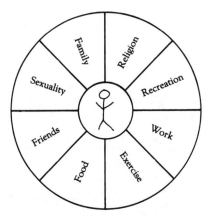

Balanced Life Wheel

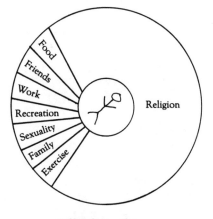

Off-Balance Due to
Obsession

Marguerite is definitely the fanatic in her family. She has five children, two of whom have health problems. Her marriage is foundering and her younger brother, who ran away from his parents' home, has moved in with her also. Yet Marguerite staffs the county Suicide Hotline, serves on three committees at church, witnesses door-to-door on Tuesday and Thursday evenings, and attends not only two Sunday services but a Wednesday evening interdenominational prayer service as well.

"I just can't seem to make her see that if she stayed home and attended to her family instead of her church, then perhaps they would be in better shape," says her sister. "But this is her escape. If she's involved with the church, then she doesn't have to deal with her problems and stresses."

The fanatic is in need of serious help and understanding, because the real problem is not one that has anything to do with religion. The religious fanatic needs to be treated like the addict that he or she is, if the wagon wheel of life is to become balanced once more. (See chapter 15).

Finally, as we have seen, while some family feuds over religion are truly over theology, most involve family roles and expectations that are all part of family life. Employing the skills of planned communication, adjusting expectation levels, humor, surrogate families, and—above all in the case of religion—tolerance will allow various religious influences to add shades to the foliage of our family tree rather than blight it.

15

Addictions

The statistics concerning addictions are startling. According to figures compiled by the American Psychiatry Association and other agencies:

- There are more than 10 million alcoholics in the United States today. Alcoholism is the country's third leading cause of death; it costs business and industry $54 billion each year in loss of production, accidents, and damage.
- Nearly 25 million (or one out of every ten Americans) have tried cocaine, many becoming addicted.
- More than 60 million have tried marijuana, with roughly 20 million using it regularly.
- By the time children reach the seventh grade, 60 percent feel strong pressure to use drugs and alcohol. By high school, 65 percent have used alcohol or other drugs, and, ultimately, 34 percent will be affected by chemical dependency, eating disorders, and other compulsive behaviors, which will be damaging to their lives.
- There are between 400,000 and 700,000 heroin addicts in the country today.
- An estimated 5 million Americans are addicted to gambling in one form or another.
- An estimated 20 percent of the population suffer from eating disorders or addictions.

What puts these statistics in a particularly startling perspective is the understanding that none of these addicts exists in a vacuum. Each addict has a family that is affected by his or her addiction—or multiple addictions. The families of addicts are part of a silent epidemic, as two or more concerned individuals in every addict's life attempt to correct, cope with, protect, or adjust to the abuser and his or her erratic behavior.

Marty grew up with an alcoholic father. She learned she couldn't bring friends home because his behavior was sometimes violent, sometimes bizarre. Although, as she grew to adulthood, she eschewed alcohol herself, she married a man who had a drinking problem. She sees the cycle repeating itself for her children; at a recent family gathering, she was terribly ashamed when she was asked to take her husband home after he violently attacked her brother during a political discussion.

Mark got his first joint from his older cousin Bill. After marijuana, Mark progressed to cocaine. In order to maintain his $400-a-week habit, he stole from family members, burglarized houses, and dealt drugs himself. When he got his sister started on drugs, his life hit bottom.

Alice is a once-pretty twenty-four-year-old who has starved herself down to eighty-nine pounds. Her brother, Nick, fits the family profile a little more closely. At five feet, nine inches, he weighs in at 252 pounds. All family discussions eventually get around to weight. Both Alice and Nick are headed for self-destruction.

Family members who have an addict in their midst assume a variety of roles to try to cope with the sick behavior, thus becoming, in many ways, sick themselves. These relatives have been termed co-dependents or co-addicts by nationally recognized self-help groups such as Al-Anon. Despite all good intentions, co-dependents do not help the addict. On the contrary, because they are so enmeshed in the relationship, even the most loving of these family members exacerbates the problem and creates a new pattern of sick behavior, which is passed down through the family chain, often for generations.

This chapter is not meant to dissect all the addictions available, their whys and wherefores, or to give you a prescription for them. There are many fine books written by experts in the various fields that are excellent reference sources. What will be dealt with here is the role the family members play in the cornucopia of addictions, and how you, as a strong individual, can take action to build bridges that benefit both the addict and the family.

Dealing with an addiction in the family is tricky business, because there are so many egos and so much other family emotional baggage involved. All the roles, "supposed to's," rivalries, and issues of family dynamics, which have been discussed up to this point, swirl about a person with an addiction; this turbulence sets up a barrier to those very people who could be the most help. For example, imagine that your brother, whom you always considered the favored child, has developed a cocaine addiction. Because of hostile feelings for him, left over from childhood, you may dismiss his wife's or your mother's comments about his erratic behavior. After all, he's had a lousy attitude since you were both adolescents. This is a natural reaction. A normal one. It is also one that may fade as we examine our own parts in the addiction drama.

IS IT AN ADDICTION
OR JUST CRAZINESS?

Do you have an Uncle Jolly? Uncle Jolly is the relative about whom family legends are made. Uncle Jolly is the one who got so drunk one time that he rolled off the roof, landed in the back of a pickup truck, and when he awoke, he was two states away! "Yup, that's Uncle Jolly," everyone laughs. "But let me tell you this one. Another time Uncle Jolly got so drunk . . ." And so it goes. The theme that ties all the stories together is Uncle Jolly's continuing drunkenness, but few want to address that fact. The stories are funny, after all. Anyway, how could Uncle Jolly have a problem? He has a nice wife, two kids, holds down a job . . . well, he has changed jobs a few times recently, but that's not so unusual.

Besides, he's not nearly as much a problem as Aunt Sandra, who is a physical-fitness freak. She makes everyone around her feel guilty every time they put something in their mouths. She couldn't attend her mother's seventieth birthday party, because she had signed up to run a marathon race. She leaves work, her own family, or family gatherings to put in her minimum three hours of workout time per day, no matter what is going on or who might be ill—including herself. She won't even go on vacation unless there's a fully equipped gym at the site. Now *she's* the crazy one of the family. Right?

Actually, both Uncle Jolly and Aunt Sandra have an addiction problem and it is no surprise that they are both in the same family. According to the experts, addictive personalities do tend to run in families; there are two mechanisms at work here: genetics and environment. Recent studies by the Harvard School of Medicine indicate that addiction to alcohol or drugs is different from other obsessions in that the former is a disease, with the susceptibility to that disease passed down through families.

On the other side of the coin is environment. The coping mechanisms that a family employs to offset stress are learned and passed down as well. In addition, those family members surrounding the addict have learned particular behaviors that also contribute to addiction. Whether the addict is an adult or an adolescent, the family changes are the same.

Dr. Miller Newton is an internationally recognized authority on adolescent addictions. Founder and director of the nonprofit award-winning program KIDS of Bergen County, New Jersey (the subject of the television movie "Not My Kid!"), he has personally dealt with 3,600 kids during the last nine years and recently supervised the opening of two additional KIDS facilities in Texas and Utah. He has also dealt with their families. Family involvement is an integral part of treatment.

"When an individual makes the choice to use a substance and begins using it regularly, it affects the family," says Newton. "At first, something doesn't feel quite right, so family members try new pieces of behavior to cope with that change. As usage progresses, the addict becomes the center of the family and literally controls what goes on. Their acting up causes everyone else's schedules and needs to change. At that point, family members develop a reactive disease. You can't live in a situation like that without going crazy trying to cope with it, so it's this reactive disease, with people trying to cope and protect their own self-worth, that inadvertently begins to contribute to the addict's disease as well."

But, you might wonder, how do we know whether Uncle Jolly really has an addiction? How can someone else tell?

Dr. Jerry Richards is the former Addictive Diseases Program administrator for Charter Hospital of Tampa Bay, a rehabilitative hospital with eight counseling centers throughout the state of Florida and the founder of the Richards Institute of Florence, Kentucky. A former Catholic priest and recovering alcoholic himself, Richards is now called upon to lecture to groups ranging from the clergy to physicians to civic organizations, spreading the need for education on addictive diseases and their effects on the family. He said that if there were some way to measure preoccupation with a substance, you wouldn't need any other signs.

"A primary sign of addiction is a total imbalance in the person's life," he says. "And by substance, I don't mean just drugs and alcohol. Food is a substance that can be an addiction, religion can be an addictive substance. I firmly believe workaholism is an addiction, because I've seen cases where a person spends incredible numbers of hours at work, early mornings, late nights. When they tell him not to come in, he develops withdrawal symptoms.

"Physical exercise can be an addiction," continues Richards. "Last year, I was in Indiana during a terrible drought. The temperature was 102 degrees and there were still people out there jogging. That is not healthy—that's an addiction."

Recalling the diagram of the wheel on page 167, we could say that a person's addiction throws off the balance of the wheel, and their life. Normal activities are neglected—family, friends, jobs, sometimes food. These are the people who are preoccupied with one facet of their lives; they revolve their days around that activity and are irritable if they cannot indulge.

These are the family members with addictive personalities. Have you ever known one who was always compulsively involved in some cause or activity to the exclusion of everything else? Perhaps Aunt Delia, who was a devout Catholic until she discovered Christian Science and then immersed herself in that religion. Along the way, she became a devotee of vegetarianism and herbalism to such a point that you couldn't discuss anything else with her. Just because Aunt Delia is indulging in socially acceptable activities doesn't mean she's completely healthy. Aunt Delia has an addictive personality. So does brother Tom, who has been married four times. Love can also be an addiction when someone is continually looking for that *high* from first romance. When it begins to wane, he or she goes to the next person for a *fix*.

Look around your family. There may be some who are attempting to find outlets for these tendencies. While some, like exercise, religion, and work are socially more acceptable and more difficult to pinpoint unless the immediate family structure is obviously affected, others such as alcohol, drugs, food, and gambling are easier to identify.

That identification requires tremendous honesty, however, and honesty is something that families of addicts tend to put on the shelf as they assume various coping roles.

ROLES FOR COPING, NOT HELPING

"It happened again!" says Frieda. "I may kill him next time! I have a fifty-three-year-old brother-in-law who is a drunk. He also happens to be president of a well-respected computer firm. At the last family gathering, he became so drunk that he attacked my husband after losing at a volleyball game. Our fourteen-year-old son tried to intervene and my brother-in-law game him a bloody nose.

"My sister-in-law tries to make up for this man by going out of her way to be generous and sweet, and she is always having to clean up his messes for him. If it wasn't for her, I would have been tempted to call the police. If it happens one more time, I swear I will!"

One of the key roles that a close family member assumes when there is an addict in the family is that of Caretaker or Rescuer. As the term implies, the Caretaker steps in to save the day. Usually assumed by the spouse or a parent, this role is one of the more visible effects of a family addiction.

The Caretaker may be long-suffering Aunt Minny who fills in for Uncle Joe when he is passed out or can't be found, because he's down at the racetrack when he should be at a social engagement or family affair. The Caretaker is the one who calls the addict's place of employment to offer excuses for his or her absence and winds up shouldering added responsibilities to compensate for the addict's unreliability.

The Caretaker has some aspects of the Diplomat, and caretaking is an easy trap to fall into, because such people don't want confrontations or trouble. They spend a great amount of time attempting to minimize the opportunities in which trouble could occur. If it wasn't for the Caretaker, the addict would be held accountable for his or her actions. And that's the trouble with this role.

"My husband not only gambled away our mortgage money, he gambled away the money for food, for doctors—you name it," says Laurie. "He just didn't seem to recognize the fact that I was trying to feed three small children and keep a minimum survival household going. If it wasn't for my father-in-law coming by once a week, I don't know what I would have done. He would bring me bags of groceries, little treats for the kids . . . most often, he would also slip me some cash. He'd say it was just 'til Johnny got himself together or hit it big. Well, Johnny is forty-four years old and I don't think he's ever going to get it together or hit it big, but at least the kids won't starve."

The Caretaker, with all the love and goodness in his or her heart, encourages addicts to continue their addictions by making their lives easier.

"Everybody sees this person as being so caring and long-suffering, but since the addicted persons don't have to suffer the consequences of their actions—they are always being taken off the hook—in actuality, it helps addicts get worse," says Newton. "The caretakers' intention is to pick up the pieces and keep the family intact, but they are adding to the sickness, not helping it get better."

Another role assumed in order to deal with the addictive situation is the Butterfly or the Avoider. (We discussed this aspect of the Butterfly's formation briefly in chapter 4.) If the addict is an adolescent, this is a role most often assumed by the father if the household is intact.

"When we started recognizing that D. J. had problems, all of a sudden, my husband found that his job was requiring more of his time," says Lillian, mother of a drug-dependent daughter. "He was working more nights, taking more business trips. He even signed up to play on two tennis teams instead of one—leaving me to face everything alone! At first I thought he was having an affair, but then I finally realized that he just didn't know how to deal with the situation, so he escaped from it."

The Butterfly might also be a sibling, and if the addict is an adult, one of the children in the household may deal with the conflicts and craziness by avoiding them. These are the ones who withdraw, who distance themselves from the problems, who are building up a silent rage inside. Some experts call this emotional distancing and isolation "psychic numbing." With enough practice, the Butterflies find it difficult to distinguish their true feelings and wind up having difficulty relating to anyone.

Since so much of the family attention centers around the negative activity of the addict, there is usually one in the family who feels the need to validate the family's good name. This person is the Hero. Usually a sibling or child of an addict, such a person continues this role well into later life.

"My mother was an alcoholic," says Gina. "I knew I was different from other kids because of it. I felt I needed to prove that I wasn't like that, too, so I worked hard to be on the honor rolls, make the teams, be the cheerleader, and all that happy stuff. Even now, as an adult, I'm still working—still proving that some good came out of my family too. It's exhausting, but I can't stop."

The trap these superachievers fall into is one of addiction themselves. They may not drink, but they are compulsive in other ways. They are the ones who can easily become the workaholics, anorexics, fitness freaks, or religious fanatics. If they do fall into the addiction trap, it is rarely recognized, because everyone expects this character to be "the most likely to succeed."

If the Hero role is already taken, then another family member may discover that a way to diffuse conflicts that occur around the addict is to become the family Clown or Mascot. Advice columns are full of letters from spouses of Clowns: "He never takes anything seriously. He always turns everything into a joke"; "We haven't had a serious discussion in years. Especially when something goes wrong, he just jokes about it."

This family member fully believes the adage "Laugh and the world laughs with you, cry and you cry alone." He or she has had plenty to cry about, but the method of coping is to divert fights and confrontations by clowning or acting cute. It becomes a way of life. These people may be the life of the party—particularly family gatherings—but you just can't seem to pin them down to a real discussion. If you did, they might just break down and cry—and then they'd be alone to face the demons that plagued them all their lives.

Finally, we have a reprise of the Scapegoat. As discussed in chapter 6, the Scapegoat serves to take the heat and attention away from the real problem in the family, the addict.

"My father drank, but that was never discussed," says Lin. "I'm the one who was always in trouble, so the attention was on me. I fell in with a drinking crowd in high school. I wasn't like my sister, Kari. She was a Tammy Twirler, worked on the yearbook—everything that I wasn't in the family. I remember driving to a counselor once with my mother. There was snow on the ground and she was in a really bad mood that day because she and my father had had another fight. She turned to me and screamed, 'Do you want me to drive this car right into the bridge?' Then she floored it. I was scared stiff. I ran away, but they found me hiding in my girlfriend's closet. When we got home, my father punched me in the mouth and then screamed at me to clean up the blood. Then he went and had another drink."

As long as the blame for all the family's troubles can be placed on the Scapegoat, then the real problem will not be confronted. Besides, who wants to admit to having a problem in the first place?

DENIAL IS THE FAMILY GAME

"I just can't seem to get through to my sister-in-law, and my husband— her brother—refuses to address the problem," confides Meagan. "His sister has two children. The boy is overweight and the girl, I'm convinced, is anorexic, yet my sister-in-law just can't seem to see it. She's constantly harping on the boy to cut down on his food intake so he can be more attractive like his sister. His sister meanwhile looks like a walking skeleton.

"Family dinners are a joke. The boy eats everything in sight in the kitchen even before the meal—I've learned to buy an extra half-gallon of milk just for him. Then the girl pushes her food around and doesn't eat anything—which is okay with her brother, who proceeds to clean the plate. Then my sister and brother-in-law get into another argument about food, but their real problem is their marriage. They don't seem to see that either."

The biggest block to getting help for the addicted person is the family's refusal to recognize that there is a problem at all. "It is not unusual for it to be more difficult to break through the family's denial than the addict's," says Richards. "Don't forget that this is an illness that affects the entire family. The family disease becomes so strong that members can't even tell anymore what is real and what is not real. A lot of people look upon addiction not as a disease but as bad people doing this stuff. It's just not true."

It is a difficult barrier to break through, however. There is a lot at stake—
all the "supposed to's" of family life are on the line:

"We have a nice family and nice families aren't *supposed to* have addicts."
(Or problems of any type, for that matter.)

"I have been a good parent; therefore we're not *supposed to* have a child
who becomes addicted. That would mean that I'm a failure."

"He's too intelligent to get mixed up in something like that. Intelligent
people are *supposed to* know better.

"If I admit we have a problem, then we may have to change, and that's
scary. We're not *supposed to* be afraid of our own family members."

"We're *supposed to* be able to take care of our own. We don't need any
stranger telling us what our problems are."

All these "supposed to's" are based on fears—the fear that the family
will fall apart if you recognize the problem, the fear that you might not be
needed as a Caretaker anymore, the fear that the changes will mean you
can't have fun anymore (as in the alcoholic's family).

"I'm convinced that the reason nobody drags my father to a clinic or
Alcoholics Anonymous is because drinking is such a part of our social life,
that they're afraid they'll have to throw parties with soda and chips instead
of beer," says Rob. "I come from a real Irish family where it's just part of
the family tree to have at least one who is known for being the family
drunk. They almost revel in that fact and protect the drunk. It's just too
sick."

Particularly in the case of alcohol or drug addiction, there is a general
feeling that there is a moral failure involved that is a reflection on the
family. Such people would rather be told that a family member has cancer
or some other illness that is nonthreatening and easier to accept. Such was
the case with Jefferson, a seemingly successful accountant. Jefferson had
always been a hard drinker but had no problems he "couldn't handle." He
also tended to lose an inordinate amount of money on various gambling
enterprises. (Addictive personalities often are involved in more than one
addiction or obsession at a time.) When his wife left him, he got into a
crowd that used cocaine regularly. He was soon hooked on that as well.
Pretty soon, he couldn't function at work, he was skimming money from
the company to pay both gambling debts and drug pushers, and he indulged
in alcohol when he wasn't high. The family reaction? They just thought
he was having difficulties adjusting to his divorce.

"By the time family members recognize that someone may have a problem, the addict has been involved for an average of two or three years

already," says Newton. "At first they tend to think it is simply a behavioral problem or a physical ailment that is making the addict act so crazy—they don't usually think of drugs and alcohol. That's tougher to accept because, then they feel it could be their fault."

Then again, some people finally face the fact that their relative has a problem, that it is not entirely normal for Cousin Steffanie to weigh 100 pounds and eat by herself in the bathroom instead of at the kitchen table, or for Uncle Sam to always insist on bringing his own bottle to family gatherings and everywhere else, "just in case the booze runs out and the liquor store is closed." But what can you do? "I knew there was a problem," says one woman whose brother is an alcoholic, "but I didn't know what to do, so I did nothing. Maybe that was wrong, but I guess I felt it wasn't my place to point the finger."

Pointing the finger is divisive. However, extending a helping hand, when you recognize a family member is in trouble, is building a constructive bridge. After all, if your cousin were drowning just three feet from you, you'd reach down and pull her out, wouldn't you? Addicts are like the laboratory mice who have electrodes wired to the pleasure centers in their brains. The mice learn that when they hit the right little button, their pleasure centers light up, and for a few moments, they feels wonderful. Pretty soon, all the other realities of life, including food, sleep, socialization, and exercise, are ignored as the little mice obsessively continue to hit the pleasure button—even to their death.

The addict's life wheel is too far out of kilter. Like the mice, the addict doesn't even recognize the necessities of the real world anymore—but you do. And there is a definite plan of attack that has been designed specifically for family involvement.

INTERVENTION: THE FAMILY PLAN

Dr. X. was a highly respected internist. He served on several professional boards, was chairman of his department for a large metropolitan hospital, and the father of three children. He was also an addict, to both pills and alcohol. Through the years he had not only disappointed his wife and children by his unreliability and mood swings, but it had become increasingly apparent in his work that he was endangering his patients.

One spring, while he and his wife were on a week's vacation in the Caribbean, there was a knock at the bungalow door. In walked his three children, his brother, and four of his fellow physicians. They calmly sat him down and for the next several hours, they took turns outlining specific ways in which his addictions had affected their relationships, both personal and professional. At the end of the session, Dr. X., in tears, agreed to seek professional help. "I couldn't believe they all cared about me so much, to do that," he still says. "They literally saved my life. I can see now that I wasted so many years."

The process used is called *Intervention*, and one of the more famous examples of its success is former First Lady Betty Ford who, after being confronted by her family members, not only faced her addictions and sought help but went on to establish the Betty Ford Clinic to help other addicts.

Intervention can be used very effectively by family members, but it should not be attempted either alone or without professional guidance, warns Richards. "One of the first most important things about Intervention is that it must be done in love. Anyone who is not sincerely interested in helping the addict should not participate," he says. "What has happened to me in a couple of cases is that one of the people involved turned out to be chemically dependent as well, and their input was certainly not constructive."

The interested family members should meet with a counselor experienced in Interventions and systematically write down all those occasions when they were present that give them an indication that there is an addiction involved. The list must be very specific. For example: "Mom, it was my fifteenth birthday, and just before the kids came over to celebrate, you sat in the kitchen drinking. All during the party you flirted with the boys and embarrassed me by acting like a stranger instead of a mother. Toward the end of the party, one of my friends told me you had passed out in the bedroom. I was so angry, I didn't even check. I love you, Mom, and I want to help you."

After the family members, who may be joined by an employer or family physician, make their lists, a rehearsal session is held so members can pull the session off in a unified and organized manner, as well as be ready for the denial they will encounter.

"Control is always an issue," says Richards. "The family will try to control the addict, which, of course, they can't. The addict will say 'I'm going to try to control my drinking,' or whatever. And they have lost it right there—you don't have to try to control something that isn't already out of control."

Once the group feels it is ready, they then approach the addict. It is best to confront the addict somewhere other than at home so he or she will not have the home-turf advantage. The group arranges itself around the addict in a semicircle and they begin what they have rehearsed.

"It is a very emotional process," says Richards. "One of the effective things about Intervention is the sheer number of individuals who are saying to the person, 'We care about you—that's why we're doing this. But you have done these things and we won't live with the craziness anymore.' Not in every case, but in most cases, the individual will finally then get help." Ultimately the decision to go into treatment must be made by the addict, as treatment will not be effective without his or her full cooperation.

Getting past the hurdle of identifying the problem and accepting the fact that someone close to you needs professional help is just the first, albeit big, step. The next logical questions are, What kind of help should I seek? and, What can I do, if anything, to head off any additional problems? Is the addiction contagious?

GETTING HELP TO BREAK THE CYCLE

There are hundreds of programs and institutions across the country equipped to deal with addictions of various kinds, from alcohol and drugs to eating disorders and "love" addictions. Those which have consistently proven the most effective over the long run, however, are those that include the family as part of the counseling and rehabilitative process.

Since, as discussed, addiction becomes a family disease, it does the addict more harm than good to return to the diseased environment after putting his or her own addiction into remission.

When fourteen-year-old Missy announced that she was going on a diet after her father laughingly called her his "little Danish," everyone in the family applauded. They continued to tell her she looked good as she dropped ten, fifteen, twenty-five pounds. But Missy didn't know when to quit. By the time her parents forcibly got her to a hospital, the 5-foot, 4-inch youngster weighed 92 pounds.

Missy was enrolled in a program close to her home after the hospital stay, which consisted primarily of pumping nutrients into her emaciated body. The follow-up program was a self-help group meeting once a week. Sometimes she attended, sometimes she didn't. Four months later, after returning to her anorexic behavior pattern, Missy collapsed again.

Remember that the addict has an "addictive personality," which he or she will have to recognize and battle for the rest of his or her life. There is good reason behind the familiar saying, "There's nothing worse than a reformed smoker" (or alcoholic, or atheist). Often an addict simply shifts the addiction from one substance to another. In some cases, the new substance is the "cure." Experts say that they have seen many a recovering alcoholic fanatically attend a dozen A.A. meetings a week. But what else do they do with their lives? Where is the balance?

Throughout the other chapters, the need for surrogate families and support has been emphasized over and over again. The only difference here is that the addict, first, needs the help of an outside surrogate family of professional counselors and support groups, and second, his own personal family must be reeducated into a healthy life pattern, so as to rid themselves of codependents' disease.

As I said before, there are hundreds of programs equipped to deal with a relative's addictions, but look for the ones that involve the family, or the sister programs like Al-Anon, for relatives of those who are attending A.A.

For example, family involvement is a mandatory part of the process at KIDS. From the child's admission to the residential center in Phase One right through to the return home in Phase Five, when the child earns the privilege of assuming family responsibilities again, the entire family is counseled, educated, and supported. In this particular aspect, KIDS differs from many of the current treatment programs. It not only uses the immediate and extended family but involves the adolescent's surrogate family of peers in the treatment.

"The most intimate peers that an adolescent has are his siblings and cousins," says Newton. "If a child has an older sibling involved in an addiction, there is a 90 percent chance that he or she will get involved too. At the KIDS program, we've been able to get that down to less than 6 percent because of our total family approach. Most people assume these are bad kids from bad homes who get involved in addictions. But the fact of the matter is that most of these kids were achieving, productive individuals before they got involved, and in 90 percent of the cases, they said 'No' the first two or three times it was offered to them. But peer pressure is relentless, so we use that also in rehabilitation."

Both Newton and Richards recommend that families consider a rehabilitative program's overall organization, plan, and counseling philosophy. "You don't want a counselor with the laid-back attitude that drinking is okay for minors, but hard drugs are a no-no," says Newton. "Believe me, they are out there. They want to be your kid's buddy. Your kid, at this stage, needs help, not a buddy, in the counselor."

Look for support and educational groups offered to the addict's family members, as well as those where participation of the entire family is encouraged.

Finally, a successful program will offer a period of aftercare; that is, support and continued counseling after the addict has left a treatment facility and during the time he or she is once again facing the stresses of the real world without the crutch of addiction.

Understanding that an addiction is a family disease, a family pattern, you can achieve the realization that you are one link in a chain of potentially troubled people. By seeking out education and help, you can be the link that breaks the chain of addiction in your family and ends the craziness.

16

Illness and Dependence

There is, I am told, an old Irish blessing that says, "May your relatives stay well and die quickly." An interesting sentiment, but not usually the case. As we travel life's highway, instead of the road coming up to meet us and the wind ever gentle at our backs, we find the road full of potholes, some wider and deeper than others, and the wind howling in our faces. One of those potholes in the road is illness. It is a fact of life for all but few, and its length, degree, and depth serve as the catalysts for determining the family's strength and efficiency in combating external assaults.

Edna's mother was diagnosed as having cancer and given less than a year to live. Two of Edna's sisters moved up their wedding dates, a brother and his wife decided to have the baby they had been putting off, and everyone made decisions based on the doctors estimate. Within six months, Edna's mother went into remission and has been in remission for three years, but her health has become a cause célèbre among most of her children. "I get scolded if I don't call Mom five times a week, if I don't volunteer to drive her places, and if I don't drop everything any time she gets a cold," says Edna. "I love my mother, but my sisters and brothers are driving me crazy."

Uncle Mike drives his family crazy. Every time he, or anyone around him, gets a headache, he speculates loudly that it's a brain tumor. If someone is pale, he's sure it's leukemia. He suffers strange stomach pains, particularly if he feels the food that's being served hasn't been refrigerated properly, and carries an ample supply of medicine around with him in his doctorlike bag, which also contains a stethoscope and a sphygmomanom-

183

eter. For Uncle Mike, illness is an event, whether it's real or imagined, and he insists on sharing the event with everyone.

After she fell and broke her hip, Bob's seventy-year-old mother moved in with Bob and his wife Marsha. While Marsha is obliged to remind her mother-in-law to take her medicines, see that she eats and rests well, and prevent her from exacerbating her asthmatic condition by smoking. Bob's mother, in turn, does nothing but complain that Marsha can't hold a candle to her own daughter Liza. Of course Liza hasn't been to see her mother, has not sent any financial help, and has called only once on the telephone.

When we deal with illnesses, from mild to serious, within the family structure, all the old family roles come into play. The Dictator knows, of course, the best treatment to follow. The Pot-Stirrer will poll the relatives on everything from the ill person's temperament to medical diagnosis, the Diplomat will scurry around trying to find appropriate materials to inform and entertain, the Scapegoat will take the blame for the illness, and the Butterfly will fly away.

Complicating these roles are the individual personality types and different approaches of the people involved, all potential kindling for an explosion. The *feeling person* will make a decision emotionally, while the *thinking person* may coolly step back and offer practical and logical suggestions. The feeling person gets angry and accuses the thinking person of not caring, who, in turn, is convinced that the other is an incapable airhead who can't handle the stressful situation.

Chaos evolves when you mix two extended families (or more in the case of blended families)—with their varied interests, rivalries, and hidden agendas—into a situation that may require a coordinated, if not unified, effort.

In addition to driving you crazy, your family can also make you sick, or well, depending upon certain genetic traits. Researchers such as Dr. Aubrey Milunsky, director of the Center for Human Genetics at Boston University, are demonstrating that even the body's response to infection, as well as its predisposition to certain illnesses and diseases, are genetically controlled.

Less controlled is the nuts-and-bolts emotional response when a relative is ill or becomes dependent. "I'm married to a physician who practices, teaches, and lectures," says Karen, "but when someone gets sick in my extended family, my parents turn to my sister, who is a practical nurse, for medical advice! I forget half the time that I'm even married to a doctor when I deal with my side of the family."

Old family patterns may re-emerge, like the us-versus-them pattern. "I don't know how much more I can take," says Carolyn, whose marriage to

Gene is a second one for both of them. "My husband's brother moved in with us last year and we haven't had a moment alone since then. Turk even comes with us on our vacations and Gene always does what Turk, his older brother, wants to do. When I disagree, I find that Gene sides with his brother against me. I may go crazy and just walk out on both of them."

Just as a photographer develops images captured on film through a system of chemical baths, the family discovers the hidden myths and many cultural "supposed to's" when illness or dependence bathe it in stress. "We take care of our own; we don't need any outside help" is a common cry. "We won't put anyone in a nursing home. That's for people who don't have families who care" is another one that sometimes heralds chaos. And "Families are supposed to join together and help out when a member is sick" is another one.

While the intention behind such sentiments is noble, our contemporary lifestyles dictate something else. That "something else" is usually guilt: guilt over the fact that since both adults are working full-time to support the family, nobody is home to take care of an elderly parent who needs help; guilt over the fact that you are living halfway across the country when a severe illness strikes a parent or sibling; guilt over the fact that you have to attend to other priorities before you help the extended family. The expectations of family members and the guilt resulting from them are a major cause of arguments and feuds at a time when support is most needed.

Of course, if you are ill, you may have tenacious relatives who will call just to remind you that your illness is a judgment and punishment. "God's punishing you for being lazy" (or promiscuous, a heathen, not serious enough, drunk, stupid, undependable). "The last time I got a phone call from my brother like that I told him that my punishment wasn't my illness, it was being related to him! And then I slammed the phone down," says one woman.

Then there are those intrepid family members who revel in every little ache, pain, and fever, particularly their own. Their throats are sorer, their coughs more hacking, and their sneezes more frequent than anyone else's; that is, if they settle for something as mundane as a sneeze or cough. They cannot perform chores because of their "condition," and they demand constant attention and support whether the illness is real or imagined.

* * *

ILLNESS AS AN EVENT

Aunt Sarah's newsletter each year never fails to draw sighs of exasperation as well as a few chuckles. "The best thing about 1988 is that James and I lived to see the end of it," she wrote triumphantly. From that point on, the sixty-seven-year-old chronicled all the illnesses she and James had suffered during the year (beginning with January, of course), what the doctor prescribed, their physical reactions to medications, and the aftercare involved. Aunt Sarah also mentions the illnesses of her grown children, although they only rate one line. She ends with a bright, "We would love to hear how you and your family are as well"—but don't make the mistake of thinking she really wants to know. Aunt Sarah has her hands full with her own "problems."

Hypochondriacs come in all shapes, sizes, ages, and family backgrounds. They are the ones who leave the house prepared for any emergency (they *always* wear clean underwear . . . just in case!), keep files on diseases, medicines, and cemeteries, and subscribe to cable television just to get the medical channel. When a new disease is in the news, you can bet the family hypochondriac will begin to develop symptoms, but this person doesn't believe in the phrase "suffer in silence." He or she is very vocal about suffering, because that's truly half the fun.

Family members, particularly those who are dealing with very real financial, medical, or emotional problems, tend to have short tempers around the hypochondriac. "I have handled unemployment and my son's learning disabilities," says Joyce. "I'm afraid I don't have any patience for my sister, who has had a comparably easy life. Everything that happens to her, she thinks, is an insurmountable crisis. I often wonder what she would do if a real illness or emergency arose. It has gotten to the point where I find it difficult to speak to her civilly."

Not only do some hypochondriacs try the family's emotional patience, but they appear to be insulting. "I have an uncle who won't eat anything that he does not watch being prepared," says Kenia. "I used to try to please him, but now I just tell him what I'm cooking, and if he can't eat it, I tell him that he might want to bring his own food. I used to get insulted because he acts as though we are all out to poison him—my mother won't even invite him over anymore, and he is her own brother! But there are too many things in life to get excited over and this is not one of them, as far as I'm concerned."

Some families may find that the hypochondria, itself, is contagious. "My father is a bad influence on the children," says Sally. "I have noticed that my twelve-year-old is beginning to become preoccupied with every little ache and pain he gets; he runs to take his temperature whenever he gets a slight headache. He is simply mimicking my father. My mother always catered to Dad and his imagined illnesses. I don't know how she did it all those years. But when my son told us that he wanted a doctor's note to get him out of soccer at school because it's hard on the joints, my husband hit the ceiling."

Most agree that hypochondriacs learn their behavior early in life. Usually, there was an original, legitimate reason for them to be concerned about their health, but that concern was either blown out of proportion or encouraged long after that reason disappeared. Such is the case in Ginger's family.

"As a young child, my aunt suffered from some sort of heart murmur. She was protected from getting upset and was even sent to a special school, although I'm not sure why that was necessary," says Ginger. "I think her frailty was exaggerated, particularly as she outgrew the problem. Now the woman is in her fifties and she makes everyone crazy reminding us that she has always had problems. If a family member gets ill, she's convinced she's coming down with the same thing—or that she must be a carrier. We all dismissed her attitude as nerves, but then she decided that she must have a nervous *condition*, so she drove us crazy with that.

"The worst part about it is that her son is now worse than she is. When he was growing up he had allergies—just your run-of-the-mill allergies that millions of other people have. But now, according to him and his mother, *his* allergies are special. They both let you know how careful he has to be of everything. All we can do as family members is listen and laugh. I mean, it really is amusing if you can put it in the proper perspective, but there are days when they can drive you right up the wall."

Here is one instance where planned communication seems to fall on deaf ears—but don't use that term or the hypochondriac will swear they've noticed that their hearing has been failing lately. Even though they may issue dire warnings ("My mother used to screech if we even touched a handrail when we were going up and down stairs," says one man. "Do you know how many germs there are on banisters?"), they are primarily interested in their own health, and all the logic in the world is not going to change their firmly held convictions that they have been singled out of the human race to suffer untold agonies. Then they proceed to tell you just what those agonies are.

All you can do is adjust your expectations for this person and use your sense of humor. If, by chance, you have hypochondriacs who are fond of ministering to others in ill health, make use of their talents, but realize that somewhere in their bag of medicines and literature are the worst possible scenarios for any ailment you might contract. But don't worry, they also come equipped with a comparative analysis of hospitals across the country that are ready to handle invalids—or relatives who have been driven insane!

While we can laugh at the hypochondriacs and their bids for our attention, *real* chronic illness is no laughing matter. Long-term illness and accidents in which other family members are involved wear away the fabric of family relationships.

ACCIDENTS DO HAPPEN

Kerry's family has been swept up in a legal battle as well as a fight for health that is tearing the family apart. Twelve-year-old Kerry, racing over the bumps and hills at his grandparents' farm on his cousin's all-terrain vehicle (ATV), hit a tree. The accident left him badly brain-damaged. In order to collect the insurance to pay for Kerry's extensive medical and rehabilitation treatments, his parents were directed by the insurance company to sue both Kerry's grandparents and aunt and uncle, charging negligence. This has spurred a family feud that has left many angry, guilt-ridden, and depressed. Kerry, himself, has told his parents he wished he had died.

The myth that we are "supposed to" be able to protect our family against the vagaries of life disintegrates in the moments it takes a car to crash, a ladder to fall, a pistol to go off, or an ATV to hit a tree. Then there is a tremendous guilt that may be further complicated by legal proceedings.

Murray was pulling out into traffic from a stop sign when an oncoming car hit him in the driver's side. His son and nephew were not wearing seat-belts, although he had reminded them to do so, and the boys were thrown onto the opposite side of the car by the impact. His son suffered a broken leg and collarbone, but his nephew suffered several cracked vertebrae and head injuries.

Once again, the parents were directed to sue their family member in order to collect insurance money to pay for the medical treatment and therapy. They not only sued Murray to cover medical expenses, but added on a hefty amount to cover "mental anguish." This divided the family. Some members felt Murray should volunteer to absorb all the medical expenses himself, although they made it clear that even that wouldn't absolve him from blame. Others agreed that the lawsuit was the only way to go but didn't endorse the additional amount. A couple of others would not speak to Murray because he had "broken their trust" by causing an accident that hurt one of their own.

What they were saying was "Your nephew was supposed to be safe with you and you let us down. You are no better than a stranger." When one is standing outside the circle, it is easy to be dispassionate and logical. When one is caught up in the family melee, however, with all the roles, rivalries, and secrets, it is difficult to separate an unfortunate incident from the person involved.

People take lawsuits very personally, particularly when a family member has to charge the already guilt-ridden party with negligence. People's feelings get hurt, and that is understandable. This public "denouncement" of one of our own family members goes against everything we are taught from birth about "us versus them": We stick together. Fight among ourselves, but stand united against outsiders. Don't criticize a family member in front of strangers.

All these commandments of our youth stand in judgment when a serious accident within the family circle occurs. "How could you say those awful things about me?" cries a grandparent. "You know I did everything I could!" vows an uncle. "God knows, I wish it had been me instead. I would never do anything to hurt him," says another. And they mean it, but the most difficult thing to remember is that the most important person when an accident occurs is the victim.

"There has to be a high level of communication among the family members," says attorney Stephen Sepaniak. "The important thing is to protect the injured party and this may mean bringing a lawsuit. What we're talking about here is really insurance coverage. If what a relative is after is protection for the victim, it's foolish not to take advantage of the policy that was provided for such a purpose. People should not forego benefits to which they are entitled simply because they are related. I know that it's easy to say that when one isn't emotionally involved, but people have to separate the insurance policy from the emotional situation."

Sometimes accidents lead to chronic conditions, which serve as an ever-present reminder of a "family sin," and become an ever-present source of conflict. In other circumstances, chronic illness places a tremendous amount of stress not only on the caretaker but on other family members as well. And even more frequently, a member's chronic illness reveals a few more of the "supposed to's" that fall by the wayside and beget arguments.

CHRONIC ILLNESS, CHRONIC GUILT

Chronic illness is, at best, very wearing for all concerned. At worst, it can be the loose thread that, once pulled, unravels the entire network of relationships. It is during the prolonged illness of ourselves or a loved one that we begin to see people in a new light. "We learned who our real friends were" is a common theme among those who have weathered such situations.

Not only do we find out who our true friends are, but we find out which of our relatives can truly be counted upon. The Butterflies will all flutter away, and left on the branch will be those who come through to varying degrees.

When Geraldine's son contracted a blood disease and was ill for five years, Geraldine felt let down by her family. Although a couple of the family members lived within driving distance, most lived out of state. Geraldine, as the primary caretaker for her adolescent son, felt overwhelmed. She was also angry at relatives for not helping out more. When her son took temporary turns for the worse, or if something in the house fell apart, Geraldine would call relatives and hysterically relate the latest catastrophe. Although her son recovered, Geraldine still refuses to speak with one of her brothers and an aunt whom she felt "didn't come across" when she needed them.

Remember, however, that just because *you* are dealing with a difficult situation, doesn't mean that your relatives are going to change their personalities. "Oh yes, my family helped out when I was down with hepatitis, but I almost wish they hadn't," says Roger, a policeman who contracted the disease during a scuffle with a drug user. "My father—who is a classic Dictator—even called the chief and threatened a lawsuit. My brother, who has never liked my wife, kept making comments about how she could go out and get a job to help relieve our financial crunch. My aunt must have told me every horror story she ever heard concerning hepatitis. This went on for six months. I was never so glad to get well! If I'm ever that sick again, I'll try to keep it a secret."

Families do tend to act out of concern for their members, but there are times when the expectations are great and the actions are few. "I'll never forgive my sister," says Lucy emphatically. "When her husband was in a car accident, I took meals over to them, I ran her boys around to their sporting events and lessons, I even did laundry for her. What happens when I need her? I fell and broke my leg in two places. It was summer and we don't have air-conditioning, so I was miserable in a cast from my toes to my hip. Not only did she not volunteer to make any meals or take my two kids anywhere, but when I asked if we could borrow their air-conditioning unit, she said no, because her husband has allergies and wouldn't be able to sleep at night without it. I felt that he could have given up the unit for a few weeks. She just wasn't there for me. We speak, but I won't kill myself to help her out again."

Because our family is where we are "supposed to" let it all hang out whenever we want, it is also subjected to continuing complaints and travails, particularly when a long or chronic illness is present. Sometimes all the complainers want is for someone to listen and pat them on the back, but even that need can be tiring to those who must deal with it continuously.

"It has gotten to the point that if I even hear my cousin's voice on the telephone, I cringe," admits Dorothy. "All she does is complain. Everything is a crisis when it comes to her husband's back problems. I used to try to come up with solutions for her, but she wasn't really interested. It took me a long time to figure out that she just wanted me to go as crazy as she was. No more! And I don't feel guilty!"

Nikki, however, did wrestle with guilt. "My aunt opted to care for my uncle at home rather than put him in a hospital," she says. "He had a form of stomach cancer, and I know it was very difficult for her for a couple of years. We all tried to do what we could, but if she called and we didn't drop what we were doing to run over so she could go to an appointment, she'd hang up on us and then not speak to us. We all felt guilty when we said no, but we weren't being mean. His care was her whole world, but we all had families to take care of as well."

BRIDGING THE GAPS

"We are supposed to take care of our own" is a family saw that can be the cause of many family feuds during an illness. It is a sentiment to which most people still cling. The problems arise, however, when the care that's available does not measure up to expectations. Because families today are generally scattered geographically, it is difficult to "take care of our own" long-distance—particularly over a long illness. Some well-meaning children persuade an ill parent to move closer to them. This places the older person in a strange town, without the friends and landmarks that mean stability at a time when the stress of illness places an extra burden on them.

This is one of those times when we must use all the bridge-building tools available to us. An honest two-way communication must be established. The caretaker should communicate what his or her expectations are and what is needed from the specific family members. Then family members can communicate with the caretaker and relate whether those needs can be met realistically. "Yes, I can drive you to your appointment on Thursday morning." Or, "I can't be there to physically help you because I can't get away from work, but call me on the telephone when you just feel the need to get something off your chest."

The primary need to be fulfilled during a chronic illness is help—help with the patient, help with the household, and help to relieve the caretaker for a period of time each day or week so he or she may make contact with the outside world and remain sane. Rather than place this burden entirely on family members, outside help should be employed, which can be arranged by another member—even a Butterfly who would rather not be around a sick person. There are numerous support groups and medical assistance agencies that provide help for free, or one can arrange for a babysitter, patient sitter, or transportation.

If there is a true illness, and the caretaker is not simply satisfying his or her own needs by "creating" an invalid (a hypochondriac in the making), then the caretaker needs real emotional support on a constant basis. We may feel as though we're "supposed to" take care of our sick parent, child, or spouse, but it is important to realize that we all have limitations and to be honest about them, rather than feel guilty for having them. It can be worse for those growing up in a household where an invalid becomes the physical and emotional center of the family.

Tina grew up in such a household. Her mother was chronically depressed. "From my earliest memories, Mom was in bed. I am the youngest of four children, so I don't really remember her as a regular functioning adult. She was just someone we all had to tiptoe around, check on several times a day, and even take turns cleaning and washing. They really didn't have antidepressant drugs back then, and my father wouldn't let anyone other than family take care of her, so our lives revolved around her inactivity."

One day Tina, as was her responsibility, came home during her lunch hour at school to make a sandwich for her mother and take it up to her room. Her mother said she wasn't hungry, so fourteen-year-old Tina just left it by her bedside. When she arrived home from school later that afternoon, her sixteen-year-old sister Anne was hysterical. She had found her mother dead.

Tina felt guilty that perhaps she might have missed some sign when she delivered the sandwich to her mother. Fifteen years later, Anne committed suicide during a bout of depression, leaving a bewildered husband and two children. "Now it's my turn, I guess," says Tina, her dark eyes cloudy. Tina has just come through three years of treatment for depression. During the course of the three years, she has received shock therapy and psychological counseling, and is on a variety of medications. She swears that she doesn't want her children to go through what she went through as a child.

"I think they have as good an understanding of what's going on as anyone can," Tina says, referring to her three children, who range in age from ten to fourteen. "They have had their ups and downs just as I have, and we try to laugh about it—Oh, Mom's getting her crazies again! Certain members of my extended family have helped, some haven't. One sister took my children for part of the summer when I was in the hospital. My brother hasn't come to visit once in three years and another sister hasn't even called. Sure it hurts, but I can't dwell on that. They are probably dealing with their own fears."

Because of those private fears, Tina emphasizes that outside support is vital to long-term care, rather than reliance on family members to fill in. This also relieves the patient of some of those guilts involved in making continual demands on relatives.

But what if the ill person is Mom or Dad, and you determine that the best avenue of care is to have them move in with you?

PARENTING YOUR PARENTS

For the first time in American history, the average married couple is said to have more parents than children and could, conceivably, spend more years caring for an aging parent than a dependent child.

According to the census bureau, the number of people over age sixty-five increases by 1,600 per day. There are approximately 28 million people classified as elderly, 3 million of whom are over age eighty-five, comprising the group most likely to require some assistance.

Through the miracles of modern medicine and nutrition, our senior citizens are living longer, but not necessarily more healthfully. Between health problems and the cost of living, many couples are finding as they become free of dependent children, they must care for dependent parents.

This is the situation Mac and Emma find themselves in. Their two children are out of the nest, Mac took an early retirement from his engineering firm, and the couple planned to travel the world in fulfillment of youthful dreams. Then Emma's widowed mother developed kidney disease. Neither could see putting her in a nursing home, so Emma's mother has moved into Mac and Emma's home. She depends upon Mac and Emma like a child, requiring trips to the hospital dialysis units several times a week and help with very basic tasks. Not only has this kept the couple housebound once more, but it has precipitated arguments and resentments toward other family members who are "not pulling their weight."

"I love my mother, I want that clear from the beginning," says Emma. "There was no question that she could count on me for help, but I have begun to feel that I'm in a no-win situation. Not only does my brother not help out with expenses, but my mother treats me like a jailer. I am the one who has to tell her *no*, she can't eat certain foods, and *no* she cannot smoke, and *yes* she must take certain medicines, and so on.

"All she does is argue with me like a rebellious child. I even overheard her tell one of her friends on the telephone what a boss I am—nothing about what I try to do for her, or the fact that I'm trying to keep her healthy and alive. Yet let my brother call and you would think she got a call from the king. As far as I'm concerned, talk is cheap. If he really wanted to help, he'd be here doing something!''

Unrealistic expectations need to be adjusted if families are to cope successfully with this new multigenerational lifestyle. This is a lesson that Marco and Ramona learned the hard way. Marco and Ramona invited Marco's widower father to live with them when it became difficult for him to get around his small house. Their two children, age ten and fifteen, were pleased that their beloved Grandpa was moving in. His visits had always meant fun. But the fun was not to be.

During the first couple of weeks, Marco and Ramona tried to see that Grandpa was part of all the family activities. But Grandpa needed naps during the afternoon, the only time the ten-year-old could have friends over after school. The fifteen-year-old began to resent the household's revolving around his grandfather's schedule and started to rebel. And Marco and Ramona began to quarrel with each other and then with Marco's brothers about their father's care.

"What I thought was going to be one big, happy family was falling apart,'' says Marco. "I began to dread coming home because I couldn't stand the bickering anymore. I finally realized, when we all sat down to talk, that we were each expecting something different out of the situation from what we were getting.''

Ideally, the decision to bring an elderly relative into the household should be a family one. Experts advise that a meeting be held with all family members, including the elderly person, to discuss expectations and such practicalities as schedules. By understanding some of the compromises that will need to be worked out, all family members, and particularly the younger ones, can benefit from the presence of a grandparent, rather than focus on the negative aspects. Not only will the family then learn to communicate and adjust their expectations, but they will learn tolerance as well.

THE NURSING HOME HURDLE

One of the dilemmas that adult children face on a more frequent basis is how to handle a parent's diminished capabilities and increasing illnesses. Not only must they accept that the man or woman who used to ride bicycles with them can no longer walk up the stairs, but they wrestle with the guilt that they, personally, cannot provide the twenty-four-hour-a-day care that many illnesses require.

There have been numerous articles dealing with the decision to place an elderly parent in a nursing home, so I will not dwell upon this aspect of the problem. What has been often repeated to me, however, is that once families work through the emotions involved in making the decision and then telling the parent, the ultimate results are usually gratifying as long as family members can cope with the new lifestyle.

"For awhile I was the big monster in the family because I did all the groundwork for placing my mother-in-law in a nursing home," says Susan. "She needed medical supervision and none of her children could accommodate that, but they all kept saying 'Well, there should be something else we could do.' Well, when the doctor said she should go, that took some of the guilt away and she went.

"It's a wonderful facility and I made sure all her friends and acquaintances would know how to contact her. The problem now is the family. They were quick to criticize me for wanting to move her to a home, but few of them will go to visit her. I've tried to call and tell them, and they always say they will go, but they don't show up. It hurts me to see her hurt by them. Once again, I'm the bad guy. Now I'm the nag on the telephone. I have been told that in so many words."

I have stressed here that you cannot change others; all you can do is change your own attitudes and actions in your dealings with them. You will not suddenly turn a self-centered adult-child into a caring and giving son or daughter—at least not overnight. All that can be done to prevent further aggravation is to assess the situation realistically and then adjust expectations accordingly. If your brother and sister aren't pulling their weight, and all your best guilt trips, lectures, and pleas haven't worked, let go of those expectations, because the only one who will go crazy harboring the "supposed to's" is you.

DECREASED CAPABILITIES, INCREASED VULNERABILITY

What if the person who is driving you crazy isn't a sibling, but the parent who is becoming increasingly disoriented and doesn't realize it? Dementia of some kind affects approximately 20 percent of senior citizens today, with 2.5 million suffering from Alzheimer's disease. These victims' vulnerability sometimes makes them the target for unscrupulous relatives or caretakers.

"All of a sudden my father's younger brother has decided to become buddy-buddy with him," says Cliff. "After practically ignoring him for forty years, this is a real turnaround. I would be happy for my father, except for the fact that his brother is a snake who's just zeroing in on my dad because he's in the early stages of Alzheimer's and has a fat checkbook. I've seen checks that my father has written to his brother for hundreds of dollars at a time, and if I question him, he says " 'So what? It's my money, my brother.' I agree, of course, but I can't help thinking that my uncle is using my dad's illness to finance his gambling."

Joan's seventy-one-year-old father married his nurse, who then proceeded to transfer all the retired financier's assets to her name. Suffering from multi-farct syndrome, a disease similar to Alzheimer's, the old gentleman was sometimes aware of what was happening and sometimes unaware. Joan's new step-mother then sold off much of Joan's mother's furniture and many personal items without offering any of them to Joan, an only child. Joan even caught the landscaper smuggling china out of the house in peat-moss bags.

"We were able finally to get my father declared incompetent—that was the easy part. My husband was made executor of my father's estate, but Lila was attempting to be made his guardian, which would have given her complete say over all of his legal and personal affairs. She also moved her twenty-six-year-old son from one of her previous four marriages into the house, which was now empty of furniture. Then my father began having accidents."

Through the ensuing three years, Joan fought her way through the legal system, going through several changes of attorneys and judges, hiring several outside aides to assist her father, and finally placing him in a nursing home where he died soon after one of Lila's visits.

"I learned that the system doesn't work—it's too unwieldy," says Joan. "The people who would really listen often didn't have the power to get anything done—and nothing is done quickly. I learned you also have to be very nervy when it comes to looking out for your elderly parents."

If you feel that your parent is being taken advantage of due to illness or incompetence, whether by another family member or an outsider, you would do well to consult an attorney first. States may vary as to their guidelines for incompetency, but generally, if people know who they are and what they own, they can choose to waste their money or assets in any way they see fit, whether during an alcoholic binge or a reunion with a "long lost relative."

As parents or other relatives move into the final stages of their lives by passing through the storm of terminal illness, other family frictions develop.

* * *

DEALING WITH TERMINAL ILLNESS—
AND EACH OTHER

Andrea's brother-in-law arrived in Detroit for her daughter's wedding with a new girlfriend in tow. Andrea and her husband Dean had heard for the last six months how his brother Donald and his wife of twenty years had separated after much marital discord. They didn't particularly relish the idea of his girlfriend at their family event, but they didn't want to upset the bride with family squabbling, so they didn't object.

Donald and his girlfriend flaunted their relationship, falling all over each other throughout the weekend. But Andrea finally exploded when Donald's wife called from her hospital bed where she had been suffering with terminal cancer for three months, wondering if Donald was there. She knew nothing about the separation story that Donald had spread among all his out-of-state relatives. "That man will not step foot in my house again!" says Andrea. "His poor wife lay dying, and not only did he not tell us, but he's out partying with some floozy!"

When family members step on each other's toes during the normal course of a relationship, there is usually the feeling that the disagreements are wrought in an infinite sphere of time and that resolution will eventually take place. No hurry; it's more important to make a point, take a stand, be king of the mountain, or show disapproval by withholding affection and attention.

When someone is critically, terminally ill, however, every little slight is viewed through an emotional microscope. This microscope, which magnifies every action or slight, becomes even more powerful as the ill person's impending death draws nearer. Since everyone is usually dealing with their own set of emotions, ranging from guilt to protectiveness, family members can either be bound together or pushed further apart at this stressful time.

"You'd think she'd come to see her dying father, wouldn't you?" demands Jack. "My brother and I were there, but my father kept looking for our sister. She said she didn't want to remember him ill, she wanted to remember him when he was strong. By the time she finally started thinking about someone besides herself, he was dead. He died unhappy and it's all her fault."

It's so hard to know what to say to someone who is dying. The Puritan work ethic to which so many subscribe impels us to be on the move, doing something, working at making a situation better. It is difficult to face the truth that when a relative is dying, there is very little we can do but just *be* there. The Diplomat can't negotiate the illness away, the Dictator cannot banish it, the Pot-Stirrer cannot change the outcome through talk, and the Scapegoat is not at fault. But the Butterfly?

"I felt that if I went, I should know what to say," says Paul. "But I didn't, so I made up excuses not to go sit with the family when my uncle was ill. I did go to the funeral, but they were very cold to me. I just left quickly."

This is one situation in which we have to adjust our expectations for ourselves as well as those around us. The relatives who are dealing with guilt over cheating the patient out of his share of the company business may be falling all over themselves to "make up for it" while they can still get absolution from the dying partner. The college student who is studying abnormal psychology may deal with his or her own feelings by treating the entire family as a psych experiment and ask what some may consider to be insensitive questions, like "What do you think Uncle Benny would say to you now if he wasn't hooked up to the respirator?" This, of course, will drive sister Elsa, who is trying like mad to deny that Aunt Jenny is dying, crazy: "I know she's pale—she always uses a strong sunscreen. She'll be fine, you'll see."

And then there are those who show up to atone for past feuds, only to be turned away by the family. "Get that S.O.B. out of my sight and away from this poor dying man! What, did you come to see how fast you could kill him off? Got any more lies to tell him?"

Looking for someplace or someone to blame when a loved one is dying is natural. Sometimes contemporary medical equipment and options only add fuel to the fire.

DECISION TO TERMINATE

Newspaper headlines trumpet the more controversial of these cases: "Parents Petition to Unplug Daughter," "Husband Files to Remove Wife from Life Support," or "Children Tell Court—Let Our Mother Go Peacefully." There are many such heart-wrenching family dramas being played out on a weekly basis with much less fanfare. When a relative is terminally ill and parts of his or her body have already shut down, then the next of kin and the medical staff may agree to terminate life-support systems. Such termination is not decided upon lightly. One of the requirements of termination is that it must be a unanimous decision by the family, the attending physician, and the appropriate hospital committee. Conflicts can arise, however, if the family itself is not in complete agreement.

Ninety-one-year-old Martha had been unconscious and on a respirator for four weeks. A five-year struggle with emphysema had been complicated by pneumonia. Her kidneys had shut down, her liver was deteriorating, and the doctor's prognosis indicated that Martha's time on earth was limited. After wrestling with their anguish, her two sons agreed with the doctor that a termination was appropriate. Martha's daughter, however, threw a fit and accused her brothers of trying to kill their mother. It took nearly a month of legal maneuvering in order to obtain the termination because of the daughter's opposition.

Situations surrounding terminations are, from the family viewpoint, fraught with tears, unresolved guilts, and old family roles and expectations. There is no formula for making this decision other than keeping all lines of communication open among those involved. If all members are in agreement, then the order can proceed. If a family member threatens opposition, there are two avenues of action. The family can inform the opposing member that since the doctor, hospital, and the rest of the family are for the termination, it will be carried out unless he or she does something to stop it. Should that member move forward to take legal action, then the family can petition the court, informing it that the order has the blessing of the doctor, the hospital, and the majority of the family. It will then be up to the court to resolve the issue.

If handled efficiently, a court order can be obtained within a couple of weeks but, cautions attorney Sepaniak, it is critical that family members seek out someone who specializes in health and hospital law, for otherwise, the attorney may waste time learning about the procedure at the family's expense.

This advice and information is based on New Jersey law, which has been recognized as being at the forefront of liberal termination decisions. Since termination law varies from state to state and each case is decided on an individual basis, family members will need to seek local counsel before proceeding with termination petitions.

It's not easy, but if we can tolerate the sometimes irrational and very human behavior of our relatives (whether we endorse it or not) when a loved one is dying, then the death can serve to connect us more deeply to our family roots, rather than becoming a blade that slices off a branch of the family tree.

Bridging gaps during times of illness and dependence means lowering our expectations all around, for both ourselves and others. Family members are not magically "supposed to" know the right things to say and do. We must communicate what we need, accept what is offered, and then take advantage of outside support systems. Even though we are family, it is unreasonable to expect that we are "supposed to" do everything and remain strong throughout.

With the proper medical and legal cables in place, our expectations adjusted, and surrogate supports activated, then communication can keep the bridges of our relationships strong even while the members are weakened.

17

Death, Loss, and Guilt

A death in the family is traumatic, whether expected or sudden, whether young or old are involved. Deaths can precipitate family arguments and feuds for a number of reasons. Perhaps the deceased was the mortar holding the bricks of the family together. Sometimes family members find that all they had in common was that one person, parent or grandparent. When that person dies, the family "bricks" gradually begin to tumble, unless another member steps in to fulfill the "mortar" function.

When Rachel died, everything in the family seemed to fall apart. Rachel had been the one who served as the Communicator and Diplomat for an extended family scattered across four states. Her death also unleashed a series of rifts that had lain below the surface for years, held in check through her peacekeeping efforts. After some bitter words at Rachel's funeral, many family members have since lost touch with each other.

Sometimes a family death serves as the backdrop for old rivalries and acts of manipulation. Linda was twenty-three years old when she was killed in a car crash involving one other car on a deserted stretch of highway. Linda's cousin Emily, who had always been jealous of her, spent the days following the accident spreading rumors concerning Linda's drinking, boyfriends, and drug experimentation. So thoroughly had Emily done her pot-stirring, that she caused a split in the family for more than a year.

Sometimes death (particularly in the case of an accident) provides an excuse for assigning guilt to the survivors. Dan was slightly intoxicated when he and his wife Diane drove home from a holiday party on a snowy

December night. The car hit a patch of ice, spun around, and plunged into a creek, partially sinking into the icy water. When Dan dragged Diane from the car, she was dead. Dan must not only deal with his guilt but the animosity of Diane's family, who hold him responsible for her death. When his children visit Diane's family, Dan is not welcome. He hopes it will change, but it has been this way for more than two years.

The way the deceased was treated while he or she was alive is often scrutinized and criticized by family members. "My father and my maternal grandmother got in a big fight at my mother's funeral," says one man. "My father accused her of never showing my mother enough love and affection, and she accused him of traveling all the time on business and not being there when my mother needed him. It was a nightmare. Pretty soon, other relatives were dragged into the arguments and half of them walked out of the funeral home. They attended the funeral, but they stood by themselves and didn't come back to the house."

Perhaps so many family arguments and feuds flare up when a family member dies because, aside from reminding us of our own vulnerability and mortality, a death in the family gives many an attack of the I-should-haves, as in "I should have visited her more often," "I should have told him how much I loved him," or "I should have just overlooked the stupid things he said and mended fences ten years ago." Guilt is intensified by grief, leaving people with a low tolerance for the weaknesses and insensitivities of others.

"I was standing by the coffin looking down at my favorite uncle when a distant cousin came up to me and said, 'So you're the one who gave poor Jimmy here a heart attack when you changed your name. I've heard all about you!' " says Marie who, five years before, had legally Americanized her Slavic name. "It took all the willpower I could muster to keep from punching him right in the mouth," she says. "I looked over and there was my aunt nodding and pointing. I was furious that they brought up my changing my name when I was so broken up over my uncle."

AN END OR A PASSAGE?

On a trip to Egypt a few years ago, I was both amazed and impressed by the Egyptian view of death. From the time Egyptians are born, they are in preparation for their death, which they consider the doorway to eternity, the most important aspect of their existence. As you drive along Cairo's highways, you can gaze out over the hundreds of acres that make up the necropolises, the cities of the dead. They are much more than mere cemeteries, as our guide pointed out.

He proudly showed us the houselike tomb where he and all the members of his family will finally rest. Surrounding the sarcophagus area is a kitchen where female members of his family can prepare nourishment for visitors. There is also a meditation room where visitors and family members can sit, pray, or even do quiet work. While their existence on earth is temporary, as are the injustices they suffer, Egyptians discuss and look forward to their death as a permanent and happier state.

Not so with most of us. We view life as the only state that matters. Insults are forever, and death is something to be feared and grudgingly accepted. The widespread denial of death in American society is examined in such texts as *Death Be Not Proud, The American Way of Death,* and the much-quoted *On Death and Dying* by Elisabeth Kübler-Ross. When a family death occurs, it can either draw members closer together, bonding them together, or death can tear the family apart through the selfish acts of the surviving family members.

A major conflict of "same versus different" often rears its ugly head at times like these. It is a time when everything from the funeral arrangements to the way a person mourns may be discussed and judged. Ethnic customs, religious rites, personal desires, and control issues all become the focus of attention as the family gathers for one of the most stressful family gatherings.

THE FAMILY GATHERS TOGETHER

There's something about a funeral that brings even the most distant relatives out of the woodwork.

Aunt Bertha, who changed her name to Sunflower Sweet when she joined a hippy commune in the sixties that she never left, will arrive bearing homemade elderberry jam, wearing sandals even though it's only forty degrees outside. Cousin Ted, who's been officially married four times and lived with so many others that relatives have ceased trying to keep up, will arrive with a flourish and be particularly solicitous to pretty, young friends. And no matter that your Uncle Gus told your father six years ago, "I hate your guts and never want to speak to you again!" He'll show up and tearfully accept the condolences of your friends declaring, "We were so close. No one could have asked for a better brother!"

It's enough to make you nuts at a time when losing a grip on reality is a very real possibility for some family members. We like to think that all members will be joined together in a loving circle of connecting strength. *That* is the ideal. That is the "supposed to." While the good intentions are usually present, and the circle is formed, the lines may waver and occasionally break—or at least include a few curlicues.

"When my mother died, everything turned into an argument," says Paula. "One sister said Mom wanted to be cremated. My brother argued that he had never heard her say that and besides, he wanted her buried where she spent most of her life—which happened to be up north near him, instead of Florida where she retired.

"Then there were the arguments over the religious service and what I call the 'pre-argument arguments.' You know—those are the ones that go 'If Uncle Max says this, then I'm going to tell him off once and for all!' Those, of course, prompt another argument—and the situation hasn't even happened! My father was no help because he was in shock. He couldn't make decisions. Fortunately, he was also oblivious to all the tensions between other people as well."

Shock *is* Nature's way of helping the bereaved get through a tormenting time but, again, everyone's level of mourning and shock is very individual. This, too, can cause barbed comments as others try to work through their grief.

"It took me a year to be able to speak to my father civilly after my mother died," says Helen. "She had cancer of the liver and mercifully went very quickly. My father would act the part of the sad widower for everyone else's benefit, particularly strangers, then flip to his jovial old self when he wasn't 'on.' I just couldn't believe it. It was almost as if he were playing a role that he was enjoying—and I was so crushed that my mother was dead!"

Some find that a death in the extended family is the quickest detour to sliding back into old family roles, a situation that inspires resentment and frustration at a time when both are little tolerated.

"It was amazing," says Edith. "With my sisters and brother, it was almost as though we had never left home, although we were all in our thirties and forties when my mother died. My oldest sister just took over and started making decisions. The rest of us either listened or argued like we did when we were children. I particularly found it frustrating because I am the baby of the family and that's how I was treated every time I made a suggestion, despite the fact that I now run my own business. It was almost as though I hadn't spoken. I found myself throwing a temper tantrum—in other words, reacting like the baby of the family. It was crazy!"

Others use the death as a barometer of family loyalty—and God help them if they don't pass. "I was in graduate school facing final exams when I got a call from my sister that said to come home right away, because our father, who had been in the hospital with cancer for several months, was taking a turn for the worse," says Jan. "This was a Wednesday and I had to take exams on Thursday and Friday. I thought about it a long time and told her I could get home by Saturday afternoon. She raised hell, but we had been through this with my father before. Well, I got home Saturday afternoon to find that he had died that morning. I'm sure my family viewed me with disgust because it has been brought up a few times over the years. But you make certain decisions in life and sometimes it's not a good call. You have to live with that."

Issues of loyalty and control were what Angela had to face when her uncle, the family patriarch, died in another part of the country. She could not get away from work for the funeral, because she was due to make a presentation that day. "My mother ranted and raved on the phone for a half hour that she was so embarrassed because her other sister had all of her children there," says Angela. "Everyone else had their sons and daughters there to support them and *she* was the only one who had a daughter who was too busy to attend the funeral. And that poor Aunt Grace really missed me, was asking about me, and was very hurt that I wasn't there.

"It's a good thing I spoke with my brother, who assured me that Aunt Grace was in shock and didn't even realize who was there, so I don't feel as badly as I might have. But it's a control thing with my mother—we have to jump when she lifts her hand, no matter what's going on in our lives. As long as I can do a reality check with someone else and recognize the situation for what it is, I can distance myself from it and keep peace."

Yet how do you keep peace when it's the deceased who gets the last laugh? Betty was two years younger than her sister Jane, but at some point during adulthood, Jane began telling everyone that she was two years younger than Betty. This would make Betty crazy. The final straw came, however, when Jane died before Betty. She had everyone so thoroughly convinced that she was younger that both her death certificate and tombstone reflected the error. An irritated Betty spent the rest of her life trying to refute the age discrepancy. Her dedication to this goal drives the other members of her family to distraction.

DEALING WITH LOSS AND GUILT

Milton was considered an infuriating, abusive, manipulative Dictator when he was alive. He bullied his wife, children, siblings, and even his grandchildren. When he died at age seventy-six following a massive stroke, there were few tears shed. The family drew closer together during the funeral and agreed among themselves that Grandmother Adele was going to enjoy peace and quiet for the first time in forty-five years.

Fortunately, most of the extended-family members lived close by and would drop in on Grandmother Adele to visit. That's when they began to notice the shrine. First it was just a photograph with a candle in front of it. Soon it progressed to a series of photos, mementoes, and articles of clothing. What had begun as a simple remembrance soon took an entire corner of the living room. Grandmother soon began extolling Milton's virtues for hours on end, dragging friends and relatives into her home to pay homage at the shrine.

"She would speak so glowingly of Grandpa that we began to think *we* were crazy for not appreciating this saint who had walked among us—never mind that he used to blacken Grandma's eye," says a grandson. "She drove everyone crazy with special holiday celebrations—his birthday, Father's Day, you name it. We indulged her as much as possible but nothing could make her stop."

The old adage that you should not speak ill of the dead crosses all cultures and generations. Sometimes the bereaved cope with their loss by idealizing their spouse, parent, grandparent, or sibling—however undeserving the deceased may have been.

"What drives me crazy," says Kevin, "is that when my father was alive, my mother ruled the roost and was verbally abusive to the man. She would tell anyone who listened what a wimp he was, how inept he was, and that he was nothing without her. Then he died in a car crash, and my mother has canonized him. She goes on and on about how wonderful he was. I just wish she had told *him* that when he was still alive to hear it! I'm afraid I have to leave the room when she gets on that kick."

It is nothing new to say that people deal with their losses in a variety of ways, from the person who doesn't cry to the one who sobs continuously, from the one who never speaks of the deceased again to the one who enshrines him or her. All are facing grief, but not all are dealing with it. Such was the case with Pat when she and her husband Michael lost their young son, Allen, in a car crash.

Michael sobbed and mourned throughout the ordeal. Pat did not cry and could not relate to those around her. "I remember standing in the hall of our home and watching my father look around Allen's room for the last time before he left to go back home. I'll never forget the look of pain on his face, but I couldn't go to him—couldn't reach out.

"In the weeks that followed, I had never been invited to so many luncheons and activities. So many people felt it was their sole duty to keep me busy fourteen hours a day, and I let them. The only feeling I could feel was guilt," says Pat. "Guilt that Allen was not seat-belted in and that his reminding me to fasten my seat belt actually saved my life. And then there was another guilt I had over a feeling that I was not able to recognize for a long time. I realized suddenly that I had been relieved of the responsibility of raising a child and that realization brought a sense of relief in many ways, because I married late and had experienced a life of freedom. Now through this tragedy, I was going to feel that freedom again—and that realization also made me feel very guilty."

Although Pat had another child within two years after Allen's death, she lived her life in a manic state. For nearly ten years, she pushed away thoughts of the child and the need to confront his death. Then, suddenly, she began to unravel emotionally. Her marriage to Michael began to suffer and she finally sought professional help.

"What I wish someone close to me had done at the time of the funeral or shortly thereafter was slap me across the face and say 'You're not in the real world' and drag me to some professional help," says Pat. "If this happened to a relative or even close friend of mine now, I would handcuff them if necessary and get them help. There are also many support groups out there, depending upon your personality, whether you function well in a group or if you prefer the privacy of a one-on-one session. . . . But the key is to get help. Everyone thought I was coping because I wasn't falling apart outwardly. What they didn't realize is that I had frozen inside and stayed that way for ten years."

Depending upon their inclinations, many relatives decide that this time of mourning is the appropriate time to remind the bereaved of God's love, that there are other fish in the sea, and that at least they won't have to put up with the deceased's dirty socks on the floor anymore. These relatives, though well meaning, may find themselves frozen out, punched out, or thrown out: "It was the day after the funeral, and my brother wanted to set me up on a blind date!"; "One of my cousins, who I thought should know better, came up to me at my eleven-year-old's funeral and said, 'Well, at least you won't have to go through the agonies of teenagerhood.' My God! I'd give anything to go through those so-called agonies!"; "Every time I bring up my dead sister's name, my aunt reminds me that it was God's will. I don't know who I hate more—my aunt or God!"

Elisabeth Kübler-Ross, in her landmark book, *On Death and Dying*, states that families of those who have died go through the same five steps of *denial, anger, bargaining, depression,* and *acceptance* as do dying patients. She states further that the biggest help relatives can offer to the deceased's immediate family is to support them as they work their way through those steps at their own pace, without blame or judgment. "If we tolerate their anger," she writes, "whether it is directed at us, at the deceased, or at God, we are helping them take a great step towards acceptance without guilt. If we blame them . . . we are blameworthy for prolonging their grief, shame, and guilt, which often results in physical and emotional ill health."

* * *

Communication, adjusting your expectations, understanding the difference between tolerance and endorsement, and a sense of humor will help you to get through the funeral process and enable you to remain on speaking terms with your relatives.

First and foremost is the reminder that emotions will be running high and relatives may act and react and overreact in unpredictable ways. Now is not the time to make judgments, to try to "get it right" as far as other relationships are concerned, or to play power games. But should you find your relatives doing just those things—remember tolerance. You will not win by trying to change their behavior, but you can stay somewhat sane by accepting their temporary insanities as just that—temporary.

Some may deal with the death by focusing on the sense-of-humor coping tool. This can be jarring to other family members, but it seems to occur with regularity. "At my mother's funeral, an old acquaintance of my parents showed up," says Don. "He was always rather strange and my sister and I latched on to a couple of mannerisms. During the entire three-day ordeal, we'd twitch our noses at each other in imitation of this man, which would send us into gales of laughter. My aunt got really angry at us, but it was one of those things we just couldn't help. It broke the tension."

Family members can truly provide the healing salve for the bereaved if they can just remember to put aside their personal rivalries and agendas. Researchers such as Ruth O'Brien of the University of Rochester have found that while supportive family networks can't decrease the stress a death creates, they can help the bereaved member cope and adjust better than those without those support systems.

Remembering the term *support* is important, because it indicates that we should be standing behind or providing strength for someone else—not drawing attention to ourselves. Support means, too, that practical and *specific* assistance should be given. Many people indicate that the help they appreciate most from relatives is the kind that helps routines to continue despite the emotional upheaval. For example, picking up bank and Social Security forms, paying bills, answering letters of condolence, taking children to lessons, grocery shopping and cooking, answering the telephone and keeping a log of who has called, and housecleaning.

"It really hurt when my son died that my sister didn't pitch in and help," says Monica. "Oh, she asked if there was anything she could do, but of course I said no. To tell you the truth, I wasn't thinking very straight. I had friends who did the chores and practical things while my sister waited by the phone, I guess. She's probably still waiting for me to call—and it's been nearly a year."

Sometimes even the most supportive and loving of family networks is not enough to lift a member out of the quagmire of loss and guilt feelings.

Family therapists unanimously agree that this is the point at which the modified surrogate-family bridging tool should be employed: Bring in outside support systems. In other words, we need once again to let go of the "supposed to's" and realize our very special strength as family members. We are the ones who can say what we think, we generally are the closest to the people in question, and we can determine whether they are indeed putting up a front for others while they are falling apart inside.

If we can tolerate the temporary insanities brought about by the death of a relative, yet remain sensitive to individual differences, we can help our family heal and continue to grow.

18

Feuds for
Growth

Not all family feuds arise out of a negative conflict. Being different and
making different choices from our parents' family code is often an essential
pathway to growth. It can also be the quickest route to hysterical confrontations, threats of disinheritance, and forty-seven strangers calling to tell
you that Aunt Agatha put you on their prayer list for desperate cases.

Joan came from a family where the women were all housewives. Joan
wanted a family, but she also had an artistic talent that she wanted to
develop as a career. Because of her family's active opposition, she had to
put herself through college and upon graduation she moved to a city far
from home. Today, Joan is a graphic artist with a national magazine; she
has two children and a supportive husband. She happily juggles the different facets of her life. That does not protect her from being criticized by
her mother and sisters if she has to miss one of her children's school
events.

Max saw his father work himself into an early grave attempting to support his family on a tailor's salary. When Max's uncles were pressuring
him to learn the trade, Max would hide and study for his college courses.
Today, he is a leading oral surgeon in a major metropolitan city, but his
extended family constantly makes fun of his clothing, lifestyle, and vocab-
ulary.

Phillip took what his family considered a step down. Born into a wealthy,
well-educated family circle, Phillip found early in life that he could not
take a serious interest in their sports, monetary pursuits, or even their

stringent educational demands. Talented with his hands, his efforts at creating images out of wood were always met with a polite "That's very nice dear, but . . ." Today Phillip is with the forestry service as a ranger, which leaves him plenty of time to create both furniture and figures out of wood. He avoids family gatherings.

Some families encourage and reward growth and change, while some view any kind of deviation from their family tradition as traitorous. Even within a large, extended family, one branch may encounter opposition from another in an attempt to curb errant meanderings, this pits flexibility against rigid expectations.

HOW DOES YOUR TREE GROW?

When you look at trees, which is more likely to capture your imagination and attention, the slender spruce with its cool symmetry or the exotic banyan with its maze of roots and thousands of branches that bend and twist, soar and dive, curl and straighten? While the spruce exhibits a controlled beauty, the banyan fires our imagination.

A healthy, progressive family can be compared to the banyan tree. From the single, sturdy trunk grow myriad branches, ever extending and sending new roots down into the ground. Rather than take away from the main trunk, these branches add beauty, interest, and dimension. Similarly, each of us needs from our family the feeling of belonging to a group, yet enough support to be an individual growing our own way.

Growth means change and risk, two of the scariest words in the English language. Where do we absorb our ideas about change and risk? From our silent navigators. Some families will tolerate very little change. Most will tolerate change within certain prescribed boundaries. The very rigid will attempt to stifle any change, and the results can be disastrous.

Emily came from a very rigid family where girls left the nest only as brides. Although Emily had yearnings for a career, her upbringing won out and she married during her second year at college. "I know it sounds ridiculous now, but I essentially married to get out of the house. I knew that after I graduated from college, I would be living at home. When I announced my intentions to marry, everyone was so happy because I was continuing the family tradition. I wasn't strong enough to break tradition. Marriage was my escape. What a mistake!"

Emily's marriage broke up after ten years and one child. Although her divorce—"the first one in the family!"—rocked the foundation of her family's tradition, Emily was finally strong enough to withstand the well-meaning pressure. She went back to school, went to work at a bank, and is now supporting herself and her son. She recently acquired a live-in significant other and is again having to fight the family "supposed to's" regarding what they describe as "settling down the right way by getting married."

One may be tempted to criticize Emily's initial choice and say, "Well, she should have just stood up to them in the first place," but that's easier said than done. The world-renowned psychologist and author Erich Fromm recognized this in his work *To Have or to Be?* "The growing person," he writes, "is forced to give up most of his or her autonomous, genuine desires and interest, and his or her own will, and to adopt a will and desires and feelings that are not autonomous but superimposed. Society, and the family as its agent, has to solve a difficult problem: How to break a person's will without his being aware of it."

In this respect, families do their job rather well through a system of rewards and punishments as children are growing up. But even in the most rigid of households, there occasionally arises an adventurous and rebellious soul. What follows is enough conflict to drive you crazy!

TAKE A RISK!

When we are babies, our lives are full of risk. In learning to walk, we struggle to stand and take a step and fall. We pull ourselves upright again and fall and repeat the process until we walk across the room. As children, we also take risks as we stretch and grow: learning to ride a bicycle through numerous falls, learning to socialize and make friends despite being bopped on the head with a Tinkertoy, and expanding our mental horizons in school by trying, failing sometimes, and trying again.

As we get older, however, we can become more fearful of taking risks, of bruising, perhaps, not only our knees, but our fragile egos as well. We thereby limit our growth. The *what if* questions take precedence over the possible results: What if I fail? What if I look stupid? What if it hurts? What if they don't like me? What if they get angry? What if I find out that I really can't do it? What if I find out that I *can* do it?

All of these will involve change, some good, some not so good. What people forget is that the results are rarely fatal. We just act as if they are because somewhere along the way, we were not rewarded for taking risks: "What do you mean you're going to try out for cheerleading? What makes you think you can do that?"; "You don't have a coordinated bone in your body—you take after your Uncle Charlie. You'll never make the soccer team!"; "Who said you were good in math? What does he know? I think you're crazy for trying for that job!"; "What will our friends and family

say if you decide to go into construction? Women can't build houses!";
"Don't be such a fool. You'll fall flat on your face and then you'll come
crying to me. Forget it!"

There is a whole different aura around risk-takers and that's pretty scary
for some people too. Look at the opposition that Christopher Columbus
encountered when he announced his intention to sail westward in search
of a route to the Indies. I can just see his Uncle Luigi popping an olive
into his mouth and saying, "You crazy boy! You'll fall off the end of the
earth. Everyone knows the world is flat!"

Whether we are looking at the pioneers, who left the comfortable East
Coast settlements to venture into the untamed West, or the NASA astro-
nauts, who have expanded humankind's understanding of space, there are
always the naysayers standing at the sidelines saying, "You crazy person!
Don't you know you'll fall off the end of the earth?" But risk-taking, with
all of the conflict it may bring about, is as American as the proverbial
apple pie. Even the historian Max Lerner, in his classic *America as a Civilization*, states that it is part of the American heritage to have a "spirit
that hates a cribbed confinement. The American will not tolerate the fate
of being boxed in like a trapped rat. He will somehow break free, even if
the new independence he must win is an independence from vested power
groups."

But what if the "vested power group" includes Dictator Grandpa Ar-
chibald, vociferous Aunt Clara, and your mother? The "supposed to" which
has to be let go of here—and it is sometimes very painful—is that our family
is "supposed to" be supportive of our growth, despite what anyone else
may say.

"I was offered a tremendous promotion, but it meant I would have to
relocate my family to Europe for two years," says Ted, a chemical engineer
in his forties. "When I called my parents with the news, you would have
thought I told them I had an incurable disease! Instead of focusing on the
wonderful experience my children would have, my mother kept telling me
about the inferiority of the schools. My father would make comments about
my mother's ill health and that she might die while I was so far away.
Here I expected congratulations and all I got was grief. I took the promotion, moved my family, and it really was a growing experience for all
of us. But even my parents' letters kept up the sour note. Since we've
moved back to the States, I'm afraid I just don't feel as close to them as I
used to. I was hurt by their attitude and now find it difficult to share other
successes with them."

In adjusting your level of expectation, and realizing that your family's
endorsement is not necessary for survival, you will be able to see their
opposition for what it is, an issue of control. You may have the old refrain

"it's tradition" thrown up at you. "Your grandfather attended Harvard, your father and uncles attended Harvard; it is a family tradition. What do you mean you want to go to the University of Hawaii?" You may be layered thick with attempted guilt trips. "If you become a deep-sea diver, the stress will kill your mother!" Or you may find the old standby, inciting sibling rivalry, tossed out at you. "We always go to the lake house for two weeks as a family every August. Your brother and sisters and their children will be there. *You* will be the only one not attending and making your grandfather miserable."

As these arguments are hurled at you, appealing to your emotional heartstrings, family loyalty, and genuine desire to please, remember one thing: These people are stronger than they seem. It takes incredible strength and energy to labor at *not* changing. What you are dealing with here is not just a relative or group of relatives who are trying to control your actions, but people with very real fears. The biggest fear is the fear of change.

CHANGE MEANS REASSESSMENT

As adults, we each have a particular image of ourselves. That image may be positive or negative, but we expend a lot of energy protecting it— sometimes even subconsciously. When someone or something forces us to view ourselves in a different way, it can be startling.

A very simple example of that occurred to me in recent months. During a press interview for my previous book, *The Phantom Spouse*, a reporter looking for a local tie-in ascertained that I had been born in Manhattan but raised in Miami. "So you are a native New Yorker," she commented. This is hardly a startling statement, but since my family moved to Florida when I was four years old, I had always considered myself a Floridian. Yet here were the facts and they forced me to reassess my self-image to a degree. For the rest of the day, I wondered if anyone could sense my transformation. Gosh, a native New Yorker. I guess I am!

This was not a change that affected any other member of my family, but often growth and change within the family are most difficult to deal with because they force other members to look at themselves in a different light. They may have to question their roles, their past decisions, even their own judgment. This breaks the comfort of the behavior patterns in which families operate.

"In looking for patterns in my family, I realized there was a definite pattern of control among the women," says Katherine, age thirty-eight. "My grandmother, at eighty-eight, still controls or attempts to control my mother. She can still make my sixty-two-year-old mother feel guilty that she's not hovering over her elderly mother.

"My mother religiously attempts to control my brother and me. We clash constantly. Most recently, it was over my breaking the pattern," says Katherine. "I signed my twelve-year-old son up for sleep-away camp and my mother went through the roof. But I firmly believe that part of loving is to help our loved ones be free. I'll be damned if I'll continue the pattern of control by controlling every aspect of my son's life. The cycle has got to be stopped somewhere. This is a small step, but it's a first one."

When a family member strikes out on an individual path of growth, rather than be supportive, it is usually those closest who put up the greatest opposition. This was addressed by the father of psychotherapy, Sigmund Freud, who lamented that family members were usually more interested in keeping his patients as they were, rather than see them grow and get healthy.

Why don't we simply take a firm stand and declare confidently that we are right and such-and-such is what we are going to do and damn the consequences? Because growth is not comfortable for the one experiencing it either, and our confidence wavers.

Have you ever attempted to learn a new sport, such as tennis for example? Your coach may begin by teaching you a certain stroke and how to move laterally across the court. The next day, you wake up and your arm and legs are sore from using your muscles in unfamiliar ways. "Should I be sore?" you wonder. "Am I doing it right?" During the next lesson, your coach may modify a move and teach you a new one. Again, you wake up sore and wondering why you are going through this masochistic experience. As you progress through your lessons, you find yourself incorporating those moves more fluidly and with less soreness until, wonder of wonders, you can play a game. Your confidence soars. The aches and pains were worth it—you now have a new skill. You have grown. But what if, during those early lessons, someone close to you had said, "Oh, you're doing it all wrong. That's why you're sore. You're heading for tennis elbow, water on the knee, and damaged brain cells from the heat of play. Better take it easy." You just might have listened. After all, your process of growth and change were painful in a very tangible way at a time when you were not far enough along in your development to defend its eventual benefit.

Divorce attorneys are all too familiar with those cases where one partner in a marriage has grown while the other has not. The conflict becomes centered on the "Go for it!" philosophy, clashing with "Let's stick with the comfortable."

Also, if your deviating from a family path becomes the source of conflict, that deviation and conflict becomes an important topic of conversation in the family, which can involve numerous people.

"I had been divorced for about a year and I decided to buy a small house," says Sharlene. "This became the major topic of discussion to the point where I felt like a small child who was doing something bad. My brother decided to go to the closing with me—I guess to protect me or something. As I picked up the pen to sign the legal documents, I suddenly felt like I had this baby—which was really me—stuck to my arm. I was going through the motions like an adult, but I wondered if anyone else in the room could see the baby that was really there."

When we are children, grades in school serve as one form of benchmark for growth. As adults, those benchmarks are more nebulous. Are you growing or staying comfortably stagnant?

TEST YOUR GROWTH

One of the first laws of physics is "A body in motion tends to remain in motion; a body at rest tends to remain at rest." This can also apply adequately to our emotional growth. Answer the following questions to determine if you are in motion or resting.

PROFESSIONAL GROWTH

During the last five years, have you . . .

1. changed your field of employment?
2. voluntarily changed jobs, even within the same company?
3. started a new business?
4. relocated due to a job?
5. discussed a point of disagreement with your boss?
6. presented a new idea to your boss?

SOCIAL GROWTH

In the last two years, have you . . .

7. taken the initiative and said, "I'm sorry?"
8. confronted an irritating relative or friend and told him or her specifically why you are angry?
9. said "no" instead of "yes" when you really meant "no"?
10. let someone else have the spotlight without contributing or interrupting even once?

11. asked for help instead of insisting on doing it yourself?
12. spoken out to defend another relative to a Dictator or Pot-Stirrer type?
13. paid an honest compliment to someone who usually inspires your jealousy?
14. spent an hour with a relative who drives you crazy and maintained your dignity and sense of humor?

PERSONAL GROWTH

In the last year, have you . . .

15. spoken up for a controversial idea you believe in?
16. chosen to do something because it appealed to you, rather than because it was expected of you?
17. changed your hairstyle or haircolor?
18. moved to a new residence or town?
19. purchased a new or different car?
20. voluntarily begun or ended a significant relationship?
21. kept your mouth shut and listened when confronted with unsettling information about yourself?
22. traveled farther than 100 miles from home?
23. met five new people?
24. learned a new skill, sport, or hobby?
25. tried a new restaurant or cuisine?
26. updated your clothing style?
27. rearranged some furniture or redecorated a room?
28. spoken to a stranger in public?
29. read three books or more?
30. gone somewhere by yourself for at least an hour, just to think and re-evaluate your life and goals?

TO SCORE: Give yourself five points for every *yes*.

A Score of 120–150 Points. Change and growth are a way of life for you. You are the fearless adventurer, the one who will continue to grow unless the parachute doesn't open when you go skydiving. Any conflict that your lifestyle causes within your family rolls off your back. The conflict is *their* problem, not yours.

A Score of 100–120 Points. You are changing and growing, but you struggle through the conflicts it brings about. Opposition and the opinions of others influence you, and you need to feel that the risk of change is worth taking before you cautiously venture forth. Your growth is slow but enjoys a few spurts along the way.

A Score Below 100 Points. Wake up and take a few more risks! You sometimes find yourself in a rut and get frustrated but are shy about reaching out. The biggest risk you face is stunted emotional growth, so throw away those negative things you may have been told about yourself. Get out there and make some changes—you will be happier for it!

GROW WITHOUT GOING CRAZY

I had a psychology professor in college who discussed a case she once encountered of a woman in her forties who suddenly developed agoraphobia, the fear of open spaces. Mrs. X. would not leave the security of her home even to go out on the front porch. It had all become too frightening for her. Her family pleaded, cajoled, ridiculed, and yelled. Yet she wouldn't budge. Her husband promised trips to exotic locales, her children laid guilt trips on her because she had dropped out of their lives outside her home, and her extended family offered to take her visiting, dining, or anything else that would move her from home. But the change and the noise were all too terrifying for her.

Through a number of therapy sessions, the psychologist finally got Mrs. X. in motion. First, Mrs. X. practiced going to the front door and turning the handle. The next week, she opened the door and then closed it. Two weeks later, Mrs. X. stepped into the doorway and then back inside. This slow process continued for weeks, through minute steps: walking out onto the front porch, stepping off the porch, walking the fifteen steps to the mailbox, and finally crossing the street. It took nearly a year and much agony for Mrs. X. to take her first car ride in more than two years.

Sometimes when we undergo revelations, transformations, or periods of growth, our families may seem as unmoving as Mrs. X. Like Mrs. X., they may be experiencing fears related to moving out—even, or especially, to our movement. Although we may mean well, we tend to throw this newfound knowledge into the faces of those closest to us, expecting them to swallow it wholeheartedly, while slapping our backs with congratulations. For a few, it may work that way. For most, it presents conflict.

Like the therapist, we must move our resisting families through the process slowly, step by step. Planned communication will help bridge the gap between your growth and your family's fears.

Let people know where you are in your growth process. Are you thinking of changing religions, jobs, spouses, sexual identities, or just vacation plans? Communicate your thoughts little by little. Shock value rarely works to your advantage in the family tree. Gardeners know that any plant or tree that has experienced a shock will go into a state of trauma that must be overcome. Family trees are no exception to the rule.

Realize, however, that there will be times when you will simply have to face your family's opposition—which is usually well-intentioned, though misguided—and don't always expect their endorsement of your decisions. Hopefully, they will tolerate your path of growth, but if not, change your expectations and rely on those outside the family tree to provide the meaningful and confidence-boosting support you need and want. Brother Jerry may never warmly embrace your decision to become a karate instructor and practice Zen Buddhism, but so what? If you are growing in a path of your choice, you are adding to the family tree in an interesting and banyanlike way.

Nongrowth is stagnation. The beauty of life is in its constant evolution, so all you can do to preserve your sanity is equip yourself with coping tools. That is exactly what you're doing in reading this book. All any self-help book or therapy will do is equip you with the coping tools with which to confront those conflicts in your life. The more coping tools you have, the stronger and more confident you will be, and, I hope, the more empathetic toward others who may lack the skills that set you free.

Part V

CONTRIBUTING CIRCUMSTANCES

19

Burning Your Bridges

Most families have a cache of old home movies, which they enjoy pulling out and viewing at various gatherings. Through the miracle of modern video technology, those old black-and-whites can now be strung together on a two-hour tape, thus preserving for posterity a time period when Grandpa's hair was still brown, Aunt Louise still weighed 110 pounds, and Uncle Joshua looked just like the gangly teenager who could be your son's double.

In my family, it is also a record of who wasn't speaking to whom.

Although I vaguely remember some of those traditional Thanksgiving and Easter dinners when all the family branches pushed themselves, seven card tables, and sixteen additional folding chairs into my godmother's living room right next to the fish tanks, I have become intimately acquainted with them over the years by viewing these celluloid pieces of family history. "Oh look," my mother will laugh. "This is the year that Aunt E. and Aunt C. aren't speaking to each other. See how they're sitting with their backs to each other? Ha, Ha. Look! There's Aunt C. sticking her foot out to trip Aunt E. who's carrying the mashed potatoes to the table!"

Fast-forward to the next year and it's Grandma who's not speaking to Uncle M. "Hee, hee! Look at the gesture she's making at the camera when she saw your father taking the movie of her putting the cigarette ashes in Uncle M.'s stuffing! And right there's where he's refusing to pass the cranberry sauce that she asked for. Isn't that funny?"

Of course, every year the combatants changed, and as children it was sometimes difficult to remember who was speaking, who wasn't, and who it was that our particular branch of the family was angry with at the time. These trips down memory lane are all very humorous now, but it's difficult to remember the humor when a family is in the throes of screaming "Drop dead! I never want to speak to you again!"

One doctor told me that in his family, it was called "being on the outs." "Someone was always on the outs with someone else," he says, shaking his head. "Sometimes it lasted a few months, but sometimes it lasted a few years. Then, of course, other members took sides, so you had all these people lined up against the others and half of them weren't exactly quite sure why they were supposed to be angry."

If communication and the other coping skills are bridges across individual differences, words that set fire to those bridges and destroy communication become obstacles themselves. In some families, the practice of burning one's bridges is the method of communication. The implicit warning is, "If you don't do as I think you should, I'll never speak to you again!"

The "never" time period in family language can be anything from two hours to twenty years, but it's the ultimate threat, to be cut off from the group that gave you birth and heritage. The practice of cutting off a branch of the family tree (although it can be disturbing) is viewed as a tool to cope with any or all of the stresses and conflicts that arise in families.

There are really two levels at which this method of coping is practiced. In a *level-one* feud or situation, the splitting off of a family member comes about because of a disagreement. Perhaps brother Bob ducked out of his financial responsibilities and directed his creditors to your house—again. Or perhaps you are sick to death of Aunt Jane always striving to be the center of attention, and the straw that breaks the camel's back falls when she screams at you in front of your in-laws. These are situations that can set your blood boiling and impel you to strike back.

A *level-two* feud or situation is more serious in terms of affecting your emotional or physical well-being. Level-two situations are those in which continued contact with a particular member or family branch will prevent you from functioning in a normal and healthy manner. Level-twos are usually premeditated and carry long-term consequences. These will be discussed a little later in the chapter.

Most family fights occur on a level one, however. To deal with a particularly aggravating member or situation, it is easy to turn your back, slam the phone down, shut the door, or return mail stamped "I am dead to you! Remember that next time!" But does it really solve the problem?

One woman who had not seen her parents in nearly twenty years recalled the incident that split them apart. "I was home on college vacation, right before graduation," she says. "I announced my intention to marry a boy I had been going with and whom my parents didn't like. I would also be moving to a neighboring state instead of going into the family business. Well, my father was so angry that after three hours of yelling, screaming, and threats, he screamed at me to get out, consider them dead, and never contact them again. So I left that night, got married, moved away, and didn't see them again until about a year ago. What a lot of wasted years!"

If It Hurts, Cut It Off!

"When someone had a blowup with another member in my family, the solution was just to cut that member off," says Lanie, a forty-six-year-old English teacher. "My whole family was that way. I grew up not knowing whole sections of the family. As a kid, you wonder about them. As an adult, to try to contact them looks like an act of treason. As you can imagine, I have a very small family now!"

As a veteran observer of family feuds that lasted from three months to twelve years, I am always amazed at the reasoning that goes into solving these level-one arguments by alienating various family members. It is the same reasoning that dictates if your arm hurts, you should cut it off. Never mind that the source of the irritation could be neutralized with a little salve. Or maybe all that needs to be done is remove the rubber band that you have wound tightly around your wrist, thus blocking the flow of blood. Or just make the effort to extract the thorn from your thumb.

To cut off one's arm will, of course, solve the immediate problem, but the results will present a long-term problem of greater magnitude. Life goes on, and sometimes ends, during a period of noncontact, and no amount of remorse can recapture those moments that contribute to the full picture of family life.

Family members who resort to cutting off others with whom they are displeased do so for three reasons. First, by rejecting their relatives, they are punishing them—"If you make me angry, I will cut off our contact." Leo got tired of finding that the books he loaned his brother usually came back damaged in some way. When his brother Jerry returned his pictorial World War II volume with a blob of chocolate ice cream on one of the inside photographs, Leo went crazy. "That's it! He knows how I felt about this book. Now I'm not going to speak to him. We'll see how he likes it!" Instead of communicating to Jim why he was angry, or simply refusing to loan him books in the future, Leo punished Jim.

Second, breaking off a family relationship is a weapon of control. This is regularly practiced by elementary school children: "If you don't play the game I want, I won't be your friend anymore." It is also practiced in adolescence: "If you don't join in and drink a beer with me, you'll be out of the gang." Unfortunately, some people never seem to grow up: "If you don't come over to our house for a family dinner every Wednesday night, I won't speak to you"; or, "If you join that band, I won't speak to you"; or, "If you marry that boy, you can forget you're a member of this family."

Third, cutting off a relationship is seen as a solution if someone has not learned any other coping tools. When we slam a door in someone's face "forever," we have cut off discussion. We have thrown up an obstacle to resolving the problem. The communication that should take place, however, may make the parties involved feel uncomfortable, so it's easier to put time and distance between them than deal with the real issue.

Such was the case with two sisters, Jenna and Rose. Jenna had been jealous of her younger sister Rose all her life. When they were children, Rose was favored by their mother because she was vivacious and funny. As adults in their thirties, the two sisters had never gotten past the family-encouraged sibling rivalry. They never worked through the "supposed to's," so when Rose inherited the family-heirloom silver candlesticks, Jenna couldn't "forgive" her. "You brat! You've always gotten everything you wanted all your life. I'm never speaking to you again!" she screamed and stomped out of her sister's life. Rose, who was weary of Jenna's poor attitude, retorted with "Good riddance!" The sisters haven't spoken for three years.

Had either of them developed better coping skills, they could have used this final insult to open some meaningful dialogue, built some bridges across those years of differences, and arrived at a more honest, if not closer, relationship.

Cutting off family members can be a negative tradition. How can we break it and create a healthier cycle of building bridges instead of burning them? We can begin by remembering the building supports that have been discussed in this book and by taking a tip from the child-guidance professionals.

As most young mothers are told when reading books on child discipline today, when a child has done something displeasing, we should separate the person from the deed. If Johnny spills his grape juice all over your handmade quilt because he was drinking it in the bedroom instead of the kitchen, you scold him because what he *did* made you angry. Johnny himself is not a bad, unworthy, or unlovable because he spilled juice. What he did in disobeying and possibly ruining your quilt is what was wrong.

In dealing with family members whose coping skills are limited, we are in a sense dealing with children, or at least beginners in the process of learning healthy skills. So when a family member makes you crazy, once again, although the temptation may be to cut him off, a more productive solution would be to separate the person from the action and focus on the issue, the action, or the role that is irritating you. By addressing the problem, rather than the person, you can make an attempt at resolving it. If you attack the person, the problem will not be resolved. Even if you don't speak for six months, the pattern of behavior and the problem will re-emerge and you'll be repeating the cycle once more.

Remember communication. A family involves long-term relationships. Whether we want them there or not, whether we speak to them or don't, whether we even acknowledge their existence or not, their navigation is as much a part of us as our veins and arteries. It is much less taxing to be on friendly, or at least civil, terms with our relatives, so we can put our energies to more productive use than figuring out how we can avoid running into sister Shirley at the grocery store or declining to attend a wedding because cousin Fred is going to be there.

Should you find yourself "on the outs" because one of your relatives who cannot cope has decided to cut you off, you can, as the now stronger and more savvy member, set a teaching example by extending those lines of communication first, thereby opening a pathway. This, I realize, is easier said than done.

"I figured that I had nothing to lose," says Marie, a twenty-eight-year-old beautician. "I come from a large French family and somebody's always fighting or throwing somebody out of their house. Most of them don't even speak anymore and we're all scattered across the country, so when my sister slammed the phone down on me over some stupid disagreement, my first reaction was to see red. After I calmed down, I realized that I didn't want to be cut off from someone that I valued, even if most of the time she drives me nuts. It took two tries of my calling back before she wouldn't hang up on me. We both wound up crying and talking about things we had never discussed in our family before. It was really something. I almost feel as though I have a new friend."

That feeling of being cut off, isolated, or abandoned in the world is why the bridge-burning threat is often successful in controlling a family member's behavior. It is also a reason why some hesitate to cut off a family relationship when they should.

WHEN IS ENOUGH, ENOUGH?

There are some situations that are so traumatic for the individual involved that to continue the family relationship would destroy their mental and physical health. These are the level-two feuds, and professional therapists will cautiously counsel terminating those family relationships. Elaine's is one such level-two feud.

Elaine is a thirty-five-year-old mother of two, who is self-employed as a freelance graphic artist and also gives piano lessons at night. Her marriage has been a happy one, but two years ago she suddenly begun to experience panic attacks. Without warning, she would find it difficult to breathe; she bordered on hysteria and found it difficult to sleep at night. After several months of these frightening changes, Elaine sought professional help.

What emerged as the cause has changed her life and separated her from her extended family.

Elaine had suffered extreme physical abuse from her father and verbal abuse from her mother when she was growing up. Her mother told Elaine it was her own fault that she made her father so angry. Many of Elaine's relatives were also very abusive in their own families, so there was no source of help for the young girl. After she grew up, Elaine moved away, married, and began to raise a family of her own, shutting those sad and terrifying years away in a corner of her mind. But any time the large family would plan to get together, Elaine would experience violent headaches, stomach cramps, and nervousness. Then came the panic attacks.

Finally, at the encouragement of the therapist, Elaine wrote her extended family a letter explaining that she could no longer remain in contact with them if she were to survive with any degree of sanity. She recounted numerous incidents, cruelties, and hurts, which they denied, and then cut off contact. Two years later, Elaine has begun to resume relations with an aunt whom she always felt was sympathetic, and with a cousin, but just thinking of her father can send her body into uncontrollable tremors.

"If a relative is going to be constantly emotionally abusive—and constant criticizing is emotional abuse—then maybe it's not healthy to be involved in that relationship anymore," says therapist Kurtz. "These people have to do a reality check if they are constantly abused and not buy into it. It is also crucial that people know it is all right to seek help, and when to seek professional help, because very often the feeling is, I must be crazy or a bad person if I can't handle this myself—after all, it's my family."

When something in a relationship is interfering with a person's highest level of functioning, then there's something very destructive going on that needs to be addressed. If a fight with your mother keeps you awake at night for a week while you worry over possible courses of action, that's probably a level-one situation. If fear of your mother is preventing you from functioning at work, carrying on a meaningful relationship with the person of your choice, *and* you can't sleep at night for weeks on end, then you have a level-two situation and should consider seeking outside help.

Benny and his wife Liza did not seek professional help, but came to the conclusion that they needed to cut off a family relationship in order to preserve their own sanity and nuclear family. "Liza's brother walked out on his wife and four children when the kids were really little," says Benny. "He couldn't handle the responsibility. He just drifted around the country doing odd jobs, but whenever he showed up at the front door, Liza let him in. He would stay for awhile, we'd think he was getting himself together, and then he'd take off again—a real Butterfly. You couldn't rely on him for anything.

"Well, after three marriages and his kids growing up, he decided that he wanted to establish relationships with them again. As usual, he was very charming and eventually his daughters were happy finally to have a father who was interested in them. The problem was, they were all messed up. Their mother was pretty flaky and they had practically raised themselves. One girl is twenty-two with two illegitimate children, the nineteen-year-old has drug problems, and the other two are a little unstable. But old Sal wanted to be a part of his daughters' lives, he said. They made elaborate plans to visit from California, using our house as the meeting place. The one daughter started planning to move near here to be with her dad. My wife Liza was spending all her emotional energies on counseling the girls and running around finding apartments. Then Sal decided that things were getting to heavy for him again and he left.

"He just picked up and left everyone in the lurch," says Benny. "He hasn't lived up to his responsibilities as a father, a brother, even a man. This has thrown the whole family into an uproar. Sal flits around and then every once in a while, he lands at our house and throws everything and everybody into an uproar. A three-day visit turns into five months, people change plans, even their lives, and then he takes off again. I told my wife this just can't continue."

Liza realizes that what Benny says is true, but she feels guilty. And that is one of the prices you pay when you do cut someone off, whether you are confronting a level-one or a level-two feud.

"There is tremendous guilt in turning your back on a family member, even if the relationship is killing you," says Kurtz. "You really pay for it internally, but you have to decide which is worse—to let the situation continue or deal with the guilt."

The other long-term ramification, being isolated from your family tree, can be very scary. "I'm a recovering alcoholic," says thirty-year-old Andrew. "Both my parents are alcoholics, and my brother died because of alcoholism. Because my parents are not in recovery—in fact, they put me down for going to A.A.—I have had to cut off my relationship with them. It's frightening to be fighting my problems alone, to feel that I can't turn to the people who were closest to me. But if I want to survive, I cannot be around them and their attempts to bring me back down into that alcoholic cycle. I hope that one day, at least one of them will go into a recovery program, but until then—they have to be out of my life."

Those who are involved in level-two feuds are in particular need of building a strong surrogate-family support system. Nobody wants to be alone in the world. Most people feel that even if they don't have friends, they at least have family. When that family has been cut off, it is vital to have the surrogate system, a place where you can be nurtured, encouraged, and made to feel welcome, all things our real families are "supposed to" do.

If all families did all the right things they were "supposed to" do, there would be little need of therapists, self-help books, or family services. Until that utopia arrives, however, we will have to use all the coping tools at our disposal to fill in the gaps, or at least try to build bridges over them so our families can flourish and grow.

20

The Ethnic Influence

The wonderful thing about being part of an American family is that the landscape of personalities is never dull. Because America is made up of so many different nationalities, some family conflicts are influenced by the ethnic backgrounds of those involved, whether we realize it or not.

In order to discuss ethnic differences and how they might contribute to family conflicts, it is necessary to deal in generalities. Sometimes the generalizations may seem prejudicial, but they are not intended that way. The fact that I feel impelled to make this disclaimer only goes to show how one family member can be sensitive—and maybe overly sensitive—to comments that are not meant personally, but rather stem from our ethnic heritages.

Sean doesn't trust his brother-in-law, never has. How can he trust a man who refuses to take a drink? Try as he might to tease, goad, or shame the poor excuse for a man into imbibing, all Sean seems to accomplish is making his sister mad at him.

Elvira has watched her daughter-in-law take advantage of her son Colin in many ways. She's walked out on him once, is extravagant with his money, goes out with girlfriends while expecting Colin to clean house and babysit, and at the last family gathering, the girl sat talking and drinking with the men of the family instead of helping with the food and children. Though Elvira turns a cold shoulder, she holds her tongue. She feels it would be improper for her to say anything.

Anthony, on the other hand, doesn't stop to think what would be proper or not. If something angers him, he lets everyone know it—loud and clear. Of course, five minutes later, the incident has been erased from Anthony's mind as he gregariously dispenses hugs and tickles to any family members around. Most of them seem to bounce back from Anthony's tirade . . . except for his new son-in-law, who's still shaking from the blistering tantrum.

Although America is commonly and idealistically referred to as the melting pot of cultures, Dr. Monica McGoldrick, director of family therapy at the Rutgers University Medical School and pioneer author in the field of ethnicity, objects to this myth. "Ethnicity remains a vital force in this country, a major form of group identification, and a major determinant of our family patterns and belief systems," she says in *Ethnicity and Family Therapy*. "The premise of equality, on which our country was founded, required us to give primary allegiance to our national identity, fostering the myth of the 'melting pot'—the notion that group distinctions between people were unimportant. Yet, we have not *'melted.'*

"There is increasing evidence that ethnic values and identification are retained for many generations after immigration and play a significant role in family life and personal development throughout the life cycle."

Our ethnic backgrounds, like our extended families, are part of the silent navigational system that guides us through our lives. Whether we are first- or sixth-generation American, our unique status of having another nationality involved influences everything from how we deal with illness, children, the elderly, how we recognize and celebrate holidays, how we express our emotions, and even our attitudes toward seeking help.

I am told that there is a joke among therapists that says if you ask an Irish family what the problem is, a great silence will descend over the room, but if you ask a Jewish family the same question, you won't be able to get a word in edgewise.

When I relayed this quip to a "very" Irish friend of mine, he said, "That's right. We take care of our own. We don't need any help from the outside." You can see how this particular attitude might conflict with Italian Aunt Tessa's, or Cuban father-in-law Jose's, who view one member's problems as the entire family's problems and eagerly move in to help.

Not only do our views and methods in life present gaps that must be bridged, but to get down to the basics, even our definitions of family are often different, based on our ethnic backgrounds. Whereas most WASP Americans regard the nuclear unit as "family," Italians include the extended family of several generations under that umbrella term, and Asians tend to include ancestors as well.

"To do something wrong, such as get pregnant without being married, would embarrass my whole family," says one young Korean woman. "And by family, I mean all my great-grandparents for a hundred years back. What we are and what we do is considered a reflection on them—not just the relatives who are alive today."

I grew up in an ethnic household. My father was a first-generation American whose parents were born in Greece. My mother was the daughter of a man born in Spain and a woman whose various ancestors came from Italy and France. When I was growing up the noise level in our home was usually a few decibels above most others around us. Everything was loud and out in the open—loving, fighting, involvement in relatives' lives, and expressions of opinions.

I married a man who was the child of a first-generation American father whose parents came from Belgium, and a Scotch-Irish mother whose family had been in America for several generations. His home was serene. When people spoke, others quietly listened; unpleasant feelings were either held in check or kept under wraps to reveal themselves in indirect ways. During our early years of marriage, I am sure he was as much intimidated by my family's volubility as I was frustrated by his family's elusiveness. Through the years, however, the realization that there is neither a right way nor a wrong way in terms of ethnic approaches has allowed us to enjoy the similarities in our backgrounds and view the differences as an option for growth. Larry has become more outgoing and open, and I have learned to think before I speak (or at least I try).

These cultural differences, particularly if they go unrecognized, however, can lead to hurt feelings and frictions among extended family members.

DEALING WITH ALIEN BEINGS

"I married a man from a very traditional Italian family," says Vivian, who was raised in a New England WASP family. "According to custom, a first son in each family should be named after the husband's father. Now my husband had four brothers who all followed this tradition, so every other person in this family is named Roberto. It's crazy when we all get together. Since my husband is the youngest of the brothers, I figured we could get away with a different name, but when I suggested it, you would have thought I had suggested disowning the family! The arguments and hurt feelings were ridiculous! Of course, my family wasn't even considered. I mean, his father enjoys his little kingdom of 'Roberto' clones. It's so egotistical!"

There are so many little cultural customs that become part of our lives. We live with them unquestioningly, until someone from outside brings them to our attention. "I married a man with a strong German background," says Maria, a second-generation Mexican-American. "Our ethnic backgrounds have given us trouble in little ways, like the fact that I thought his parents hated me for the first few years we were married because they would always close the doors in their house—even if they were just going from the living room to the kitchen. I always felt shut out. This influenced the attitude I had about other things they said to me and I guess I developed a chip on my shoulder.

"I know this sounds dumb, but it took me years to say something about it. When I finally mentioned it, they looked at me as if I was nuts. It's just the way they were brought up in Germany, to preserve the heat in a room. Even though they don't need to do that here, it is part of the way they live. I felt a little foolish, but it just goes to show how you can misinterpret things."

Misinterpretations are common when we come together not only from different families with the "us-versus-them" attitude, but also different ethnic backgrounds, which point up the "same-versus-different" conflict. Closed doors in a home can inspire wrong perceptions; so can punctuality or lack of it, weak or strong handshakes, drinking or not drinking alcohol, or even the inclusion or exclusion of children at events.

"We wouldn't think of not including the children at a wedding in my family," says Rita, who comes from a large Puerto Rican family. "So I was really insulted when we got an invitation to my sister-in-law's wedding and a special notation was made that this was an adult function. I thought, they can't mean *my* three children, we're family—but I was wrong. I just don't think my husband's family likes children around—or maybe that's just the way the British are."

Now there are many Brits who would include children as well, but views of child rearing do carry different perspectives in the different cultures. I am reminded of a radio advertisement that featured a French mother reading a letter to her husband from their daughter who was traveling abroad in Greece. In the letter, the daughter writes of sexual escapades to which her French father reacts mildly. He goes crazy, however, when she tells him that she has been drinking Greek wine. Now had that ethnic background been reversed, the Greek father would have been on the next plane to get his daughter and would not have left until the bottles of French wine had been cracked over the skulls of the daughter's suitors—assuming she had been allowed to travel by herself in the first place, which is unlikely.

Treatment of other family members can cause frictions in a practical sense. Lena, whose Cuban family is scattered through three states, has an elderly cousin in the hospital in Florida. The cousin's illness has been the cause for numerous telephone conversations at all hours of the day and night because of the different time zones where family members live. "My husband, who is English-German, cannot understand what all the fuss is about," says Lena. "I keep trying to tell him that the phone calls are important because we are a very close family and we make a lot of decisions together. He doesn't see it that way. He sees the big telephone bills and says the woman is either going to live or die, and all of our talking isn't going to help her. But that's okay, because I've told him that many things his family considers normal aren't normal to me!"

In some families, the ethnic background seems to take precedence over the "American" aspect of their lives. Mary Ellen, a thirty-three-year-old mother of two, who was raised in a Russian-English household, says she still goes crazy when her Irish in-laws reduce every argument to an ethnic conflict. "These people live the Irish-English conflict and do not hesitate to discuss their views on the British Empire's inadequacies and cruelties," she says. "They enjoy discussing the conflicts between the Turks and the Greeks, and they have a field day with World War II—who helped the Americans, who didn't—it goes on and on. And it's not just talk. When they meet someone, they want to know what country their relatives came from and that affects the opinion they form about them. It makes me crazy!"

EMOTIONAL VERSUS RESERVED

This separating of people into "us versus them" or "same versus different" is a common practice; it may involve the subconscious exclusion of others by speaking in a foreign tongue ("I grit my teeth every time my husband's family starts speaking in French," says one woman. "I think they do it on purpose to irritate me!") or the conscious pointing out of differences.

In the comedy *The Four Seasons*, the character played by Rita Moreno constantly refers to her background when she engages in emotional outbursts or tongue lashings. "I'm Italian—I can't help it!' she says, as if that explains and excuses her actions. And actually, if the reaction of the audience is any yardstick, it does. Someone coming from a less emotional background may find the day-to-day dealings of an emotional Latin type more grating than humorous.

"There's no such thing as not making a scene," says Pennsylvania Dutch–born Trina. "My husband's family is Italian, and it doesn't matter where they are, if something makes someone angry, they let loose right there. They got into a big argument in a restaurant once, and the manager had to come over and ask that they tone it down. I was so embarrassed, but that's what you buy into when you marry into an emotional family."

Emotions and how to deal with them are the source of many ethnic generalizations, but like all generalizations, there are many exceptions. I am sure that you, like me, have met many warm British people, though they are generally labeled "reserved" and "aloof," and just as many cool Latin types who are "supposed to" be warm and outgoing. This display of emotions or lack of it can contribute to frictions in households where ethnic sensitivities interpret every nuance and tone of voice.

"We have a great combination—Japanese and Jewish," says Carlie. "We joke that if we can make it work, any two countries ought to be able to get along in peace. I can't begin to tell you the hurdles we've had to cross, even though my husband's family has been in the United States for a hundred years, and mine wasn't all that religious. My mother-in-law can raise an eyebrow and her grown children know what she wants from them and they move to do it. Me? I analyze the raised eyebrow and then start a whole discussion, which Asians tend to find distasteful. They drive me crazy with their subtlety and I'm sure I drive them crazy with my big mouth.

"But you know how we get along? We try to focus on the similarities instead of the differences," says Carlie. "Both our families had members in concentration camps during World War II, so we know what prejudice is like. We focus on the love of our children, on respect for each other's culture and beliefs, and on making a positive contribution to society. It's not easy and it involves a lot of ignoring things that irritate us, but it can be done."

Focusing on the similarities, communicating feelings, tolerating differences, and having a sense of humor are all coping supports for building bridges across ethnic crevices within our family. So maybe brother-in-law Sean is just trying to connect with you the only way he knows how when he badgers you about sharing a Bushmill's. Maybe your daughter-in-law was raised in a household where she wasn't stereotyped into the subservient female role. And maybe your father-in-law doesn't realize that you take his temper tantrum to heart, instead of dismissing it like everyone around him has done all his life.

At least by recognizing that there are other silent navigational forces at work within the family, you can lay good foundations for building.

21

The Distance Factor

When Judy didn't call her grandson for his birthday, greatly disappointing him, her daughter Kate got annoyed. The next day, she telephoned her mother, who lived 2,000 miles away, but because of Judy's busy work schedule, all Kate got was the answering machine. She left a message and sat back to wait. Kate heard secondhand that her mother took affront to the phone message, so it didn't surprise her that the phone was silent.

When Judy didn't call for her granddaughter's birthday three weeks later, Kate got irritated again and called her mother the next day to explain the children's disappointment. Again she got the answering machine. Kate told her sister, who also lived in another state, who called their brother, who lived on the coast and who took his mother's side. Pretty soon, an aunt was involved and sharp words were exchanged on two more answering machines, which resulted in Judy's calling Kate and leaving a message on her answering machine to "go to hell." Now five different family factions were involved in five areas of the country and no one had been able to make the personal contact necessary to straighten it all out.

Prior to World War II, the majority of Americans lived, raised families, and died within thirty-eight miles of their birthplace. Today, it is unusual to find natives of any given area still living near their birthplace, and even more unusual to find entire extended families residing near each other.

As our society has become more mobile and governed by corporate opportunities and transfers, families have found themselves attempting to communicate across a gulf, not only of personality and opinion but distance as well. Often, it resembles the old game of Telephone, where what comes out at one end bears little resemblance to the original message. And because of our frenetic lives, the messages are often relayed via electronic answering machines rather than responsive human contact. Small hurts or misunderstandings, like Judy's and Kate's, can escalate into major conflicts through the lack of interactive communication.

Telephone calls are fine, if you can reach your party. There is nothing more frustrating, however, than an unanswered ring or the too-bright message of an answering machine. "I feel I have more of a relationship with my sister's answering machine than I do with her," complains Erika. "I just recently got married and moved away from home—400 miles away— and it's a difficult adjustment to be that far and not to be able to participate in family barbecues or just stop in for a cup of coffee with my mother or sister. Then when I call and my sister doesn't call me back, I go through all kinds of mental exercises. First I worry that somebody's been hurt or killed, then I get mad that she hasn't called me back, and I feel rejected. By the time I do hear from her, I'm so irritated that I'm not always nice. I know she leads a busy life and can't drop everything just to stay in touch with me, but being separated by these many miles has affected our relationship."

Bridging the distance gap becomes a physical and financial challenge as well as an emotional one. One not only has to work a little harder at the relationship, but pay a little more as well. This can also be a source of family frictions. "I just can't afford to keep calling my relatives and talking to answering machines," says one man. "Telephoning gets expensive and frankly, I don't like talking on the phone anyway. It always feels so artificial and unsatisfying. I've gotten to the point at times that I've left nasty messages and then there's this gap of silence for months on end. That doesn't help a relationship much."

If you are separated from your extended family by distance and are very lucky, you will have a relative who is a good letter writer. Most of us, though, because of busy schedules, resort to store-bought cards or quickly scrawled notes—if we write at all. Particularly when there is an argument brewing, however, a letter can be a sword rather than a balm, as the written word can be misinterpreted and cause hard feelings without the author's ever knowing or being able to amend a statement.

While many feel the physical separation contributes to family stresses, there are just as many who view it as a means of survival. ("Are you kidding? If I lived in the same town, I'd kill him!")

* * *

WHEN DISTANCE LENDS ENCHANTMENT

"My parents, and my mother in particular, are the kind of people who like to stay in control of their children's lives," says Lynne. "My mother still tries to run my life even though I'm thirty-eight years old. For example, I'm constantly being cross-examined. 'Why don't you get involved religiously? Why aren't you more interested in your nieces? Why don't you make overtures to the rest of the family? Why aren't you coming to the weekly dinners? Why don't you cut, color, change your hair? Why don't you join a service club? Why don't you make more friends?' The questions go on and on. She likes to play one of us off against another, like: 'You're not as good or smart or pretty as so-and-so, but I still love you.'"

"My solution was to move 1,800 miles away. She still calls and it still annoys her that I can't attend high holy services with the rest of the family, but I can deal with phone calls. And if things get too bad on the telephone, I can always hang up. I know that if I still lived in the same state—never mind the same town—we would not be on speaking terms!"

Putting physical distance between incompatible personalities is relatively easy today and is a popular method of coping with Dictator personalities and remaining sane. Periodic family gatherings must then be faced, but as long as people adjust their level of expectation, it is easier to tolerate differences and keep a sense of humor if the amount of contact time is limited.

Some of the reasons people choose to move away as a means of coping are suggested by the following anecdotes. "My father is a man who is larger than life and considers himself perfect," says one man. "I could never do anything right or measure up to him in any way, living in the same small town. By moving away, I had a chance to grow and can now appreciate his positive qualities. Had I stayed in the same town, I think I would have only felt anger and resentment."

"To my parents, a good job meant a paycheck at the end of the week—not necessarily work that you enjoy doing," says a woman. "They stayed in the same area as all their relatives. Every aspect of family life seemed to be a group decision. I broke all the family rules. I went away to college and obtained a broader view of life. I can go back for holidays, but I could not go back to the narrow way of thinking and operating. I love them, but I can't live near them."

"I come from such a jealous family," says another woman. "Everyone is always looking to see what somebody else has got and trying to go one better. I can stay out of that to a large degree since I live half a country away. They try to draw me into the pettiness at family gatherings, but it's something that's easier to cope with if you know you're only going to have to put up with it for a few days."

The Rev. Dr. Thomas Campbell wrote in the early 1800s, " 'Tis distance lends enchantment to the view," and the same principle applies today. Putting distance between ourselves and certain relatives encourages viewing their positive sides while having to deal infrequently with those aspects of their personalities that drive us crazy.

As you can see, the distance factor can work both for or against building bridges to firm family relationships. Sometimes it is a solution rather than an obstacle. Does "absence make the heart grow fonder"? Or is it, "out of sight, out of mind"? Only your relatives know for sure.

22

Bridge to the
Stars

The therapist had hit a wall. He had been working with a professional couple, married for fifteen years, whose relationship was falling apart. A well-respected veteran of the counseling profession, he had tried a number of different techniques to get at the root of the problem, but the couple did not respond. In desperation, he turned to a special consultant. Attempting to steer the consultant, he emphasized that the husband was an easygoing, quiet, and almost wimpy guy, while the wife was a screaming shrew.

After studying the charts of both clients, the consultant confronted the therapist with what was, for him, contradictory evidence. The husband, she pointed out, was actually controlling the situation by passive techniques such as withholding affection, and the wife, desperate for some interaction, was simply going crazy trying to get a reaction. The therapist laughed, thanked the "misguided" consultant, and went away. He did decide to play their taped conversation for his clients, just to show his conscientiousness on their behalf. He was amazed when the two middle-age professionals began bouncing up and down in their chairs shouting, "That's right! That's exactly what's going on!"

The special consultant, mentioned above, was Manhattan-based Linda Martin. Martin is used to such reactions from both conventional therapists and their clients. Martin, who has degrees in psychology and sociology, is a professional astrologer, lectures internationally, sits on the board of the Center for Geocosmic Research, and has published numerous papers on subjects ranging from crib death, twins, and dysfunctional families to studies on addictive behavior. In addition, she is consulted by a growing number of psychologists to provide added insight to their clients' problems.

Although the California Supreme Court, in the landmark 1986 Azusa decision, classified astrology as a "soft" science, together with meteorology and stock market predictions, there are many who view it as hocus-pocus. There are millions, however, who do consider astrology to be part of their lives, and consult astrologers with questions about relationships. When dealing with relatives who drive them crazy, all helping tools are worth considering.

"A lot of people lump astrology with the Madam Zazas who hang out their shingles for palm reading, fortunes told, *and* astrology," says Martin. "The fact is, professional astrology has the potential to be the great integrator, because there is a nonmoral quality to the planets. Just as we can see the physical evidence of the movement of the moon on such things as the tides, astrology can reveal the pushes, pulls, and paradoxes of an individual personality. I emphasize 'professional astrology,' as opposed to the popular horoscopes one reads in the newspapers, because professional astrology depends heavily on precise mathematical calculations of the positions of all the planets in relation to the earth. While it will not prevent conflicts, it can help a person understand where those conflicts might arise and how to channel their energies in a more positive manner. Astrology should not be used in place of therapy, but as an adjunct to it, an objective diagnostic tool that adds another dimension to the understanding of an individual's problems."

Martin, who confesses to being a skeptic herself when she first came across astrology in her studies nearly thirty years ago, says that traditional psychological thought is based on a series of behavior models or sociological predictions about people—most Irish-Americans will probably vote Democratic, for example. It was through years of personal research, however, that she found that astrology supplied the missing components in understanding individual personalities.

How can astrology be used to help keep your overbearing brother-in-law from driving you nuts with his "expert on everything" directives? Or how about your mother and sister who clash after being in the same room for thirty minutes? Or your father who still tries to control your life even though you are forty-four? It may not stop the clashes or lectures, but it can help you learn to deal with them differently through some additional understanding.

* * *

WHAT'S IN THE STARS?

In a recent study, two French scientists, Dr. Michel Gauquelin and Dr. Françoise Schneider-Gauquelin (a psychologist and statistician, respectively), studied 20,000 birth charts and came up with what they called the "Mars effect." This connected the planet Mars as it appeared in the same position in those charts with extreme and demonstrated athletic ability.

Similarly, certain planetary positions have repeatedly pointed to addictive behavior. "An article in the *New York Times* said that 20 percent of the population, at some time, will suffer from an addiction," says Martin. "A predisposition to an addiction can manifest itself at the psychological level rather than the physiological. Sometimes a person can have a temporary addiction, and addictions vary in type. Depending on the school of thought, one can have an addiction to drugs, alcohol, food, and gambling, but there are also addictions to sex, romance, exercise, or religion. There are indicators in one's chart that can reveal this, just as if you were trying to diagnose diabetes."

Not only can addictions be pinpointed, according to Martin, but so can conflicting personalities. Perhaps you come from a rowdy, outgoing family. If there's a party, a game, or just a lively discussion, you are used to everyone's just jumping on. Everyone except for your brother-in-law Ike, that is. Ike rubs everyone the wrong way with his standoffish, supercilious attitude. The more you try to entice him to participate, the colder his behavior. What does your sister see in him anyway? Eventually, you either blow your stack or just cut him out—and your sister too, which doesn't sit well with your parents, but after all, it's your house and you don't need that kind of aggravation.

In family dynamics, there are several ways of viewing a situation. And at the risk of encouraging everyone to go around as in the sixties and ask, "Hey baby, what's your sign?" one's approach to integrating into the family situation can be influenced by one's birth sign and chart.

A gregarious Sagittarius can go into a chaotic situation, immediately assess what is important, and join in. A more rigid Virgo may look at the same situation and say "This is madness!" and remain on the fringes, usually irritating the others, as Ike does. And then you have your Capricorn, who will watch for a while, assess the activities, and then join in slowly.

Conflicting needs can also be pinpointed, according to Martin, particularly in several generations. "I've studied some families as extensively as seven generations back and can see the same planets in certain combinations," she says. "If a family constellation is around material wealth and achievement—and your personal chart varies—you may wind up feeling that you are constantly disappointing your family, and this causes conflicts."

Using astrology as a tool to differentiate personalities and needs, strengths and weaknesses, we are able to keep predispositions and family patterns in perspective. Astrology is not a means of controlling the behavior of others or even one's life. Former First Lady Nancy Reagan incited a heated controversy when it was revealed that she consulted an astrologer regularly. You don't have to check the newspaper or consult an astrologer to see whether you should get out of bed in the morning or buy a new car, but when used as an auxiliary source of information, astrology might—in conjunction with the bridge-building supports already discussed—help you stay sane when reaching across a "relative" divide.

23

A Challenge to
Grow Close

At any given time, Joann Sheptock's sprawling home in Interlachen, Florida, houses from twenty-one to thirty-five children. While seven are her biological children, the rest are adopted, referred by adoption or state agencies. These are the "hard-to-place" children—sibling groups, handicapped children, and those who have seen tragedy beyond their years. They come from a variety of races, creeds, physical needs, and backgrounds.

Surely, that many personalities living in close quarters, each placing special and emotional demands on the others, must cause some conflict, yet Joann rarely seems agitated. Her secret? A devout belief in "the grace of God Almighty and forgiveness," she says energetically. "He forgives me and I forgive others. Family relationships are difficult, but they can work. We humans carry so many things over from one day to the next. Today is the day you can do something about because tomorrow may never come. It's human nature to want something we can't have. The world keeps setting standards that no one can reach. People want to get there and they keep struggling, and then they lose hope. It's the same thing with relationships. People set standards for others that they themselves cannot reach, and then they become frustrated and lose hope when those impossible standards aren't met. We have to learn to forgive others and forgive ourselves."

That philosophy not only works for Sheptock but would benefit the general population, according to a study by the sociology department of

Duke University. Entitled *Peace of Mind*, the study reveals a number of factors that are found to contribute greatly to emotional and mental stability. They include:

1. The absence of resentment and suspicion. Nursing a grudge was a major factor in unhappiness.
2. Living in the present rather than with an unwholesome preoccupation with the past and past failures.
3. Not wasting time and energy fighting conditions one cannot change.
4. Forcing oneself to stay involved, rather than withdrawing in times of stress.
5. Acceptance of the fact that nobody gets through life without some sorrow and misfortune.
6. The cultivation of old-fashioned values such as love, honor, compassion, and loyalty.
7. Adjusting one's self-expectations. When there is too wide a gap between self-expectation and ability to meet goals, feelings of inadequacy and depression set in.
8. Finding something bigger than just oneself in which to believe.

I find these results fascinating because they reflect several of the bridge-building supports, including adjusting one's expectation levels, tolerance, and value of the family unit. God, for many, is something bigger in which to believe. Family is also something bigger than any single member. For that reason, its influence, impact, and silent navigation in our lives are pervasive and far-reaching.

If you purchased this book thinking it would fix your family, I hope you realize by now that no book can fix your family as such, or change its many disparate personalities and quirks. What it can do, however, is equip you to change your perspective and build bridges across those gulfs of misunderstanding and differences that cause conflicts and sever relationships.

So many of us, in relation to our families, live with the resentments and guilts from yesterday and fears about tomorrow that prevent us from functioning fully today. And today, as Joann Sheptock says, is the day we have a chance to do something about. Making that first torturous step and using planned communication, adjusted expectations, tolerance as opposed to endorsement, surrogate family relationships, and a sense of humor, we can build strong bridges to our relatives. Without those bridges, we stand separated by a rushing river of differences that, through erosion, will only become wider.

When the Romans finished construction of the Pons Sublicius over the Tiber River in 621 B.C., they celebrated by throwing people into the river as a sacrifice to the gods. Contemporary construction jobs may end with the workers celebrating by hoisting a tree to signal that the bridge (or building) has reached its final height. This "tree topping" is seen as a sign of good luck and is often met with applause by a gathered crowd.

The difference between bridges made of steel, however, and bridges made of personal dynamics is that steel bridges connect static objects while emotional bridges connect people whose relationships are continually changing and evolving. These emotional bridges need to be even stronger than their metal counterparts in order to withstand the turbulence of growth and change.

It is a strong temptation to emulate the Romans and simply throw our relatives into the rushing waters—and many do just that. How much more rewarding it would be, though, to be able to hoist a tree instead.

It requires more strength, planning, and hard work, but our tree, our family tree, can rise in celebration of the ongoing construction of strong bridges.

BIBLIOGRAPHY

BOOKS

Berne, Eric. *Games People Play*. New York: Grove Press, 1966.

Bloomfield, Harold, and Felder, Leonard. *Making Peace with Your Parents*. New York: Ballantine Books, 1985.

Boszormenyi-Nagy, Ivan, and Spark, Geraldine. *Invisible Loyalties*. New York: Brunner/Mazel, 1984.

Bramson, Robert. *Coping with Difficult People*. New York: Ballantine, 1981.

Carnegie, Dale. *How to Win Friends and Influence People*. New York: Pocket Books, 1964.

Conroy, Pat. *The Prince of Tides*. New York: Bantam, 1987.

Cooper, Cary L. *Executive Families Under Stress*. Englewood Cliffs, New Jersey: Prentice Hall, 1981.

Cowan, Paul, and Cowan, Rachel. *Mixed Blessings*. New York: Doubleday, 1987.

Dyer, Wayne. *Pulling Your Own Strings*. New York: Avon, 1977.

Faber, Adele, and Mazlish, Elaine. *Siblings Without Rivalry*. New York: W. W. Norton, 1987.

Feldman, David. *Why Do Clocks Run Clockwise?* New York: Harper & Row, 1987.

Fisher, Roger, and Brown, Scott. *Getting Together, Building a Relationship That Gets to Yes*. Boston: Houghton Mifflin, 1988.

Friedman, Edwin H. *Generation to Generation*. New York: The Guilford Press, 1987.

Fromm, Erich. *To Have or to Be?* New York: Harper & Row, 1976.

Gaylin, Willard. *Feelings, Our Vital Signs*. New York: Harper & Row, 1979.

Ginott, Haim. *Between Parent and Child*. New York: Macmillan, 1965.

Hanson, Peter. *The Joy of Stress*. Kansas City: Andrews and McMeel, 1985.

Jaffe, Dennis. *Healing from Within*. New York: Alfred A. Knopf, 1980.

Jarvik, Lissy, and Small, Gary. *Parentcare*. New York: Crown, 1988.

Kroeger, Otto, and Thuesen, Janet. *Type Talk*. New York: Delacorte, 1988.

Kübler-Ross, Elisabeth. *On Death and Dying*. New York: Macmillan, 1969.

Leman, Kevin, *The Birth Order Book*. New York: Dell, 1985.

Lerner, Max. *America as a Civilization*. New York: Simon & Shuster, 1957.

Menninger, Karl. *The Vital Balance*. New York: Viking, 1963.

Nelsen, Jane. *Understanding.* California: Prima Publishing & Communications, Rocklin, CA: 1988.

Newman, Mildred, and Berkowitz, Bernard. *How to Be Your Own Best Friend.* New York: Ballantine, 1986.

Scarf, Maggie. *Intimate Partners.* New York: Random House, 1987.

Tatelbaum, Judy. *The Courage to Grieve.* New York: Harper & Row, 1980.

U.S. Department of Health and Human Services. *Study of National Incidence and Prevalence of Child Abuse and Neglect: 1988.* Washington, D.C.: Government Printing Office, 1989.

MAGAZINES AND PERIODICALS

Ansberry, Clare. "Kids Are Often Losers in Joint Custody." *The Wall Street Journal* (September 22, 1988).

"Births, Marriages, Divorces, and Deaths for 1988." *Monthly Vital Statistics Report* from the National Center for Health Statistics (March 28, 1989).

Cocores, James A. "Co-Addiction: A Silent Epidemic." *Fair Oaks Hospital Psychiatry Letter* (February 1987).

Cohen, Susan. "The Distended Family." *Parenting Magazine* (April 1987).

Cole, Diane. "Grief's Lessons: His and Hers." *Psychology Today* (February 1989).

Collins, Glenn. "Stepfamilies of the 1980's: Forming New Ties, Old Stigma Is Disappearing." *The New York Times* (September 24, 1987).

Fissinger, Laura. "Sisters, Brothers—But Strangers." *Redbook* (July 1988).

Goleman, Daniel. "Agreeableness vs. Anger." *The New York Times Magazine* (April 16, 1989).

Hales, Dianne. "Understanding Your Personality." *McCall's* (March 1989).

Kantrowitz, Barbara. "How to Stay Married." *Newsweek* (August 24, 1987).

Kantrowitz, Barbara. "Who Keeps 'Baby M'?" *Newsweek* (January 19, 1987).

Kaye, Kenneth. "Turning Two Identities into One." *Psychology Today* (November 1988).

Knaub, Patricia, Hanna, Sharon, and Stinnett, Nick. "Strengths of Remarried Families." *Journal of Divorce* (Spring 1984).

Manning, Anita. "The War Against Diseases That Run in the Family." *USA Today* (January 12, 1989).

Marks, Jane. "We Have a Problem." *Parents* (April 1987).

Medical Essay: "A Long Goodbye: Coping with Alzheimer's Disease and Other Forms of Dementia." *Mayo Clinic Health Letter* (January 1988).

Newton, Miller. "The Teenage Drug Epidemic." *The El Paso Physician* (November 1983).

Ostling, Richard. "The Intermarriage Quandry." *Time* (October 3, 1988).

Peterson, Karen. "It Takes Work to Turn 'Yours and Mine' into 'Ours'." *USA Today* (October 29, 1987).

Prince, Dinah. "Marriage in the '80s." *New York Magazine* (June 1, 1987).

Pruitt, Dean. "The Controversy over Caucuses." *Psychology Today* (December 1987).

Rosenblatt, Paul. "Family Inc." *Psychology Today* (July 1985).

Rubin, Carol, and Rubin, Jeff. " 'Tis the Season to Be Fighting." *Psychology Today* (December 1988).

Secunda, Victoria. "Marrying out of Your Faith." *New Woman* (December 1988).

Secunda, Victoria. "Should You Divorce Your Mother?" *New Woman* (November 1988).

Slewka, Stephanie. "One Baby's Price." *Life Magazine* (September 1988).

Smilgis, Martha. "The Big Chill: Fear of AIDS." *Time* (February 16, 1987).

Spann, Paula. "Whose Holiday Is It, Anyway?" *Glamour* (December 1988).

Tavris, Carol. "No-Fault Psychology." *Vogue* (January 1989).

Taylor, Susan Champlin. "A Thoughtful Word, A Healing Touch." *Modern Maturity* (December 1988).

Tucker, Dorothy. "Guess Who's Coming for Dinner Now?" *Essence* (April 1987).

Victor, Richard. "Equitable Parent Doctrine Adopted in Michigan." *Legally Speaking,* Stepfamily Bulletin (Winter 1987).

Walker, LouAnn. "What Comforts AIDS Families." *The New York Times Magazine* (June 21, 1987).

Watts, Judy, and Lapinski, Susan. "When Divorce Divides a Family." *Redbook* (April 1983).

"When a Loved One Has AIDS." *Mayo Clinic Health Letter* (October 1988).

Wilder, Rachel. "Selfishness." *Self* (June 1986).

INDEX